Michael Veitch is well known as an author, actor, comedian and former ABC television and radio presenter. His books include the critically acclaimed accounts of Australian pilots in World War II, *Heroes of the Skies*, *Fly*, *Flak*, *44 Days*, *Barney Greatrex* and *The Battle of the Bismarck Sea*. *Australia's Secret Army* is his eleventh book. He lives in the Yarra Valley, outside Melbourne.

## Also by Michael Veitch

*44 Days: 75 Squadron and the fight for Australia*

*Barney Greatrex: From Bomber Command to the French Resistance – the stirring story of an Australian hero*

*Turning Point: The Battle for Milne Bay 1942 – Japan's first land defeat in World War II*

*The Battle of the Bismarck Sea: The Forgotten Battle That Saved the Pacific*

# AUSTRALIA'S SECRET ARMY

### THE STORY OF THE COASTWATCHERS, THE UNSUNG HEROES OF AUSTRALIA'S ARMED FORCES DURING WORLD WAR II

## MICHAEL VEITCH

hachette
AUSTRALIA

hachette
AUSTRALIA

Published in Australia and New Zealand in 2022
by Hachette Australia
(an imprint of Hachette Australia Pty Limited)
Gadigal Country, Level 17, 207 Kent Street, Sydney, NSW 2000
www.hachette.com.au

Hachette Australia acknowledges and pays our respects to the past, present and future Traditional
Owners and Custodians of Country throughout Australia and recognises the continuation of cultural,
spiritual and educational practices of Aboriginal and Torres Strait Islander peoples. Our head office is
located on the lands of the Gadigal people of the Eora Nation.

 A catalogue record for this
work is available from the
NATIONAL
LIBRARY National Library of Australia
OF AUSTRALIA

ISBN: 978 0 7336 4847 2 (paperback)

Cover design by Luke Causby, Blue Cork Designs
Cover photographs courtesy of the Australian War Memorial (AWM OG0606C, 094668)
Map by Raylee Sloane, Kinart
Author photograph by Gina Milicia
Typeset in Simoncini Garamond by Kirby Jones
Printed and bound in Australia by McPherson's Printing Group

MIX
Paper | Supporting
responsible forestry
FSC® C001695

The paper this book is printed on is certified against the
Forest Stewardship Council® Standards. McPherson's Printing
Group holds FSC® chain of custody certification SA-COC-005379.
FSC® promotes environmentally responsible, socially beneficial
and economically viable management of the world's forests.

# Contents

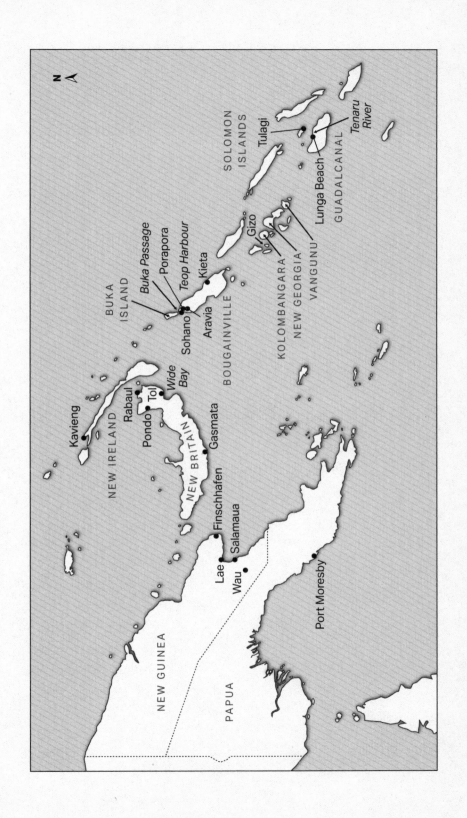

# PROLOGUE

Just before eleven in the morning of 8 February 1942, a little steamer suddenly appeared around the headland and swung its bow towards the wharf. A single shout rose up from the mass of humanity crammed onto the dock, a cry – more a sob – like the wounded moan of some gigantic beast. Since well before sun-up, several hundred men, women and children had been waiting. Now, drunk with suppressed panic, and sweating under the awful tropical heat, they fought off the gnawing terror that maybe – even now – they might not get away.

Nothing about this sultry morning was normal. The usually idyllic tropical harbour of Tulagi, a tiny island serving as the administrative capital of the dreamy British protectorate of the Solomon Islands – replete with palm trees, blue water and a majestic mountain backdrop – was today the setting of human desperation. Whimpering children, dressed in their Sunday bests, clutched a favourite toy with one hand and the sweating palm of a parent with the other. Some of the planters' wives were likewise absurdly overdressed, wearing whatever couldn't be packed into the single case the army had permitted them to take. Some had ignored the edict and stood surrounded by expensive luggage, daring the marshals to do their worst, and enduring the furious stares of those who had complied with the order.

Even the ship, the familiar old Burns Philp steamer *Morinda*, with its cheerily painted funnel and porthole trim, looked more like a cruise boat for a load of holiday passengers rather than the last hope of escape from the all-conquering, unstoppable Japanese.

Outside the perimeter, the native islanders stared into this mass of departing Europeans. To think it had all come to this. The bosses, the masters, missionaries, the patrol officers and administrators, along with their wives and families, all of them chucking in the towel and taking their manicured world of high teas and gin and tonics with them. No more formal Sunday lunches in white suits, no more tennis matches or carols about snow and reindeers.

With them would go all the old colonial assumptions which for a century or more had stood fast and inviolable: that they would somehow always be the ones in charge; that the gold, the rubber and the oil ultimately belonged to them; that to superimpose their culture and their religion onto those they regarded as inferior would always be their God-given right.

Now, on this little wharf, the whole ramshackle system was crashing down around their ears.

Blank-faced, the islanders looked on. They weren't going anywhere. Many of them had been brought over from other islands to work here for the Europeans and now they were being abandoned, stranded with no income, no food, and no way to get back to the protective bond of family and village. There would be no escape for them: the only faces on this last boat out of the Solomons would be white.

Even now, some of those Europeans departing cursed themselves. If only they had listened. Weeks – *weeks* – had passed since the offer of leaving on their own terms was raised. The stories of Japanese brutality had trickled down in terrified whispers from Malaya, Borneo and then, unbelievably, Singapore. But no, the Japanese will never come here, not those little men, those imitators with their wind-up toy army and aeroplanes made – according to the rumours – from bamboo.

They were not nearly so smug now – this macabre, shuffling carnival of humanity.

A whistle sounded. People edged towards the water as the gangways loomed closer. Australian soldiers appeared, walking rapidly down the quickly disintegrating lines. 'Leave that … leave that … get rid of that,' they grunted, kicking an army boot into a tightly packed trunk or valise, any remonstration ignored or met with a shove. Approaching the gangway, one burly uniformed man tried to rip a toy from a child's grasp until the mother put her body between them and glared him down with a white-hot gaze. The man spat a four-letter word at both of them and waved them through, the child hugging the toy tight to her little chest. 'Essentials, only essentials. You've all been told!' shouted a thin young officer through a tin megaphone. People at the back surged, fearing they would be left behind, held back only by a thin line of khaki. Scuffles broke out. One man – a doctor, or so he said – dislocated his shoulder.

Then, incredibly, at the top of the gangway, a single arriving passenger. The crowd, momentarily distracted, quietened. He was a slight man, dressed in a perfectly pressed pale suit, holding a small, ivory-coloured case. He resembled a salesman or an office clerk. Calmly, he began to make his way down the gangway. The crowd drew back as he stepped onto the dock. He politely thanked those who made a passage for him so he could pass to the rear. For a bewildered moment, all eyes followed his progress, then turned again to the gangway and forgot him completely.

With remarkable haste, the dock emptied, leaving behind a detritus of abandoned luggage, handbags, books, government forms, papers and fluttering administrative records. As the last of the passengers fought their way onboard, the man with the pale suit headed towards the town's colonial government building with a confident gait.

Martin Clemens, Coastwatcher, had arrived for work.

# Chapter 1
# BEGINNINGS

By 1922, Eric Feldt had had enough. With a heavy heart, he reluctantly put his name to the letter resigning his commission in the Royal Australian Navy. If the navy was not going to allow him to see the world, he would have to go and see it for himself.

Eric Feldt was born in 1899, the eighth child of immigrant parents who had uprooted themselves from Europe in the 1870s to seek a better life in tropical north Queensland, a place so alien to their native Sweden that his mother, Augusta, could scarcely believe the two places inhabited the same world. Feldt had toiled on his father's struggling cane farm near Ingham, but from an early age hankered for adventure in the wider world. His parents, luckily, knew the value of education, and Feldt's natural intelligence came to the notice of a teacher at his modest country government school. His parents were encouraged to apply for a scholarship to the prestigious halls of Brisbane Grammar, where the boy excelled at everything he tried. After only a year at the school, Feldt learned that the new Australian Navy was seeking its first intake of officer cadets for the following year, 1913. Thinking a life sailing the seas would be to his liking, Feldt applied and was selected as the sole Queenslander among 28 successful candidates from 137 applicants.

Inside the austere bluestone edifice of Osborne House, Geelong, Australia's first naval officers' college, Feldt rose to become Chief Cadet Captain – a position he later said meant almost nothing – graduating in time to play his part in the greatest war the world had ever seen.

Eric Feldt had only just turned eighteen when, along with most of the other boys of his Pioneer Class, he set sail from Brisbane in the first week of 1917 on the steamer RMS *Omrah*, landing in Plymouth on a grey afternoon in the middle of a British winter, from which point Feldt later said he would 'not be warm for another four years'.

Assigned to one of the mightiest of His Majesty's fighting vessels, the super-dreadnought *Canada*, Feldt's dreams of exciting action followed by quick promotion completely failed to materialise. Seemingly permanently at anchor with the Grand Fleet at Scapa Flow, the *Canada* spent the war primed for a showdown with a German Grand Fleet that never showed up. Feldt spent most of his first year fighting boredom, attempting to digest awful navy food and nurturing a deep loathing for the British class system which would stay with him the rest of his life.

Even when promoted from lowly midshipman – the worst of all ranks, engendering neither respect from officers above nor sailors below – to the single stripe denoting him a sub-lieutenant, Feldt and his original classmates stuck together, finding strength in numbers while enduring the prejudices of the English to whom they were nothing but 'colonials' or simply 'those bloody Australians'.

On the few occasions Feldt was at sea, he was assigned to the 'spotting top', a small cupola atop a tripod mast 120 feet above the water, where he worked a range-finding instrument known as a dumaresq, which plotted with relative accuracy the speed of a moving enemy vessel. No such vessel was ever sighted, and Feldt described the job as 'cold, windy, dreary, and with very little shelter'.

Only once did Feldt play at least some part in an actual battle, albeit a confusing and inconclusive engagement known as the Second Battle of Heligoland Bight. In dreadful November weather, *Canada* joined the dozen or so ships of the First Battle Squadron, part of a larger force heading across the North Sea to Denmark to intercept a German fleet trying to clear British sea mines. So dire were the conditions that the admiral in command remarked to his officers, 'I don't know where we are. I don't know where the enemy is. If I see anything, I'm just going to ram.' Nothing, fortunately, was seen, and the closest Feldt came to the fight was listening to the distant boom of gunfire somewhere up ahead through the fog. Feldt's sole injury came courtesy of an iron fitting on a coal sack which struck his head while he was on loading duty.

When the war ended in November 1918, Feldt felt he had come a very long way to see very little of the war indeed, and had little to do but draw his meagre pay and wait.

As 1918 passed into 1919, a fellow officer suggested they apply for a short intelligence officers course in Greenwich, though more as a means of getting off the ship as much as a desire to imbue themselves in the world of naval intelligence. While Feldt later stated that he learned not a lot, it was the first step in the direction of the world he would inhabit during the next war, twenty years later.

Fed up with being unable to greet their beloved son at an Australian dock, Eric Feldt's parents made the trip to Europe themselves – their first since emigrating forty years earlier – reuniting with him for a few weeks in London. It would be two years before the navy's glacially slow 'last in, last out' policy would return Feldt to Australia on the ocean liner *Orsova*, which had recently resumed its prewar London to Australia service. Finally, a week before Christmas 1920, Feldt stepped ashore into blissfully warm weather in Fremantle, Western Australia.

Choosing to remain in the peacetime navy, Feldt was assigned to the RAN's flagship, the light cruiser HMAS *Melbourne*, where his fleet commodore transpired to be no less than John Dumaresq, the brilliant and mercurial Australian-born admiral and inventor of the eponymous range-finding instrument through which Feldt had spent the war peering over a slate-grey North Sea. A true visionary who fought constantly with the Australian defence establishment, Dumaresq would succumb to a sudden bout of pneumonia just a year later.

Feldt's first voyage onboard the *Melbourne* took him up the east Australian coast, then north on a journey that would blow open Feldt's horizons and pave the path of his future. Calling first at Tulagi in the British Solomon Islands, the ship's course then took in some of the smaller, outlying places with exotic names such as Tikopia, Utapua and Vanikoro. Feldt had never seen anything like them, sensing a rugged majesty, inhabited by people unbound by the laws and parameters of his own upbringing. At Port Vila, he met a Melanesian man and was delighted to converse in some of the rudimentary Pidgin he had learned as a child from the islander cane-cutters on his family's farm. Walking the streets of Noumea, Feldt swore to himself to return. His days as a naval officer were numbered.

Back in Australia at Jervis Bay, while overseeing torpedo-firing exercises, Feldt came to the realisation that, in this postwar world, his chances of the travel and promotion he longed for were rapidly evaporating. In April 1922, he made the decision to resign the commission for which he had toiled so long by placing his name on the Navy's Retired List. He was twenty-three years old.

After packing his bags, he travelled to Sydney, reflecting later that, 'The sun was still shining, the breeze was blowing, the trees were green and the world was just the same, although I wasn't any longer in the Navy.'

•

The adventure Feldt sought would indeed come to pass, not on the high seas but in the great mass of jungle to Australia's north, New Guinea. At over 800 000 square kilometres, New Guinea ranks as the second largest island in the world, surpassed in scale only by the northern hemisphere's Greenland. For centuries, its misty valleys, wild rivers and impossibly high mountains remained impenetrable to the outside world. One of its hundreds of tribes, the Dani people of the Baliem Valley, first encountered outsiders only in the 1930s. For millennia they had believed themselves to be the only people on earth and were convinced that the astonished party of white-skinned Europeans who had finally broken the seal of their remote valley were the spirits of their own long-dead ancestors.

Since 1828 the Dutch had notionally claimed the western half of the island as part of their vast East Indies empire, attracting envious glances from Australia, particularly Queensland who, though a colony herself, fancied some empire building of her own. In April 1883, Premier Thomas McIlwraith (described in one contemporary newspaper editorial as possessing a 'barnacle tenacity to stay in office') made his move, asking Britain whether he might be allowed to annex the southeastern corner of New Guinea in the name of the Crown, to which London responded with an unequivocal 'No'. Undeterred, McIlwraith went ahead and did it anyway.

Living quietly on remote Thursday Island, the local Police Magistrate Henry Chester no doubt leaped from his comfortable chair when receiving the telegraphed order to sail over to the infant settlement at Port Moresby, run up the Union Jack over the harbour, and claim it all for the Empire as the new 'Territory of Papua'. For good measure, Chester also took the opportunity to fire off a few shells at a group of supposedly 'warlike' natives he didn't like the look of, before returning home.

The British, who in fact had no ambitions whatsoever in New Guinea, were furious at being presented with this imperial fait accompli by a cocky colonial government, but their hand was now forced into proclaiming a protectorate over their new and unsought province. McIlwraith smugly insisted he had done it to head off the Germans, who were busy building their own South Pacific empire, though the prospect of acquiring cheap labour for Queensland's burgeoning sugar industry – a ghastly process known as 'blackbirding' – may have touched upon his true motives.

The following year, the Germans did indeed help themselves to a nearly 100 000 square mile chunk of the island's northwestern corner, proclaiming it as 'Kaiser-Wilhelmsland'. This in turn required the British to formally annex their own neighbouring protectorate, which they renamed – in now unequivocal terms – 'British New Guinea'.

In 1905, after twenty years of finding no good use for the place, the British, in a fit of pique, threw it back onto the Australian government to administer entirely at their own expense – resulting in yet another name change, to the Australian Territory of Papua.

When World War I erupted in 1914, Kaiser Wilhelmsland, by now one of the most poorly defended and farthest flung of Imperial Germany's provinces, was quickly overrun by a token Australian land and naval force. At war's end, after some vociferous lobbying at Versailles by Prime Minister Billy Hughes, Germany was relieved of their colony and it was made a League of Nations Mandated Territory to be administered by Australia. Thus, only though recently a series of colonies herself, Australia found herself in the peculiar position of running two adjacent, almost identical provinces: the Australian Mandated Territory of New Guinea in the northeast of the island, and the Australian Territory of Papua to its immediate south.

Australia was not the only Pacific nation who hankered after the Kaiser's colonial spoils at Versailles. Having joined the Allied side early in the war, Japan had lent her Imperial Navy to overrun some of Germany's northern Pacific possessions, and now enquired in a voice more polite but no less forceful than Australia's as to whether she might be allowed to keep them. Having not the slightest idea why anyone would want a bunch of isolated Pacific atolls devoid of resources, the victorious powers were more than happy to let them go to appease a loyal ally. Hence, the lion's share of Germany's Pacific empire north of the equator – the Marshall, Mariana and Gilbert Islands – slipped quietly into the orbit of the Japanese Empire. One of those, Truk, a vast protected lagoon in the Caroline Islands, would later come in handy as Japan's primary Pacific naval base of World War II.

## Chapter 2
# PROBLEMS OF INTELLIGENCE

Admittedly a xenophobe who harboured a deep antipathy to all non-Anglo-Saxon races, Billy Hughes had seen through Japan's long strategic game, proclaiming that, after centuries of isolation, Japan was now intent on establishing an empire of her own through force. Had the rest of the world forgotten, asked Hughes, that less than two decades earlier, she had shocked the world when her navy burst onto the world's stage in her territorial war with Russia over Manchuria? How she had ruthlessly demolished the Russian fleet in surprise attacks on Port Arthur and Tsushima, declaring war only after their victories had been completed? The Allies, Hughes now reminded anyone who would listen, had sighed with relief at Japan's decision to side with them during World War I and not the Central Powers. But don't be fooled, he warned. This was simply their Act One. In a 1919 letter to London, he thundered:

It's a long way from Tokyo to Whitehall, but we are within a stone's throw. I desire again to emphasise that our fleet is practically without fuel, and in any case quite unequal to meet Japanese with any hope of success … that we

profoundly distrust Japan … that the experiences of Port
Arthur shows she strikes first and declares war afterwards.

In New Guinea, what the native people made of their land
being squabbled over by foreigners like hagglers at a fish
market can only be guessed at. It is reasonable to assume that
the *New Guinea Act 1920*, formalising Australia's takeover
of the entire eastern half of the island and many of its outlying
provinces, went largely unnoticed as it made its way through
the Australian parliament in faraway Melbourne.

One man, however, noticed it very closely indeed. At
nearly seventy, Captain Chapman James Clare was something
of a legend in the Royal Australian Navy – one of its original
founding figures – and a man for whom the phrase 'salt water
runs in his veins' could well have been coined. Literally born at
sea in the middle of a Bay of Biscay storm in 1853 onboard one
of his father's merchant vessels, Clare spent almost his entire
life on the water, initially as a merchant sailor, criss-crossing
the world and having adventures on every type of vessel
imaginable, from opium steamers to lighthouse-servicing
cutters, even being involved in the Boxer Rebellion in 1900.
He then joined – and later commanded – the small colonial
South Australian naval force. Upon Federation, Clare became
the second-most senior officer in the nascent Royal Australian
Navy, and was even selected as one of the dozen or so judges
tasked with choosing the design of the new Australian flag.

After service in World War I escorting Australian troop
convoys, Clare found himself during his twilight years back
at his old prewar job as district naval officer at the port of
Fremantle, Western Australia. On the eve of his retirement,
he had time to reflect on the scale of the oceans over which he
had spent his life traversing, as well as the near-impossible task
of protecting Australia's vast coastline of roughly 19 000 miles

which, if unravelled in a straight line, would stretch the entire distance from Sydney to London.

He had also noted the ease with which hostile naval forces – including countless German merchant raiders – had been able to find their way through the chain of islands to the north and sidle up to the Australian mainland virtually at will, due to a complete paucity of decent naval intelligence. Military thinking at the time speculated, probably correctly, that should an entire foreign army choose to sail up and disgorge itself onto some remote part of the Australian coastline, it would most likely be weeks before anyone knew they were there. What Australia needed, said Clare, was some kind of early warning system, particularly in this new age of smaller, faster vessels and, of course, aircraft.

In his research, historian Patrick Lindsay has uncovered a series of dispatches from the Australian Naval Board to the Admiralty in London sent at the height of World War I. In one, an anonymous Australian intelligence officer stated in early 1917 that:

> It is sometimes necessary to leave south-western Australia quite unprotected, and at times there have been no vessels available for the protection of the southern and eastern Australian waters. No attack has been made on our trade in Australian waters, but … there are on the coast of Australia and the near islands, anchorages and harbours where there are no inhabitants, and which are seldom or never visited.

Now, in the navy's postwar contraction, Clare believed there would be even less chance of preventing an encroachment from some hostile power to the north. Whether, like Billy Hughes, he assumed that power to be Japan is unclear, but as he ruminated on Australia's long and porous border, he hit upon an idea so ingenious, so logical, and yet so breathtakingly simple, that the powers of the time immediately adopted it in its entirety.

Given the navy was in no position to resource a national early warning system of its own, why not, reasoned Clare, create one from a resource that already existed? In an extensive memo, he suggested that up and down the Australian coast responsible and presumably patriotic-minded citizens from a variety of walks of life were to be found – postmasters, harbour masters, cattle station owners, prospectors, missionaries – people who could be relied upon to answer their country's call. Why could not people such as these be organised into a loose confederation of information gatherers – indeed, spies – who, in time of war, could gather intelligence of enemy activity, particularly aircraft and shipping?

Demands on the participating individuals would hardly be irksome, said Clare. They would be required to do no more than simply record their observations as they went about their daily lives. No remuneration would be offered – no funds were available in any case – but the honour of being asked to serve one's country should be payment enough. And as for the method of reporting, what better means than the post office telegraph system, which already covered vast sections of the Australian continent?

Upon Clare's suggestion, a Staff Paper soon emerged from the Navy Office in Melbourne. This was brought to the attention of the Chief of Naval Staff, Admiral Sir Percy Grant, who thought the idea a splendid one, largely on account of it requiring an outlay of virtually nothing. He then sent the idea up to the Minister for Defence, George Pearce, who likewise embraced it wholeheartedly, possibly on account of him being a senator for Western Australia and acutely aware of his own state's particularly long and vulnerable coastline.

Pearce insisted on a meeting between the three services to discuss the proposal which, in a rare moment of interservice equanimity, was again met with enthusiasm all round. It was also agreed that, since the plan focused primarily on maritime security, it should be brought under the aegis of the navy, specifically the Naval Intelligence Division, which would also be charged with getting the whole scheme up and running.

In the early 1920s, however, Australia's Naval Intelligence Division was incapable of doing anything much at all. Following deep postwar financial cuts, support for naval intelligence had sunk to such a level that even the title 'Intelligence Officer' was dropped from the Naval Staff List altogether. A report into the state of the RAN prepared by the venerated (albeit controversial) hero of Jutland, Admiral John Jellicoe, painted an alarming picture. Jellicoe prepared the report in Melbourne while on his way to New Zealand to take up the post of Governor-General there, having already turned down the offer for the role from Australia. In his report, he appears to view Australian naval intelligence as something of a joke:

It is worthy of note that there is only one other officer shown as a 'Director of Naval Intelligence', namely, 'The Director of Naval Intelligence, Admiralty'. This title, therefore, would seem to presuppose the existence of an intelligence department at the Navy Office, Melbourne, on similar lines to that at the Admiralty, and responsible for the issue of intelligence publications to the Royal Australian Navy. The machinery for carrying out this all-important work at the Navy Office does not exist at present.

'It is considered,' Jellicoe went on to suggest, 'that in order to place the Intelligence Department of the Navy Office on a firm basis, the services of an officer of the Royal Navy possessing qualified experience in the Intelligence Division of the Admiralty Naval Staff should be obtained.'

The situation was further brought to a head when the British Admiralty called upon the RAN to supply information on former German Pacific colonies to assist in the production of a series of geographical intelligence publications, and were shocked to discover that Australia could supply almost nothing of value. This prompted the Secretary of State for the Colonies to politely suggest that the appointment of an experienced British intelligence officer might be a good thing all round. Australia quietly agreed.

In 1921, a Royal Marine officer, Lieutenant-Colonel Francis Home Griffiths, arrived in Melbourne to take up a three-year posting of Imperial Liaison Intelligence Officer with the RAN, a title that was soon upgraded to Director of Naval Intelligence.

Griffiths found the division rundown, starved of both funds and staff, and regarded so poorly by the wider defence community – particularly its own Naval Board – that there was initially very little for him to work with. One of his first initiatives was to relocate the division to Sydney, ostensibly to be closer to Australia's largest port and naval base at Garden Island, but also to extract himself from the closeted and paranoid atmosphere of the Melbourne headquarters. With almost no staff, Griffiths buttonholed a civilian navy office accounts clerk, Walter Brooksbank, to be his assistant. Motivated by desperation though it was, Griffiths's choice turned out to be a stroke of pure genius.

Brooksbank was a former soldier, a 'short, blunt-featured, fresh complexioned-man with humorous and observant blue eyes', according to a later newspaper description. In World War I, he had served with the AIF's 7th Infantry Battalion, coming ashore at Gallipoli with the first landing on 25 April 1915, and later earning himself both the Military Medal and a field commission as an officer. Brooksbank was quiet, methodical and thorough. He ran on seemingly boundless energy, possessed a phenomenal memory and, as would be proven later on the grim battlefields of the Solomons, was utterly devoid of physical fear. He was also, in the style of a true intelligence operative, something of an eccentric. Under the pseudonym Horton Brooks, he would later write short stories about his experiences during the war and other topics, and even pen the occasional radio play. Later, when visiting Guadalcanal, Brooksbank, wearing his signature tailored Palm Beach suit and Panama hat, would visit the frontline foxholes of astonished Marines, utterly oblivious to the danger of Japanese sniper bullets.

The brief to begin work on establishing the network, combined with the arrival of Brooksbank, was a perfect juncture for the Naval Intelligence Division. Not only did it now possess its raison d'être, but it also had just the man to coax it into reality.

Selected citizens situated around the Australian coast were sought out and recruited from lists of postmasters, harbour masters, schoolteachers, railway officials, local police and government officials. Initially dubbed 'Special Reporting Officers', each man (women were not asked) was given an area of responsibility pertaining to their location. They were to supply information on maritime infrastructure, as well as sightings of any suspicious vessels. Priority telegraph access would be granted through the Postmaster General's Department.

To instruct on the techniques of observation and ship recognition, Brooksbank prepared a slim but concise volume, the *Naval Coastwatching Guide*, which would become the indispensable handbook for all special reporting officers, as well as provide the organisation with the name by which it would become universally known – the Coastwatchers.

It was at this early stage that another of Clare's initial suggestions was implemented, leading to a decision which, while unforeseen at the time, would transform the Coastwatchers from a limited domestic undertaking to one which, twenty years later, would have the power to turn the course of battles in the midst of a world war.

Why not, proposed Clare, expand the scheme into Australia's new mandated territories in New Guinea, and even the British protectorate over the southern Solomon Islands? Here, a ready and established population of 'islanders' – European settlers engaged as planters, administration officials, traders and missionaries – could be similarly employed, providing a service across the vital arc of islands to Australia's north.

It was never envisaged for the Coastwatchers to be called upon to operate in territory occupied by an enemy, or to take an active part in hostilities. The brief was to safely engage in passive observation.

Accordingly, in June 1923, Griffiths sent Brooksbank to join HMAS *Adelaide* on a five-week cruise to the Solomons where, accompanied by an experienced photographic surveyor, RAAF Flying Officer Ernest Mustar, nine anchorages and harbours were photographed and recorded in detail, as well as their potential to become seaplane bases. A second cruise by another RAN warship, HMAS *Brisbane*, undertook a similar mission to the large harbour of Rabaul on the island of New Britain, then the capital of New Guinea. The subsequent reports that would emanate from Brooksbank and the Naval Intelligence Division would be of invaluable use at the beginning of the Pacific War.

While in the Solomons, Brooksbank made initial forays into recruiting Coastwatchers from among the European community, and found many willing participants. Unlike on the Australian mainland, however, no telegraph service existed to disseminate information they might collect. The problem was partly solved by the issuing of a number of the recently invented pedal-powered radios, but these proved to be of limited success.

During peacetime, it was understood throughout the fledgling Coastwatcher system that sightings of 'suspicious' vessels would likely be rare. Even so, the network was put to good use reporting other nefarious activities such as the poaching of fishing grounds, smugglers, gun runners, drug traffickers and those seeking to enter the country illegally. In fact, any 'subversive behaviour' deemed to be unusual or suspicious by Coastwatchers was liable to be reported. The revival in Australian naval intelligence brought about by Griffiths and Brooksbank was not to last. Upon the termination of his three-year appointment in March 1923, Griffiths – no doubt relieved to be pulled from the bitter tangle that was Australian defence politics at the time – returned to England.

Despite an array of achievements – including the establishment of the beginnings of the Coastwatcher network; amassing a trove of useful intelligence regarding Australia's neighbours from New Guinea to New Caledonia; expanding the Naval Intelligence Division into new offices to undertake such work as the investigation of possible Communist cells within Australian naval ships and institutions; and the new Sydney branch being praised as 'a model example of a district Intelligence Centre' – Griffiths's position was abolished at the conclusion of his tenure. In 1923, the entire division lost its separate status within the Navy Office and was brought under the orbit of the Assistant Chief of Naval Staff back in Melbourne.

Australian naval intelligence would now go into hibernation for a decade and a half, during which time the staff numbers at the Department of Naval Intelligence would never exceed more than four people at any one time. Despite keen and qualified potential operators coming forward to volunteer their services, all had to be turned away.

As Eric Feldt observed in his seminal 1946 memoir, *The Coast Watchers*, 'Democracies neglect their fighting services in peace and pay for that neglect many times over when the disaster of war strikes them.'

Fortunately, one of those whose tenure survived was Walter Brooksbank, who busied himself producing intelligence handbooks on the regions he had visited. There was also the job of consolidating the Coastwatching organisation, which by 1928 constituted a network of around sixty people stretching in a long arc from Thursday Island and Port Moresby, east to Nauru and Port Vila.

It would not be until the very eve of World War II that the importance of intelligence would once again belatedly be appreciated, and a new head of intelligence would be appointed, the first since Griffiths's departure.

Rupert Basil Michel Long outwardly lacked the appearance of a typical intelligence commander. Long, or 'Cocky' as he was known, on account of the distinctive screech which rose in his voice when agitated, was cherubic in appearance, fond of entertaining and enjoyed a wide and influential social circle. Eric Feldt, who liked to pen vivid physical descriptions of the many people he encountered, noted Long as 'fattish … with a high, broad forehead and a small, thin-lipped mouth which was usually smiling'. Behind the deceptive charm of the bon vivant, however, was a brilliant mind, and Long's razor-sharp political acumen would eventually see him represent both MI5 and MI6 and earn the respect of intelligence communities the world over.

After brief service in World War I, Long was sent to England as a midshipman to undergo further training with the Royal Navy. For his lieutenant's course, he achieved the unheard-of maximum of five first-class certificates. He then studied the use and application of torpedoes, about which he became an acknowledged expert, and in 1934 was invited to apply for the prestigious staff course at the Royal Naval Staff College, Greenwich. This too he passed with flying colours. Rather than remain in England, Long applied for the position of Assistant Director of Naval Intelligence at naval HQ in St Kilda Road, Melbourne. The Navy Board – baffled as to why a rising star such as he would forgo an international career for this relatively minor position – were nevertheless delighted to hand him the job, particularly as no one else seemed to want it.

With the Naval Intelligence Division (NID) still a mere adjunct of the Assistant Chief of Naval Staff, Long found himself 'assistant' to no one at all. He soon discovered such a position could have its advantages. For years, he had nursed a burning ambition to unleash his prodigious intellect onto the field of naval intelligence, despite the fact that this would condemn him to spend the rest of his career as a lieutenant-commander, the highest rank the navy was prepared to attach to the position. But progressing up the naval career ladder was at the bottom of Long's list of priorities, particularly as he sensed war was just over the horizon.

Having previously served in the waters around China and other parts of the Far East, Long had read the tides of international affairs and was quietly certain that, despite the worsening situation in Europe, Australia's primary aggressor would soon be Japan and the fight would be much closer to home than anyone realised. Convincing his superiors of this threat was an uphill battle, and in the years before the war, Long and the NID struggled against lack of funding, lack of staff and lack of interest.

Despite this, he and Walter Brooksbank were anything but idle. Throughout the DNI's long winter, Brooksbank had been quietly buttressing the Coastwatching organisation from a few dozen operatives a decade earlier to nearly 800 by 1938. It still wasn't enough. Looking at the map of northern Australia and its surrounding islands, both men knew there were still gaping holes in the network, which they likened to a fence with several broken or missing gates, through which any aggressor could pass undetected.

There was also the grave problem of communication. Coastwatchers might gather the most important information imaginable, but none of it would be of any use if not conveyed, and quickly. Some, but by no means all, of the planters and other islanders were in possession of radios of their own, but there was no guarantee their signals would be picked up as far away as the Australian mainland. What was needed, Long realised, was a new intelligence station in Port Moresby where messages could be received and the entire organisation managed. Much of his pleadings for more resources fell on deaf ears.

In late 1938, a new Assistant Chief of Naval Staff and Director of Naval Intelligence was appointed in the figure of Captain John Collins, one of Australia's greatest naval commanders who also happened to have been in the Pioneer Class with Long and, luckily, a man who was prepared to listen. Upon briefing Collins, Long laid out in stark terms the problems facing the DNI. Collins was aghast, and promised to take the matter as far as he could.

By 1939, Collins's influence, as well as the international situation which everyone could now plainly see was deteriorating, finally resulted in more funding for the DNI, as well as its reinstatement as an independently functioning department. Now forced to cram many wasted years of work into a few months, Long immediately put the new resources towards the purchase of a strong and sturdy radio for each of his Coastwatchers operating outside the Australian mainland. The establishment of a new Naval Intelligence Centre in Port Moresby was, thankfully, granted.

In August, barely a week before the firing of the first shots of World War II, Collins was given an active command at sea, and Long named as his successor as director of the Department of Naval Intelligence.

Long knew there was precious little time to build up the Coastwatchers into an effective intelligence network. Even more importantly, he needed to find the right man to lead them.

# Chapter 3

# FELDT TAKES CHARGE

Eric Feldt paused and turned. Signalling with a slow wave of the flat blade of his machete, he urged the line of men behind him to be vigilant. His outward appearance of calm authority hid the cold dread in his veins. God knew what lay up ahead on this impossible mountain track for his little group of a dozen or so native police and a few local bearers who seemed to grow more nervous with every step. Sampson, Feldt's deputy and the man in charge of the police, caught whiff of the boss's tension and hissed at one of his men to stop talking.

For eight days now, they had trekked up into the mountains, through the Bulolo Valley, and then deeper into one of the most remote corners of one of the most inaccessible parts of the New Guinea highlands, the Upper Watut Valley. In March 1931, this was a place few outsiders had ever ventured, and for good reason. Of the many hundreds of New Guinea tribes, the Upper Watut was the domain of perhaps the most feared – even dreaded – tribe, one whose name struck fear into those living on the slopes below their inviolable mountain eyrie. Eric Feldt and his little party were entering the world of the Angu, though in this part of New Guinea they went by another name, rarely uttered, and then only in a tremulous whisper, *Kukukuku*.

Although rarely taller than 5 feet in stature, the Kukukuku were a New Guinea warrior tribe like no other. The Kukukuku pierced the septums of their noses with bone or bamboo and the men shaved their heads leaving only a top-knot from which a cloak of beaten bark – a *Mal* – hung to their knees. This not only protected them from the savage mountain winds and rain but could wrap around their entire body as camouflage. It was said to be almost impossible, even at close range, to detect a hidden Kukukuku waiting still in the jungle. With their bows and arrows, they were superb marksmen. Their primary weapon, however, was a stone axe, attached to a wristband and concealed behind their *Mal*, but which they could whip out in a flash to disembowel or crash down onto the skull of an enemy.

The Kukukuku were quick to anger, could kill suddenly and without apparent motive, and were entirely unpredictable. They were also one of the last of the true New Guinea headhunters, venturing out on raiding parties to surprise the inhabitants of a neighbouring village, whom they would kill at random then behead. After carrying off their macabre souvenirs, they would boil the heads down and decorate them as trophies.

The Australian and British administrations of New Guinea and the Solomons had done their best to stamp out the ancient headhunting practice and, by the 1930s, had been largely successful. But the Kukukuku were a different matter again. The discovery of gold had seen an influx of outsiders – particularly Europeans – into previously unknown parts of the country. A special permit was required to venture into the Upper Watut, and it was granted only to 'experienced men of good character'. One of those was Helmuth Baum, a German prospector for many years in New Guinea, who, at the beginning of World

War I, had vanished into the bush rather than surrender to the Australians, only to emerge again after the war. Baum claimed to have had friendly dealings with the Kukukuku, even occasionally trading with them. He loudly professed he held no fear of them.

In the mid-1930s, Baum and a party of eight native workers travelled through Kukukuku country in search of new gold-bearing deposits in the hills, but Baum was laid up for a few days in a nearby village with fever. In his vulnerable state, he was surprised by several Kukukuku warriors; all semblance of friendliness was dropped and Baum was clubbed to death in his bed. His native workers fled into the jungle but were all tracked down and killed.

In silence, sitting in his office at Wau, Feldt had listened as two breathless villagers recounted the news of the massacre – or what they had heard of it on the jungle grapevine. As warden, and an experienced district officer, Feldt knew that it would fall to him to take action, and that it would be by far his most dangerous undertaking in the more than ten years he had spent in New Guinea.

•

If, by the mid-1930s, Eric Feldt could no longer remember what it was that had inspired him, in 1923, to write to the then Minister of Home Affairs and Territories applying for 'any subordinate position offering' in New Guinea, he was even less certain as to why he had been accepted. A few weeks after his letter, he was onboard a ship bound for New Britain and the administrative capital of Rabaul to begin work as a junior clerk, the last to be accepted in an intake of ten.

Having never set foot in an office before, Feldt had no idea what he was doing, though took comfort in the fact that nobody else there did either. As it transpired, Feldt was at something of an advantage with the smattering of Pidgin English he already knew, and began applying himself to mastering this peculiar, hybrid language.

Despite its wide streets and relative comfort, Feldt disliked Rabaul and the petty snobberies of its closeted colonial society. He longed to venture off the island to the 'Territory' instead. Luckily, those at the lowest rungs of the administration could enter the patrol officer stream. From the get-go, Feldt was a natural fit.

In a short time, he found himself venturing up New Guinea's longest river, the mighty Sepik, in a small schooner with a Chinese engineer and four natives as part of an expedition to investigate tribal fighting that had broken out upstream.

For Feldt, this first trip was an eye-opener, introducing him to the magnificence of New Guinea, its beauty as well as its savagery. Over the next decade, he would rise through the ranks of the administration and be rewarded by being made *Kiap* – a Pidgin word derived from the German *Kapitan* – or simply patrol officer. He would contend with malaria, familiarise himself as best he could with the various strands of internecine tribal politics, be called upon to administer justice, conduct marriage ceremonies and dispense medical treatment for tropical diseases such as yaws, scrub typhus, and even the dreaded blackwater fever.

Feldt soon developed a calm and natural authority that would see him ascend to patrol officer, assistant district officer, district officer and on the eve of World War II, warden of the goldfield settlement of Wau. He would witness mystical mountain waterfalls so tall that their tops were permanently hidden in cloud, and the wonders of grass islands: vast floating sections of riverbank torn off by the mighty currents, still with upright trees and even animals attached. He was told a man could walk across one of these, but if he stopped his feet would sink straight through. He would be called upon to quell native wars, venturing deep into the jungle to administer the white man's laws. Once he saved a woman's life by gathering up her infant twins, placing one on each hip, and shielding her from a group of belligerent warriors from a neighbouring tribe, daring them to do their worst. They paused, lowered their spears and retreated back into the jungle.

When promoted to district officer, Feldt collected taxes and organised the census. In order to know the country and its people better, he spent more time than usual with the natives, even learning a handful of the more than 500 languages spread across every corner of New Guinea. Only rarely had he been required to withdraw from administering justice, such as when he was laying down the law to a warring hill tribe and instructed his native interpreter to explain that they were to stop fighting their neighbours immediately or face the consequences. The interpreter paused and surveyed the line of spear-wielding men before him. 'I'm not going to tell them that,' he said warily. Sensing weakness, the tribesmen advanced, and for once it was Feldt who had to beat a prudent retreat.

Despite this, nothing in his years as the face of order and law in New Guinea could prepare him for encountering the Kukukuku.

•

As the wary party made its way along the valley, the Kukukuku took to the hills, slapping their rumps in the time-honoured gesture of disrespect and defiance as they scrambled away. From somewhere, the deep-throated syncopation of the garamut – a native drum carved from a hollow log which, in skilful hands, could convey a message as complex as any letter – telegraphed their progress. There would be no element of surprise today, thought Feldt. Nor was he clear as to what he was expected to achieve. Reports on the attack on Baum indicated that several villages had been involved and Feldt was unlikely to discover which they were, let alone the individuals, nor how they would react to this risky display of authority. In his own mind though, his duty was clear:

> A District Officer has a further duty than the punishment of a single crime, however serious that crime may be. The country has to be brought under a rule of law, so that men may go about peacefully in the future. To walk away and do nothing would not bring that condition nearer.

Instead of being confronted, Feldt found a series of empty Kukukuku villages, the locals deciding to avoid punishment by hiding in the bush until the patrol's provisions were exhausted. Feldt ordered his men to forgo their rations and help themselves to the Kukukuku's village gardens instead. The garden was a New Guinea villager's most treasured possession and, after a few days, the Kukukuku – observing from the jungle – could no longer stand to watch their gardens being pillaged and slowly began to return.

When seven tribesmen turned up, Feldt ordered his men to arrest them immediately. When the other tribesmen returned, they were confronted with the sight of their fellow warriors in handcuffs, having apparently been overpowered by this mighty white warrior. Feldt's grand bluff had won. The next day the Kukukuku were led to Baum's campsite in the village where the killing had taken place and were made to re-enact what had happened. Through sign language, all denied their own involvement, but Feldt could see 'guilt in their eyes'.

Eventually, a small group of Kukukuku were jailed in Salamaua, any further punishment both pointless and counterproductive. Not many months later, they were released with a stern lecture, which seemed to keep the peace. Feldt's trek had lasted six weeks, at the end of which he had lost much of his body weight and was unrecognisable behind a bushy beard.

Bringing the Kukukuku to heel would be Feldt's magnum opus until the war began the most dramatic chapter of his life. In the middle of 1939 in his office at Wau, reading yet another headline concerning the deteriorating international situation, he pulled out a clean sheet of paper from his desk drawer and penned a letter to the Naval Board in Melbourne, stating that if they could find a use for him, he would be happy for his name to be transferred from the 'retired' to the 'emergency' list.

In August, with his new wife, Nan, Feldt travelled to Brisbane for some much-delayed long service leave. Stopping by a shoe shop one afternoon, he was pleased to find a pair sturdy enough for the harsh climate of New Guinea. As he left the shop, he caught notice of a newspaper poster announcing the signing of a non-aggression pact between Hitler and Stalin. Cursing quietly to himself, he knew that he would not be returning to Wau anytime soon.

•

In Melbourne, the new Director of Naval Intelligence, Lieutenant-Commander 'Cocky' Long, had to look twice at the name on the latest naval emergency list, then slapped his desk with glee, not quite daring to hope that his luck might be starting to turn. Now, finally, he had found the man he had been looking for, his old classmate from the original Pioneer Class of the Royal Australian Navy, Eric Feldt. Not only did

Feldt know New Guinea, its islands and its people, but he was also familiar with that very particular community of European 'islanders' who had made the tropics their home, and who would form the core of the Coastwatcher organisation. 'Eric Feldt!' Long repeated to himself.

Though Feldt's and Long's careers may have diverged over the years, they were now destined to come together in the gravest hour of their country's need. Further enquiries revealed more good fortune, in that Feldt was reported to currently be visiting Brisbane. His digs were quickly located, phone calls were made, and a telegram dispatched advising him that the navy had accepted his offer to rejoin their ranks and could he kindly report to Naval HQ in Melbourne as soon as possible.

On 8 September 1939, with the war less than a week old, the two former navy classmates were reunited in an office behind the imposing bluestone edifice of Melbourne's Victoria Barracks. With a warm handshake, Long greeted his old friend with his customary 'Have a cigarette, old boy', before Long and Brooksbank laid out the Coastwatcher system, its development over the past twenty years, and the gaping holes which urgently had to be filled by new operatives, who, he added, had yet to be found. 'Yes,' admitted Long with a heavy sigh, anticipating Feldt's reaction, 'all this should have been sorted out years ago but … well, here we are.'

All agreed that the conflict would not be contained to Europe, and that Japan would at some stage launch its bid to build a Pacific empire by force. Long outlined the importance of the civilian-based information-gathering Coastwatcher network to the north, and indicated how it was woefully incomplete and that any enemy could currently approach Australia almost without fear of discovery. His vision, he told Feldt, was for the chain to be complete, and the gate to Australia closed. He confessed though to having little idea how to bring that vision to fruition. 'That, old boy,' he said to Feldt, 'is where you come in.'

Indicating what he was about to say was strictly 'hush-hush', Long revealed that a new intelligence office was being established in Moresby which, in all likelihood, would become a vital link in the defence chain north of Australia in the event of war. He believed Feldt was the perfect man to set it up. Reporting directly to Long, Feldt would be charged with recruiting as many new Coastwatchers as he could find to plug the holes and 'close the gate'.

There was more. Feldt was not only being asked to expand the network but to run it as he saw fit. If he accepted, he would be appointed Moresby intelligence staff officer with the rank of lieutenant-commander. As Long spoke, casually sitting on the edge of his desk, cigarette in hand, Feldt became aware of the weight of the responsibility being slowly lowered onto his shoulders. He was being asked to set up and command a large and complex intelligence organisation – as yet nebulous and incomplete – stretching thousands of miles across Papua, New Guinea and the Solomon Islands, through some of the most undeveloped areas on earth, in which there was no telegraph, not a single rail track and less than 500 miles of useable roads.

He agreed at once.

As Long later reflected, 'Eric was the logical – but nonetheless inspired – choice for this pressing task.'

A few days later the Coastwatcher organisation was ordered to commence functioning.

# Chapter 4
# THE FAR-REACHING NETWORK

In September 1939, three weeks after his first meeting with his old friend – now his boss – Rupert Long in Australia, Feldt had travelled by plane to Port Moresby. After barely an hour's inspection of the beginnings of what was to become the navy's new intelligence centre as well as his own HQ, Feldt boarded another plane which took him on to his old stomping ground of Rabaul. Here he would begin a whirlwind mission that would span hundreds of miles of tropics to enlist every man capable of performing the role of Coastwatcher, especially those already in possession of a radio. It was a daunting task, underlined with the urgency that the war currently raging in faraway Poland would one day reach these peaceful islands and possibly Australia itself.

The administrator in Rabaul, Sir Walter McNicoll, possibly sensing his vulnerability far out into the Pacific, received Feldt warmly and promised every assistance. He was good for his word. McNicoll provided a Chinese schooner, the *Magau*, and its crew, enabling Feldt to reach New Britain's even less developed neighbour, New Ireland. Arriving at Lambu on the island's west coast, he visited and signed up several plantation owners, before taking a truck as far as the rough island roads would allow. Then he got out and walked. 'Taking a sheaf of printed coastwatching instructions with me,' Feldt wrote later, 'I set out to visit every man who had a Teleradio, to teach him how to code in Playfair, to tell him what to report.'

Having been allotted a parsimonious 200 pounds by Long for the entire venture, Feldt nonetheless had reason to thank Walter Brooksbank, whose instructive *Coastwatchers Guide* was handed out liberally. Accompanying this was a further set of guidelines regarding the language that Feldt had chosen as the Coastwatchers' means of communication, the Playfair cipher, a nearly century-old manual encryption technique based on substituted letter combinations or 'bigrams', which was familiar to many schoolchildren of the time. Today, a computer could break Playfair in microseconds, but in 1939, this low-grade code could be easily learned and required no equipment except a list of agreed keywords and pencil and paper. Feldt developed his own 'Playfair-Feldt' variation to increase the code's security and speed. Because speed, as Feldt was at pains to point out to every Coastwatcher he enrolled, would be of the absolute essence.

On New Ireland, Feldt somehow acquired a bicycle on which he completed a 25-mile journey the first day, followed by a slightly longer one the next to the town of Namatanai on the island's east coast. He then managed to borrow a car – or possibly even hitched – to New Ireland's far northern tip, again stopping at various plantations and missions along the way. Here, he was given use of another vessel, the MV *Leander*, to take him to Pak and Manus islands, far out in the Bismarck Sea.

Everywhere he could, Feldt enlisted civilians by meeting them personally and impressing upon them the simple yet vital role they had to play in the coming defence of Australia. 'Throughout,' he observed later, 'personal contact was of greater importance than the official relationship.' Many were friends or acquaintances from his time in New Guinea, happy to see him once again, albeit as a man reinvented, and on the most urgent of missions. Property and plantation owners, customs officials, missionaries and several district officers from his former life were all sought out. Almost all agreed to become part of his Coastwatcher scheme and were signed up there and then before swearing the oath that Feldt had printed and ready. He even worked his powers of persuasion on the captain of the *Leander*, managing to sign him up while he was his passenger.

'My travels took me all around the area by ship, motor boat and canoe, boot, bicycle and aeroplane, so that I saw nearly everybody, and nearly everybody saw me.' He signed up Coastwatchers at the Maka Island group and Ulawa Island, then it was east to Bougainville and south through the Solomons, where he signed up Coastwatchers in the towns of Numa Numa, Kieta and Buka. At no time did Feldt attempt to hide the dangers of what his Coastwatchers were signing up for. When asked by one candidate if there were any special benefits which went with the duty, Feldt's answer was blunt. 'The only thing I can promise you,' he said, 'is the promise of certain peril.'

Only once was he forced to turn back, when trying to reach Vanikoro, an outlying island of the Solomons on a vessel the acting resident commissioner, a Mr Johnson, had lent him for the purpose. 'A raging south-easter' rose up, blew bitterly for twenty-eight hours, and created seas savage enough to stove in the ship's port bulwarks, forcing them to shelter at San Cristobal. Running low on fuel, Feldt reluctantly agreed to turn around.

Aside from collecting Coastwatchers, Feldt took the opportunity to gather information. Much of it confirmed his and Long's belief that the islands were being prepared as a future war zone. Already reports of 'strange ships and aircraft' sighted off New Ireland and the Admiralty Islands were filtering through. Then there was the schooner *Edith*, whose Japanese captain, supposedly a trochus fisherman, brought in suspiciously small amounts of shell while spending extended periods in various ports from where letters were regularly mailed back to an address very close to the Imperial Naval Headquarters in Tokyo.

There was also the 8000-ton passenger-cargo vessel *Takaichiho Maru*, which ran regular trips between the Marshall Islands, Rabaul and Port Moresby but never seemed to be carrying many passengers and never loaded more than a handful of freight. 'Inference was clear that she ran only to keep account of our developments,' said Feldt.

The principal means of communication for the Coastwatchers would necessarily be via personal radio sets but Feldt found the distribution of these to be patchy, and many potential Coastwatchers, though equipped with copies of the *Coastwatchers Guide*, lacked the means to report their observations. Instead, they would need to rely on native runners to deliver information to the nearest radio by hand, which might be days away.

Upon returning to Port Moresby, Feldt reported to Long that he had travelled '600 miles by sea, 200 miles by car and about 90 miles on foot or bicycle'. The uptake had been high, and he expressed confidence his new Coastwatchers would quickly become proficient with his adapted Playfair cipher.

While many of the holes in the chain could now be plugged, a nearly 120-mile gap of clear Pacific Ocean between the southern tip of the long island of New Ireland and Buka, the northernmost island of the Solomons, was of grave concern. This, believed Feldt, was a potential Achilles heel, through which enemy vessels and aircraft could pass unnoticed. Only two small island groups existed in the gap, the Anir, or 'Feni' Islands, and the Green Islands, a series of atolls with tiny Nissan Island at its centre. 'Without observers on these islands,' wrote Feldt, 'our island screen was like a fence with the gate open.' These isolated specks of volcanic basalt and limestone on the one hand, and flat sandy atolls on the other, were undoubtedly some of the loneliest spots on earth but of enormous strategic importance. As luck would have it, a former plantation manager, C. C. Jervis, was in place with a Teleradio on Nissan, but as volcanic Anir was closer to the preferred navigational routes for both ships and aircraft, that too would need a watcher. For this lonely task, Feldt chose the first of what would become many men recruited into the Coastwatchers from the military, Chief Yeoman of Signals Stephen Lamont, an old sailor and, according to Feldt, 'as Irish as Paddy's pig'. He was a complete stranger to conditions on an isolated island, but 'a resourceful and dependable man'. After some rudimentary training, Lamont was dropped at Anir with a radio and left to himself.

Having exhausted all other means of transport, Feldt then took to the air to gain a greater understanding of the Coastwatchers' territory and to test their efficacy. Signalling his watchers to take particular note of any unusual aerial activity, he lifted off the surface of Rabaul harbour in a flying boat, then headed southwest on a course that took him over Anir, then down the passage of water between the double island chain which forms the Solomons. Passing over Gizo, Gaisi and Kieta, Feldt could not possibly have imagined the scale of destruction soon to be unleashed upon these pleasant tropical havens.

By the time he had landed at the capital of the British Solomon Islands, Tulagi, he was pleased to learn that his presence – including the speed, height and type of aircraft –

had already been accurately reported by several of his new Coastwatchers.

However, upon returning to Port Moresby, Feldt bluntly informed Long that, despite his success in recruiting, considerably more resources would be needed for the Coastwatchers to operate effectively. More people were required and the policy of relying on islanders already in possession of a radio was not sufficient. More radios and other equipment had to be purchased and delivered to men operating from some of the remotest places on earth. He also dropped a bombshell that would create a serious headache for Long.

Though old friends, the respective personalities of Long and Feldt could not have been more different. Long was a diplomat, whose softly-softly modus operandi relied on tact, influence and persuasion. Feldt, by contrast, was intense, driven, hated 'chair polishers', and was forthright to the point of bluntness. Long was becoming used to Feldt's directness, but was still shocked by what he now proposed.

It was all very well, he argued, to compel civilians to gather and disseminate military intelligence in peacetime, but should they be overrun and their territory occupied by an enemy, they would be regarded simply as spies with no protection from the government they served. And captured spies in wartime – Long needed no reminding – lived very short lives indeed. If, however, they were brought into the armed forces – even notionally – some protection may be afforded them. Feldt proposed that every one of his Coastwatcher civilians be given an immediate commission as an officer in the Royal Australian Navy.

While Long agreed, he knew that a service as imbued with tradition as the navy would be loath to simply hand out commissions – no matter how worthy the recipients – and rated Feldt's chances as practically nil. Nonetheless, it was a battle he was prepared to take up, suspecting it would be long and hard fought.

Securing new radios was only marginally less difficult, but Long pressed the men of the Naval Board to find the budget from somewhere, despite them failing to see the point of bolstering the Pacific when war was raging in Europe. Long secured funding for a further eighteen brand new Teleradios to be distributed through New Guinea, the Solomons and the New Hebrides.

To today's eyes, the AWA Teleradio 3B transmitter/receiver appears to be the most cumbersome of communication dinosaurs, yet this most unlikely piece of equipment would become synonymous with the Coastwatchers' operations throughout the Pacific War.

Amalgamated Wireless (Australasia) Ltd (AWA) had formed as a fusion of the Marconi and Telefunken interests in Australia in 1913 and had been taken over with a 51 per cent share by the Australian government in 1923 to provide wireless service across Australia and into the new Mandated Territory of New Guinea. This development proved a fortunate one, enabling the islands to be connected by a series of radios manufactured by AWA dubbed 'Teleradio'. The first of these sturdy units was introduced in 1935 as the Teleradio Series 1, and featured the typical Bakelite housing of the day, but by 1940 the radically redesigned 3B model was released, originally developed for use with the Australian Flying Doctor Service over the long distances of the Australian outback. They would be equally effective in the islands.

The revolutionary 3B model dispensed with the Bakelite, instead encasing the workings inside three pressed steel boxes each measuring 1 foot by 1 foot and 2 feet long. In these were housed the receiver, a transmitter and loudspeaker held in place by new quick-release steel spring clips. They featured rounded corners and were sealed to hold back the inevitable tropical moisture and humidity. There was also a small Briggs & Stratton petrol-driven engine plus generator for recharging the power supply of two 6-volt batteries linked in series for 12 volts. Add to this the standard 200 feet of aerial cable, an Ericsson headset, Morse code key, microphone, spares and various other bits and pieces.

The 3B covered the 0.2 to 30 megahertz wavelength over four crystal-controlled transmission frequencies which could be tuned to incredible accuracy via a slow-motion tuning wheel. In reasonable daytime conditions it could transmit a voice signal up to 400 miles and throw a Morse signal up to 600 miles. It was also given an extra, specially cut crystal allowing it to broadcast over a fifth, 'secret', channel, dramatically dubbed 'Frequency X'. This rarely used frequency proved highly difficult to detect, as the Japanese would later discover when they feverishly scanned the airwaves, searching in vain for the Coastwatchers' signal.

Unsurprisingly, the main drawback with the 3B was its gargantuan size. The charging engine on its own weighed over 66 pounds, and this was not even the heaviest item, those being the two wet cell batteries – each as large as car batteries – which together weighed 100 pounds. The fuel, aerial, power cables and ancillary equipment brought the entire weight of the set to between 285 and 330 pounds. It took time to assemble and reassemble, and when Coastwatchers had to relocate to avoid capture by the enemy, between twelve and sixteen native bearers were required to transport it. The charging engine was also noisy, and often had to be partially buried in pits then covered with banana leaves and other debris to muffle the sound, which could carry easily through a quiet jungle. The engine also devoured oil and benzine fuel, which had to be carried, and every Coastwatcher needed to become quickly adept in administering maintenance, as well as learning each Teleradio's individual foibles.

Nor were the casing clips as effective at keeping out the rain and moisture as the large instruction book would suggest, and many times Coastwatchers would remove the cases to dry out the workings.

At the beginning of the war, the 3B's lack of portability remained moot, as not even Feldt could envisage that the radios would need to be frequently disassembled and hauled across the hills and jungles of the Solomons and New Guinea, often in desperate haste, with an enemy in pursuit.

Thanks to AWA's government-given monopoly, the 3B became the standard set among those islanders lucky enough to possess any kind of radio, though many of these were not owned but leased from AWA.

In July 1940, with the war situation resulting in a collapse of the price of copra, many of the islander plantation owners suddenly faced bankruptcy, and were preparing to abandon both their properties as well as their roles as Coastwatchers. Aghast, Feldt begged of Long a further favour, naming seventeen stations facing collapse without financial support. Long's persuasive powers once again carried the day, and the farmers were given a monthly stipend of 15 pounds, apparently enough to stave off bankruptcy as well as disaster for the fragile Coastwatcher network. Still others gave notice that they could no longer afford AWA's hefty annual leasing fee of 30 pounds per radio. The persuasive Long appealed to the head of AWA personally, who directed that all leasing payments from New Guinea and the Solomons be suspended for the duration of the war.

Feldt's unwavering dedication to the program in the islands, combined with Long's unquestioning support back in Melbourne, established the Coastwatchers on a solid footing when they were needed most – at the beginning of the war with Japan. But even Long's charm could not shield him from the jealousies – even scorn – from other branches of the service who were also scrambling for resources.

Some of Long's friends were at pains to understand why he was being allocated funds and equipment for a 'scheme for civilians with little wireless sets and a schoolboy cipher' in a part of the world not even at war, when blood was being shed battling the Germans and Italians in the Atlantic and Mediterranean. In some cases, friends turned into 'highly placed personal enemies'.

As efficient as the Teleradio was, its signal could not always be relied upon to reach the Australian mainland, so receiver stations manned by members of the Royal Australian Navy were set up at Rabaul, Tulagi Harbour and Port Moresby, from where information would be relayed to Townsville. Each Coastwatcher would be given a special 'key' or series of coded letters to mark their identity, and be required to report at specific times. These 'schedules' quickly devolved to the universal term, 'skeds'.

All intelligence systems are only ever as good as the quality of information they provide, and for the first part of the war, the Coastwatchers – with little to report – were held in low regard by many sections of the Royal Australian Navy who viewed any kind of civilian participation as interference. After December 1941, however, the Coastwatchers' regular skeds proved so accurate and reliable, they quickly acquired 'a gilt-edged reputation'. Henceforth, all Coastwatcher reports were automatically granted the highest level of importance, the information 'qualified only by any doubts which the watcher himself expressed'.

Granting the Coastwatchers the protection of an officer's rank was another matter entirely. The navy left it up to the

Coastwatchers themselves to decide whether to continue broadcasting if and when their territory was overrun by the enemy.

This mixed and disingenuous message freed the navy of the odious task of handing out officer commissions to civilians, but slyly relied on people's sense of duty to continue operating in the face of danger. Vague rumblings about support, recognition – even pensions – were made, but the navy took great care to avoid anything that might be interpreted as a commitment. It is a sobering testament to the Coastwatchers' fortitude that, when the Japanese came, almost all elected to keep broadcasting, even though many would pay with their lives for doing so.

## Chapter 5

# WAITING FOR WAR

By mid-1941, Eric Feldt's work was as complete as it could be. His Coastwatcher organisation had grown to 100 individual operators placed strategically along a 2500-mile arc stretching from the western border of Australian New Guinea to Vila in the New Hebrides. Having been granted permission to extend the scheme beyond its original parameters of New Guinea, Feldt had, in just a few months, placed eight Teleradio stations in the Solomons, two on Bougainville (belonging to New Guinea but geographically part of the Solomons), one in the New Guinea Central Highlands and three on the island of Guadalcanal.

As proud of the organisation as he was, Feldt was at pains never to describe it as an active military force or even guerrilla army. As far as he was concerned, the Coastwatchers were to adhere strictly to the principles along which they had been established, that of passive observers. Hence, they were given no training in weapons handling, combat or tactics and were expected, as their name implied, to sit and watch. To emphasise his point, Feldt coined a new descriptor for the organisation, borrowing from, of all things, a children's book and cartoon. In

1938, Walt Disney had released an animation based on the story of Ferdinand, the peace-loving bull who preferred to sit under a tree and smell the flowers rather than fight. Hence, 'Ferdinand' would be the codeword of the entire Coastwatcher organisation.

There was no 'frivolous purpose' behind Feldt's choice, as he pointed out:

> Besides serving as one of its cloaks of secrecy, this name was an order to the coastwatchers; a definition of their job. It was a reminder to them that it was not their duty to fight, and thus draw attention to themselves; like Disney's bull who just sat under a tree and smelled the flowers, it was their duty to sit, circumspectly and unobtrusively, and gather information. Of course, like Ferdinand, they could fight if they were stung.

As the war went on, occasions would emerge when Coastwatchers indeed were forced to sting, and sting hard.

Having devoted such energy into readying the Coastwatchers for hostilities, for Feldt and Long the extended silence emanating from Japan throughout 1940 and 1941 proved somewhat of an anti-climax. The Coastwatchers' first test therefore would involve not Japan but Germany.

In December 1940, two German 'auxiliary cruisers', *Komet* and *Orion*, caused several weeks of mayhem. They sunk five phosphate-laden merchant ships on 27 December then opened fire on loading facilities at Nauru's port, before going on to encounter and sink the *Rangitane*, a New Zealand passenger liner of 17 000 tons bound for Britain.

Between them, the *Orion* and *Komet* had acquired around 500 prisoners from the passengers and crews of the ships they had sunk. Unable to take them back to Germany, the captains chose the little island of Emirau to offload them, away, it was thought, from the prying eyes of the Australian navy. No sooner had the prisoners been released onto the island than one of them found a small boat and sailed more than 80 miles southeast to Kavieng on New Ireland, where he informed the district officer – also a Coastwatcher – who radioed in his first live 'sked'. The marooned passengers and crew were promptly collected, as was a trove of information concerning the raiders, their appearance, armament and tactics, as well as the reconstruction of the routes they had followed.

'This gave the Coastwatchers some real practice,' wrote Feldt. 'With the arrival of the refugees in an Australian port, the coastwatchers settled down to waiting again, now with a feeling that they had a real role to play.'

As the first months of 1941 came and went, the rising crescendo of destruction in Europe stood as stark contrast to the peace of the idyllic Pacific. Privately, Feldt and Long began to question whether Japan intended to enter the conflict at all, having failed to act on earlier pretexts to commence hostilities. In December, therefore, the news of Pearl Harbor struck Feldt 'with just as much surprise as it did to the best informed in the United Nations'.

By the beginning of the Pacific War, the Coastwatchers were still a tiny organisation numbering a few hundred civilians and military personnel, as well as a small number of administrators both in the field and at receiving centres, handling the flow of information and organising supplies. They would, however, achieve results in stratospheric excess of their modest numbers.

Despite the passivity inherent in Feldt's edict of 'Ferdinand', this handful of civilian spies would deliver intelligence that would directly influence military actions, save the lives of dozens of stranded airmen, sailors and civilians, and provide invaluable and otherwise unobtainable information regarding enemy plans, numbers and dispositions. And all of this would be achieved under the noses of the enemy who, the entire war, remained utterly ignorant of the Coastwatchers' impact on their ambitions.

The very term 'Coastwatcher' has endured as something of a misnomer, obscuring the true scope and nature of their activities. They were, in fact, a tiny band of supreme spies, operating in dangerous and often unbearable conditions.

From their isolated mountain or treetop hideouts, or damp makeshift camps hidden deep in the jungle, they would also battle disease and malnutrition, and suffer tropical rainstorms, heat and a relentless enervating humidity. Canvas shoes would rot on their feet, paper would turn sodden and impossible to write on if left out. Mildew would form on a shirt if left on the jungle floor for even a day. The Coastwatchers would battle loneliness, near starvation, as well as countless hours of boredom, made worse by the nagging uncertainty that their efforts were serving any real purpose to the war effort.

But when a native runner burst into their concealed jungle or mountain camp with news that patrolling Japanese were mere minutes behind, that boredom would switch to a gripping terror. Then the scramble to evacuate: break down the radio to its portable parts, gather the most meagre of necessities, and vanish once again into the hills or jungle, certain in the knowledge that capture would mean torture and death.

Nor were the allegiances of the native people always to be relied upon. Many, particularly in New Guinea, had little love for their colonial overlords and sided openly with the Japanese. Others purported to be friends of the Allies but switched their loyalties and would lead, and in some cases capture and deliver, Coastwatchers into the hands of the enemy. Although in most cases an indelible relationship between native and Coastwatcher was formed.

As Feldt knew from his time in New Guinea, the Coastwatcher organisation would be utterly ineffective without the cooperation of extensive networks of the native population. The Coastwatchers relied on them utterly to carry equipment, supply food, deliver news and messages, and act as lookouts for nefarious and unpredictable actions of the Japanese. Many displayed a loyalty and courage that defies description, and some would make the ultimate sacrifice. All the more remarkable considering it was on their ancient lands that two strange and foreign peoples battled for causes that would never be their own.

The Coastwatchers' story would be one of clandestine submarine drops and midnight embarkations from hidden stretches of beach in the middle of the night; of perilous treks across unforgiving mountain ridgebacks; of downed airmen and shipwrecked sailors who, having lost all hope of surviving their ordeal, were suddenly plucked from the tiny, deserted atoll upon which they had been washed up and spirited back to safety. One marooned American sailor granted just such a second life would go on to become the most powerful man in the world.

It is the story of men gazing down from a rocky mountain eyrie onto what yesterday had been a lonely stretch of beach, witnessing it being invaded by a thousand ships of one of the greatest armed forces on earth.

It is the story of a man looking up from a damp jungle floor to count a formation of enemy bombers heading south, then transmitting a four-word message that, 300 miles away, would spare scores of lives and turn the course of a battle.

It is the story of skin-of-teeth escapes such as that of Keith McCarthy on New Britain, and cryptic final messages such as 'Unknown ship stopping at lagoon entrance' delivered in haste by C. C. Jervis on Nissan Island before he vanished forever.

Above all, it is the story of a small group of men who, in the hour of their country's greatest peril, chose not to flee but to turn and face the enemy.

To the nation they served, however, they remain – now as they did then – almost completely unknown.

# Chapter 6
# THE COLLAPSE

At 5 a.m. on 20 January 1942, a unique ceremony took place onboard the Japanese transport *Yokohama Maru* as it steamed on a southerly course from Apra Harbor, in the newly conquered US island territory of Guam. From their stifling holds below, several hundred Japanese soldiers, fully armed and equipped, were ordered to assemble on the ship's upper deck to be addressed by their commanding officer. Standing rigidly to attention as the dawn light slowly revealed a glassily calm Pacific Ocean, the men were told that it would be their honour this day to write a glorious new chapter in their country's history as the first Japanese army in 2600 years to cross the line of the equator into the Southern Hemisphere. 'We will now pay our respects towards the Imperial Palace,' the officer decreed, as the men solemnly presented arms towards the north. Despite years of brutal and dehumanising military training under a Japanese military code designed to extinguish every vestige of individuality, for some the emotion of the moment was overwhelming. As men bowed low in the direction of their beloved Emperor, their tears watered the decks of the old steamer.

Nor was the ceremony unique to this vessel. Close by in the surrounding waters, nine similar ships comprising the South Seas Transport Fleet also made south towards the line. In their holds were a further 5000 men, as well as thousands of tons of vehicles, fuel, ammunition and equipment. There were even a thousand or so horses still in use during this early stage of Japan's Pacific conquest, before the realities of modern warfare rendered their use entirely ludicrous. Soon the Japanese soldiers would be met by an armada of escorting warships, including nine destroyers and two mine-layers. Three days later, just prior to their arrival at their destination, they would be joined by an even greater force comprising four of the six aircraft carriers which had taken part in the Pearl Harbor attack, *Akagi*, *Kaga*, *Zuikaku* and *Shokaku*, which between them carried over 200 combat aircraft. There would also be battleships and cruisers, and even a detachment of submarines scouting ahead for such ships of the Allied navy as might attempt to interdict the Japanese fleet. Their search would be in vain. The great invasion force of what was dubbed 'Operation R' would arrive at its destination, Rabaul, completely unmolested.

Less than six weeks earlier, on 9 December, just two days after the attack on Pearl Harbor, the first Coastwatcher report of the Pacific War was recorded when Cornelius (Con) Page looked up from his station on little Tabar Island, just off New Ireland, 80 miles north of Rabaul, and saw a single aircraft flying due south, crossing New Ireland on a course for Rabaul. He immediately reported his observation which, on this occasion, proved to be a reconnaissance flight. Observing the dark red Japanese circle on the underside of the wing, Page felt decidedly uneasy and knew it to be a precursor of far worse to come.

Like Page, the people of Rabaul had also looked up with foreboding to the sight of Japanese aircraft ranging across their skies. As Japan's juggernaut began its unstoppable plunge down the Malay Peninsula, foreboding was replaced by dread. Two years earlier, a volcanic eruption had devastated much of the old German-built colonial town with its pleasant wide streets, bungalows and large shady European trees. Now, in hindsight, that disaster appeared as a harbinger to another.

In late December, much of the civilian population of Rabaul, including all the women and children, were evacuated onboard the liners *Neptuna* and *Macdhui*, a favour that was not extended to Rabaul's Chinese population, many of whom had lived and worked there for years. The cruelty of the decision, based purely on race, not only rankled bitterly with the Chinese but was self-defeating, as many of them would have been more than willing to take up arms as guerrillas against the hated Japanese. Instead, they were forced to stay behind in makeshift camps to look after their families.

Those who remained at Rabaul as the last shipload of refugees sailed out of Simpson Harbour looked with hope but little certainty towards the young men of Lark Force who had been sent to protect them.

Despite the passage of eighty years, the 1942 disaster of Rabaul remains a painful and still rarely discussed chapter in Australia's history, a story of ignorance, arrogance, official incompetence verging (some historians have argued) on the criminal, all of which combined to cast a stain on Australia's largely proud military heritage. And all of it was avoidable.

With its fine, deep harbour, and strategic proximity to northern New Guinea and the Solomons, it was clear to anyone in possession of a map that Rabaul was essential to the Japanese. It would be the hub of the outer rim of their new Asian empire. In the first week of the war, the Japanese were established in Hong Kong, Malaya and the Philippines. On 17 December, they took North Borneo and all its major settlements virtually without a fight. Logic dictated that Rabaul would be the next major step. To defend it, Australia sent a token force, too large to act as a guerrilla army, but too small to have any hope of success. It was, in short, a deliberate and calculated sacrifice.

Raised around Melbourne and the central Victorian highlands, the 2/22nd Battalion wore with pride the two purple and red triangles formed into a diamond on their shoulder, the same colour patch which had served the original 22nd Battalion on the Western Front during World War I. Some of those older veterans had even come to address their young successors during training, instilling in them the pride which had carried the unit from Gallipoli to the Hindenburg Line. Believing they too would be headed for Europe or the Middle East, the 900 men were bewildered when their three-troopship flotilla departed the heads of Sydney Harbour in April 1941 and turned not south, but north, and they were issued with tropical kit. Only when the ships were well underway were the men told they were headed for the island of New Britain in Australia's Mandated Territory of New Guinea, where their job would be to garrison the town, harbour and airfield. Here, they would form the main part of a roughly 1400-man composite force consisting of themselves, an anti-aircraft and anti-tank battery, engineers, field ambulance et cetera, which together would be known as Lark Force. The men listened to their officers and sergeants in silence. Most of them could barely place New Guinea on a map, and almost none of them had heard of Rabaul.

In their tropical camp in the months prior to Japan's entry into the war, the men of Lark Force might have expected to have been kept busy training in such matters as jungle warfare and tactics, or at the very least to have been given a chance to reconnoitre the large island of New Britain to familiarise themselves with its coastline and rivers, its tracks and ridges.

They may also have hoped to have been given some rudimentary instruction on how to survive in the jungle or at least learn to trade with the many native people for food, and perhaps even learn a few phrases of Pidgin. None of this occurred. In four months, Lark Force did very little in Rabaul except march around a parade ground, huddle around its town and harbour and two airfields, or observe the artillery men practising on the two 6-inch guns belatedly installed overlooking the approaches, one of which had already been rendered useless with a cracked breech block.

A newly commissioned lieutenant, Mick Smith, would in later life disclose to historian Patrick Lindsay, 'It became apparent to me, even with my limited experience, that our training wasn't good enough.'

The situation was in no way helped in October, by the appointment of Lark Force's new commander, Lieutenant-Colonel John Joseph Scanlan. Although a decorated Western Front veteran, Scanlan arrived at Rabaul nursing the delusion that this war would be a continuation of the last and began preparing for a long static war he imagined would be fought in trenches. Instead of addressing what he saw to be a lack of morale among his entirely green men by training them to the conditions, he simply parroted the order which had been cynically decreed in faraway Melbourne, that 'there shall be no faint hearts, no thought of surrender, every man shall die in his pit'.

When senior officers suggested that potential escape routes be explored, or perhaps food and supply dumps be set up inland in case of a need to withdraw, they were charged with being 'defeatist'. An offer by Keith McCarthy, Assistant District Officer at Talasea, to give the men some experience in jungle bivouacs was likewise angrily rebuffed. 'That is a defeatist attitude,' roared Scanlan to anyone who dared question his edict that even a tactical retreat was unthinkable. 'There shall be no withdrawal!' he reiterated, at once removing hope and replacing it with nothing whatsoever.

The truth was harsher still. In August 1941, a 'Most Secret' memo sent to the Minister of Defence admitted that Lark Force would most likely be unable to withstand any serious Japanese attack, in which case, 'it would not be possible to send further land forces'. Then the sober admission, '… to make Rabaul secure against any reasonably possible scale of attack would require a scale of defence beyond our present resources of materiel and probably manpower'. Thus, as far as Chiefs of the General Staff were concerned, four months before the first shots of the Pacific conflict were fired, the men of Lark Force had already been written off.

One man who had a strong sense of the true situation, as well as the prospects of Rabaul being able to withstand a Japanese invasion, was yet another of Eric Feldt's Pioneer Class naval mates, Lieutenant Hugh Alexander Mackenzie. In a career mirroring that of Feldt, Mackenzie had likewise decided to try his luck in New Guinea after service in World War I, and had done well for himself. But it would take a court case for him and his old friend Feldt to become reacquainted in the early 1930s. Owner of a copra plantation near Talasea on New Britain, Mackenzie had been caught overloading his small schooner with workers he had hired and brought over from surrounding islands. Hauled before the local magistrate, his surprise – and possibly his shame – was palpable when he discovered this to be his old pal, Eric Feldt. After ascertaining that the workers had not actually suffered, Feldt nonetheless felt obliged to fine Mackenzie, settling on a figure of 30 pounds, the cost of what would have been an extra trip for Mackenzie anyway. After the proceedings, magistrate and defendant retired to discuss complex legal matters over several beers at a local hotel.

When the war came, Lieutenant-Commander Long decided to streamline naval and air force administrations in Australia's north into a single unit, the Area Combined Headquarters, centred in Port Moresby, which would require a permanent naval intelligence officer who, among other duties, would assist Eric Feldt, particularly during his many absences establishing the Coastwatcher network. For the role, Long enquired whether Hugh Mackenzie would do. 'Would Hugh Mackenzie do?' shot back a delighted Feldt, who thought Long's suggestion of their old mutual friend 'far beyond anyone I could hope for'.

Mackenzie would not remain long at Port Moresby, as his experience of the islands better suited him to the looming danger at Rabaul. But if he had welcomed being posted back to his old stomping ground, he was quickly sobered by the parlous state of affairs that greeted him upon his arrival there in late 1941.

•

On the morning of 4 January, a clear and cloudless Sunday, Con Page once again had cause to look up from his Coastwatcher position amid the coconut groves of his plantation on Tabar. This time it was apparent that the aircraft forming a perfect V and making for Rabaul were on no reconnaissance trip. Willing his Teleradio to warm up quickly, he adopted the standard protocol for reporting aircraft, and he broadcast in plain voice that Japanese bombers were on their way. Page's warning proved ample and timely, giving half an hour's notice of the impending attack. At precisely 11 a.m. Rabaul's air-raid sirens wailed in deadly earnest, and the anti-aircraft gunners nervously scanned the northern skies.

'Can we really fire this time?' said one excited young gunner to the battery commander.

'Too right we can,' he replied, 'but for heaven's sake shut up. This is a war not a Sunday School picnic.'

The gunners opened fire with their two 3-inch heavy anti-aircraft guns, and while impressed at the noise and heat flash, they watched in disbelief as their shells exploded harmlessly way below the Japanese formation. Despite setting the fuses of their shells to explode at maximum altitude, their weapons were incapable of causing any damage to the sixteen long-range bombers whose target was Lakanui, one of Rabaul's two aerodromes.

The Japanese, never proficient at bomb aiming, were mostly wide of the mark. Many of their bombs tumbled harmlessly into Rabaul harbour, with just three striking the runway at Lakanui. Tragically, sixteen anti-personnel fragmentation bombs rained down on the Rapindik Native Hospital and labour compound with horrific results. Fifteen people were killed outright and many others suffered terrible wounds from the flying shards of metal. Native casualties did not seem to trouble contemporary accounts of the raid, which was described as inflicting little damage and light casualties. The senior medical officer at the hospital neglected to even make mention of the native casualties in his report.

The Japanese appeared again at dusk, this time a formation of giant, four-engine Kawanishi Type-97 flying boats. Again, none came within range of the anti-aircraft battery, but once again the poor-aiming Japanese missed their target of Rabaul's second airstrip, Vunakanau.

For the next several days, more raids occurred, the worst being on 7 January when, for reasons unknown, Con Page failed to provide an early warning. On this occasion, serious damage was inflicted, cratering Vunakanau's runway and scoring direct hits on parked aircraft as well as destroying the airfield's long-range RDF (radio-direction-finding) station, a precursor of radar.

The Royal Australian Air Force put up what defence they could, but as with the ground forces, they too had been given no realistic chance of surviving, let alone repelling, the attackers.

In December, 24 Squadron RAAF had arrived to take up their position alongside Vunakanau's single, unsealed runway, equipped with four Hudson medium bombers and ten utterly unsuitable single-engine Wirraways, of which roughly six were only ever airworthy at the same time.

The Wirraway, Australia's first designed and manufactured military aircraft, was a hopeless compromise from the start, and a fighter in name only. It was obsolete even before the first examples began to emerge from the factory in Melbourne. Even with sufficient warning of an impending air raid, this heavy jalopy lacked both speed and climbing power to intercept the Japanese bombers, and was so pitifully armed that, should an enemy aircraft happen to cross the pilot's gunsights, he would have barely anything to hit it with. The Japanese, by contrast, had several hundred excellent front-line carrier and land-based aircraft flown by seasoned pilots and crews, including the unmatchable Zero fighter.

Feldt would later write:

It is interesting to speculate on the possible difference this might have made in the course of the war, had there been a squadron of modern fighter aircraft at Rabaul instead of the antiquated Wirraways.

The American Hudson, for its part, was indeed a fine aircraft, but such small numbers were deployed at Rabaul that they barely mattered. It was a Hudson, however, which now performed one of the RAAF's most remarkable operations of the Pacific War.

On 9 January, two new and specially adapted long-range Mark IV Hudsons from 6 Squadron RAAF took off from their base in Richmond, New South Wales, and headed north to Townsville. After a brief stop, it was on to Kavieng on New Ireland. Here, one aircraft developed mechanical trouble, leaving the pilot of the other Hudson, 26-year-old Flight Lieutenant Bob Yeowart, a former accountant from Brisbane, and his co-pilot, Flying Officer William Green, to press on alone. Their highly secret mission would be daring, dangerous and almost certainly the only useful Allied air operation of the entire Rabaul campaign.

The flight had been ordered a week earlier from the highest level of the RAAF, upon the instigation of Lieutenant-Commander Long, in order to ascertain exactly what kind of force the Japanese had planned to use against Rabaul. The crews' briefing, in which both Long and the Deputy Chief of the Air Staff, Air Vice-Marshal Bostock, had participated, had lasted four days. Yeowart and Green were under no delusions that their mission was of the utmost importance, and their chances of returning slim.

At dawn the next morning, 10 January, Yeowart received the final prearranged signal, 'North wind', directing him to proceed from Kavieng to the final leg of the mission. Opening the throttles of his heavily laden aircraft, which had been fitted with extra fuel tanks and cameras, Yeowart bumped along the rough runway, slowly gathering speed. With flaps lowered a few degrees for extra lift, the Hudson pulled itself into the air, its underside brushing through a tall patch of kunai grass at the end of the strip before gaining height and turning its nose to the north.

Four and a half hours later, Yeowart arrived over the Japanese stronghold of Truk in Micronesia where, protected in part by a severe rainsquall, he switched on his cameras and began photographing the main island, Tol, and its large harbour. From 13 000 feet, in grim silence, he and his crew of four took in the sight of an awesome armada of warships lying at anchor below.

In a remarkable twenty-five minutes, Yeowart completed his first camera run, photographing cruisers, destroyers, merchant vessels – as well as one mammoth vessel which looked like an aircraft carrier – before making another pass over an island in the harbour which had been excavated to form a runway. Here, twenty-seven bombers and other aircraft had been parked wingtip to wingtip. Eventually, after attracting increasingly accurate groundfire and enduring worsening weather, he pulled away and headed south.

Hours later, and without further incident, he landed back at Rabaul, picking his way through recently formed bomb craters. Greeted by 24 Squadron commander John Lerew, Yeowart informed him that, from what he had seen over Truk, far worse was on its way. Lerew advised Yeowart to depart immediately after refuelling for his own safety. When he eventually reached Townsville, though exhausted, Yeowart and his crew could not rest until word had come through that their cameras had worked and the photographs had been successfully processed.

Yeowart's epic flight was eventually recorded as the longest reconnaissance trip undertaken by any land-based RAAF for the entire war, and the first active air mission ever conducted against an enemy from Australian territory. More importantly, it gave clear indication of exactly what would soon be headed towards Rabaul. Despite his skill and gallantry, Yeowart received no award of any kind.

Hugh Mackenzie, meanwhile, having just transferred from Port Moresby to become senior naval intelligence officer on Rabaul just in time for its collapse, expected to hear news of the approaching Japanese invasion force at any moment.

He was surprised therefore to instead witness the arrival of a Norwegian vessel, the freighter *Horstein*, which tied up alongside the wharf on 14 January to begin disgorging its mixed cargo of six Bren gun carriers, Thompson submachine guns and ammunition. While all this was sorely welcomed, the 3000 drums of aviation fuel and yet more aerial bombs which it disgorged onto the dock were looked upon with irony, as Rabaul's tiny number of aircraft would be barely capable of using them.

The arrival of the *Horstein* presented an opportunity for Mackenzie to embark many of Rabaul's remaining male civilians who had remained following the departure of the women weeks earlier. For the ship's own safety, Mackenzie urged it to take on people and depart as soon as possible, and cabled his superiors for permission to give the order. Amazingly, the idea was flatly denied. Instead, insisted the government, the *Horstein* was to proceed across the harbour to the Burns, Philp & Co. commercial wharf and take on a scheduled load of copra. Not quite believing what he was reading, Mackenzie sought the help of Colonial Administrator Harold Page, who attempted to intervene, telling Canberra that there may well be few other opportunities to get people off the island safely. After days of silence, Page pestered further, eventually receiving the terse reply, 'No one is to take the place of the copra on the *Horstein*.'

At midday on 20 January, Con Page reported the sky to be 'filled with aircraft', counting over twenty bombers in a large V formation. This, however, was only part of what was headed for Rabaul. The Japanese chose this day to alter their tactics: they used multiple waves of aircraft to attack from different directions. From his station on Tabar, Page was able to spot only a fraction of the nearly one hundred aircraft delivering a crushing blow to Rabaul, as well as a prelude to invasion.

Page's signal barely gave the RAAF time to intercept, and the anti-aircraft gunners were likewise unprepared. First, as usual, the bombers appeared with their long drone, but then a new note rang through the sky, and the defenders of Rabaul caught sight of the sleek outline of the lightning-fast Mitsubishi Zero fighters weaving among the towers of smoke, the pilots clearly visible in their cockpits. Deprived of Allied fighters to attack, they busied themselves in strafing runs along the beach and streets of the town. Many on the ground realised that these aircraft had, a short time before, lifted off the decks of an aircraft carrier lurking just over the horizon along with the rest of the fleet.

The bombers first hit the docks, then lined up to disgorge their load along the airstrip runways. Then the dive-bombers appeared, circling for targets of opportunity. One by one they peeled off and attacked the *Horstein*, still taking on its load of 2000 tons of copra on the Burns, Philp wharf. In a few minutes, three dive-bombers scored three direct hits and the oily copra was well alight, burning away the ship's moorings and sending her adrift into the harbour, a ghastly, smoking hulk, her steel hull glowing red from the fires raging in her holds.

Ominously, though the docks and airstrips and coastal gun emplacements were bombed, the town itself was spared. Clearly, the Japanese planned to soon make use of it themselves.

The RAAF eventually put up a gallant but doomed defence, sending aloft its remaining handful of Wirraways, and one Japanese bomber was even shot down by anti-aircraft fire. Within minutes, six Wirraways had been destroyed by the Zero pilots who casually brushed them aside, treating the combat as target practice. One witness described the fate of one of them. 'By some mischance, the slow-moving fighter came into the field of fire of the rear gunners – so it seemed – of around eighteen bombers, and literally disintegrated in the air.' Afterwards, the Japanese pilots filled in time by putting on an air show, contemptuously looping and twisting their nimble Zeros over the undefended town. In minutes, six Australian airmen had lost their lives and 24 Squadron ceased to exist as a fighting force. The stunned anti-aircraft gunners sat in silence at their guns, shocked by what they had witnessed.

Despite this, the very next day, 24 Squadron's CO John Lerew was ordered by his superiors in Port Moresby to keep the squadron operational, and to hit back at the enemy 'with all available aircraft'. This now constituted just one remaining Hudson bomber. In his famous response, Lerew drafted the old Roman gladiatorial creed, *Nos Morituri te Salutamus*. The puzzled receivers at Moresby eventually reached for their dictionaries to translate, *We who are about to die salute you.*

What Canberra had not told the Rabaul commanders was that not one but two enemy fleets had been detected by intelligence and were currently proceeding towards them. Such information, it was thought, would simply induce panic. Lark Force, and the people of Rabaul, had been cast aside and written off before the first shots of the invasion had been fired.

•

In the end, it was an elephant used to crack a walnut. A mere fraction of the firepower the Japanese brought to bear on Rabaul would have achieved the same result: a complete and immediate collapse of the Australian defences at Rabaul and the first ever occupation of Australian territory by an enemy.

The men of Major-General Tomitaro Horii's *Nankai*, or South Seas Force, landed in the dead of night at 2 a.m. on 23 January. Looking out from their widely spaced defensive positions, the Australian defenders could barely make out the small boats and landing craft before their hulls scraped the sand and the first of an eventual 5000 first-class Japanese troops and Marines poured out. Steering through the waters of the harbour carefully, the Japanese seemed to avoid a series of underwater minefields which had been laid for just such a moment. The Australians watched as the landing boats and barges made their way uncannily through the cleared passageways to arrive unmolested at the shoreline. The spies had done their work.

Already, miscommunication among the Australians was rife. Many of the men stationed on the defensive perimeter had been told they were on a practice exercise, and had not even packed rations or other equipment for an extended stay in the open. In some places, resistance was strong, but soon overwhelmed by sheer numbers. The Australians pulled back, then pulled out. By dawn, the rout was on. Having exhorted his men to die where they stood, Lark Force commander Lieutenant-Colonel Scanlan, having caught wind of the panic, then issued an order which would forever become synonymous with incompetence, blind obstinacy, and be one of the most infamous in Australian military history, 'Every man for himself'. Abandoning his responsibility to his men entirely, Scanlan fled his post and joined the stream of shattered troops heading out of Rabaul along the meagre roads and tracks stretching into the jungle and the hills. It was all over in a day.

For Hugh Mackenzie, it would now be a life on the run. When word of the approaching invasion fleet came through, he spent the whole night burning his confidential naval books and codes. All that day, a procession of civilians made their way down to the waterfront and got away as best they could in a flotilla of small boats and launches. The small ones headed for Salamaua or Wau on the New Guinea mainland or the Solomons; the larger ones hoping to reach Australia itself.

The RAAF flew out its last remaining Hudson, so jammed with ground staff it could barely lift into the air. Thankfully, it made it to Darwin without issue. A smattering of other aircraft arrived, whisking away the ashen-faced civil administration staff. Mackenzie listened as the plane took off, its engines fading away to the south. It would be nearly four years before another friendly aircraft would touch down at Rabaul.

Now, with the collapse of the civil administration, and the end of organised resistance, it would be left to the Coastwatchers to take the fight to the Japanese.

## Chapter 7
# THE COASTWATCHERS GO TO WAR

Of the thirty-six Australian Coastwatchers who were to give their lives during the long and brutal war in the Pacific, the first was most likely C. C. Jervis, the retired navy telegraphist stationed on the tiny island of Nissan, sent there by Feldt to plug the eastern end of the dangerous gap in the Coastwatcher network between New Britain and Buka. Fifty miles away on the island of Anir, John Woodroffe watched the western end. While Anir was mountainous and jungle-covered, no part of Nissan was more than 20 feet above the water.

Soon after the Japanese entered Rabaul, a blanket of silence fell over the island, leaving Port Moresby to only speculate on its fate. It later transpired that the ordnance delivered by the *Horstein* had been detonated just before the Japanese invasion to prevent it falling to the enemy. The shockwave was so extreme that it shattered the valves of the radio in Hugh Mackenzie's office, destroying the only means of communicating Rabaul's impending fate and cutting it off from the outside world.

Port Moresby could still, however, pick up C. C. Jervis on Nissan, who sent a message reporting that a ship, about 5 miles distant, was approaching the entrance of his atoll. Jervis had been told not to expect any friendly vessel and would have been under no doubt as to the reality of the visit. A further signal was sent, informing that the ship had entered the lagoon. It was the last message Jervis sent. No further word was heard from him, nor any trace ever discovered. Soon, Woodroffe on Anir would suffer a similar fate, as would Coastwatcher Guy Allen, who was stationed directly in the path of the Japanese near the entrance to Rabaul harbour on Duke of York Island. While their exact fates were never known, their deaths would have been lonely indeed. Nor would they be the last to suffer such a fate.

Despite this, there were more men willing to step up and replace them.

In the days and weeks following the fall of Rabaul, many civilians made further attempts to get off the island, finding their way to rough airstrips where outdated aircraft kept by plantation owners and district officers made a final flight. Others brought out small boats, unused for years, and made a lunge for freedom to the mainland, or even another island along the great chain, where they hoped to keep at least one step ahead of the enemy.

Others did not want to abandon their homes and everything they knew, so chose to stay and begin their work as Coastwatchers, warming up their Teleradios to commence reporting the movements of the enemy. Apart from the main town of Rabaul, the Japanese could never hope (even had they the resources) to properly occupy the remainder of the vast island of New Britain, with its 300 miles of jungle, various volcanoes and hundreds of settlements and villages. Navigable roads, in any case, extended barely 40 miles from Rabaul along the north and south coasts, and inland for only 30. Thereafter began the criss-crossing network of native tracks – rough, and suited only to foot traffic.

Once established at Rabaul, the Japanese set out to familiarise themselves with the island and its inhabitants in a way the Australian forces had conspicuously failed to do. Typically, they would arrive by sea at a plantation house, mission or other settlement to conduct inspections, search for marooned Allied personnel, occupy it briefly then leave for another further down the coast. Only at a few places would they establish any permanent occupation, such as at airfields and other bases, all of which were along the southern coast. The more rugged northern shore would be largely ignored.

Initially, the Japanese also attempted – with some limited success – to win over the native people, arriving at villages to proclaim the era of white colonialism over, and that the Japanese were their new friends and liberators. Some villagers were happy – or at least indifferent – at the prospect of exchanging one foreign colonial overlord for another. Some proudly wore the rising sun armbands handed out to them, tempered always with the solemn reminder that any assistance given to the Allies would be met with the severest punishments. The Coastwatchers would quickly gain a sense of those who were on their side and those who were not. And as Eric Feldt was acutely aware when establishing the Coastwatcher network early in the war, the support of friendly locals was to be as vital to the work of the Coastwatcher as his radio.

Following the collapse of Rabaul, many Coastwatchers still operated successfully, and now began regular contact with the station at Port Moresby. All were fully aware that overnight their roles had transformed from that of observers to active spies operating inside enemy-occupied territory, and they would be treated as such. From now on, Coastwatchers would exist on a knife edge, knowing that to be discovered in possession of a Teleradio by the Japanese would mean torture, followed by certain death. With this in mind, Port Moresby issued a signal to all Coastwatchers to relocate their Teleradios from their houses and conceal them in shacks or dwellings some distance away. If the shack seemed to resemble a privy, which was less likely to be thoroughly searched, so much the better. Some islander Coastwatchers simply returned to their lives and waited for the Japanese to come looking. And after Rabaul, there was a good deal for them to come looking for.

In the early morning of the day the Japanese were expected at Rabaul, Hugh Mackenzie, understanding what was soon to come, instructed one of his naval intelligence staff, Lieutenant Connal Gill, and an AWA radio operator, Private Stone, to set off to establish another radio station on a ridge above Vunakanau airstrip, 30 miles away at the village of Toma. Travelling along the hilly road in a truck with a badly worn clutch, it not only took them many hours, but the noise of the gunning engine prompted army personnel to report that Japanese aircraft were lurking in the area.

At Toma, where the road from Rabaul petered out, Gill and Stone awaited the prearranged arrival of a group of local bearers to take the Teleradio up to the ridge, but when they failed to show up, the pair set it up beside the road. Late in the afternoon, they attempted to contact Rabaul but were puzzled to hear only silence.

A few hours after nightfall, they were startled by the arrival of a motley armada of cars and trucks, filled with panicky soldiers who had simply driven away from Rabaul in anything they could find and had now come to the end of the road. By the look in the soldiers' eyes, Gill knew that a rout was on. More men began to arrive, this time with jittery accounts of the Japanese attack. At first light, enemy aircraft appeared and Zeros began strafing the abandoned vehicles. From Toma, men headed out along the tracks that hugged the island both north and south. Mackenzie then arrived with his party of naval personnel, confirming the worst: Rabaul had fallen, Lark Force was no longer an effective fighting unit and there was no evacuation plan.

Mackenzie made it clear there would be no rescue here. Instead, they must proceed to the coast where a boat may pick them up, but the road ahead was long and hard, and the Japanese would be hunting them all the way. He gave the collection of mismatched sailors and soldiers who listened the choice to join one of the larger parties of soldiers heading off into the jungle, where safety in numbers may prevail, or to stay with him. Unhesitatingly, they chose to be led by him. Gill enquired about firing up the Teleradio and signalling Port Moresby, but Mackenzie believed there to be no time. Besides, all they had to report was disaster.

'It is astonishing what useless things men will take with them when they hurry off,' Mackenzie later reflected. In preparing the men's packs, he was forced to discard everything except what they would need most: food. One man had even carried a heavy album of family photographs, which had to be tossed into the jungle to rot.

With no native bearers, Mackenzie instructed the radio be relayed in stages, a mile at a time. A car full of senior officers, including the CO of the 2/22nd Battalion Lieutenant-Colonel Carr and the superintendent of police, arrived, informing them the Japanese were only twenty minutes away. A large Kawanishi floatplane passed low overhead, 'blazing away at anything that looked as though it was capable of movement'. Realising the radio would now simply slow them all down, Mackenzie made the agonising decision to instruct one of his men to pick up an axe and smash it to pieces. Then, rounding up his men, he headed south into the jungle and the mountains.

With ten days' supply of food in their packs, the little party decided to live off the land as much as possible, using their tinned food sparingly and buying from native gardens where they could. With foresight, Mackenzie had thought to bring 100 pounds in heavy New Guinea shillings taken from a safe in his office at Rabaul and he was able to hire native bearers, who eased the load considerably.

The plan was to make for the south of New Britain, where hopefully a boat would take them away to the Trobriand Islands, off the east coast of New Guinea, or even Lae or Salamaua on the New Guinea mainland, then on to Port Moresby, provided that these places had not already fallen to the Japanese. Days of agonising trekking lay ahead, scaling terrain where linear distances have no meaning. 'To go forward one mile,' wrote Gill, 'you often have to travel four or five nearly vertical up and down.'

In a few days, Mackenzie's party had swelled to twenty-one, and included some of the senior officers from Rabaul. Mackenzie led at a steady pace, resting the men in the bush and jungle where and when he could. Somewhere ahead of them were the panicked and unprepared mass of Lark Force soldiers who had bolted into nowhere, many of whom now started to believe the leaflets being dropped by Japanese aircraft exhorting them to surrender. One of them read:

To the Officers and Soldiers of this Island, Surrender at Once and we will guarantee your life, treating you as war prisoners. Those who Resist Us Will Be Killed One and All … you can find neither food nor way of escape in this island and you will only die of hunger unless you surrender
January 23, 1942
JAPANESE COMMANDER-IN-CHIEF

Mackenzie didn't believe a word of it, but many of the soldiers began trickling back to Rabaul to give themselves up to whatever fate the Japanese had planned. At one stage, near a place called Adler Bay, Mackenzie encountered the bizarre sight of two officers coming the other way, leading a private who was carrying a large white flag over his shoulder. As they drew closer, Mackenzie and Gill realised that the senior member of the trio was the Lark Force commander himself, Colonel Scanlan. Stunned, all they could manage was a 'Good morning, Sir', to which Scanlan returned the salute but did not utter a word. 'I never saw a more dejected trio in my life,' wrote Gill.

Later, Mackenzie learned that, after he had made his way back to Rabaul, Scanlan had washed, shaved, and put on his best pressed uniform complete with red gorgets, cap band and Sam Browne belt to formally surrender the garrison with a crisp salute to the Japanese commander.

Another surrendering soldier of somewhat lowlier rank remembered the spectacle as being 'in startling contrast to our ragged shorts and shirts, battered boots and scrubby beards'. Scanlan would survive more than three years of Japanese captivity and return to Australia to be appointed Governor of Hobart Gaol. Hundreds of his men were not so fortunate.

Mackenzie decided to avoid the direct route to the south coast and proceed along the tortuous inland tracks, then strike south further along the coast. First, however, he needed to reach a Teleradio, and according to the specially marked map he kept close at all times, one of those was located at a place called Waterfall Bay. If he was quick, he might be able to reach it before it was discovered and destroyed. The team split up, planning to meet up again along the coast at Wide Bay after Mackenzie's smaller party made their side trip over the mountains.

For days, the men trekked over the hills, bodies permanently soaked in the cloying heat of a tropical summer, clothing beginning to rot while ulcers formed on shins and legs after brushing the agonisingly sharp barbs of the wait-a-while bushes which snared flesh and clothing alike. The only relief from these was the native remedy of a pawpaw skin, if one could be found. The nights in the ranges, by contrast, were cold, and there was little escape from the malarial mosquitoes. Thankfully, Mackenzie had once again had the foresight to bring along a thousand quinine tablets, but these would not last long. It was becoming clear that one of the men in the party was already starting to lose his mind.

Then rumours began to filter in from native villages they passed that the Japanese had murdered, in cold blood, an entire group of men. The men had apparently been captured along the coast, at a plantation further down the track called Tol at Wide Bay. According to his map, Mackenzie's party would be passing right through it.

On 21 February, the little party reached the site of the plantation. Gill dismissed the rumours of the killings, but, being a lawyer, sought his own proof. Arriving at the eerily still coconut plantation, they cautiously ventured in, and soon found three heaps of discarded steel helmets, webbing gear and torn paybooks. Gill and Mackenzie estimated there were about 120. 'We then went looking for bodies at the back of the plantation,' recalled Gill, 'but did not find any. We did find the remains of about six large and apparently fierce fires. I sifted through the ashes and found a few pieces of bone, but too badly calcined to identify as human or animal.'

Their estimation was out by forty. On the evening of 2 February, 160 Australian soldiers who had surrendered earlier that day were tied together in small groups, thumbs bound behind their backs, then butchered by grinning Japanese soldiers, mainly by bayonet. Incredibly, some managed to play dead among the corpses and survive to tell the story, such as Private Billy Cook of the 2/10 Field Ambulance.

'The first stab knocked us down. The Japs stood over us stabbing madly. I received six wounds in the back, two just missing the spine, two more breaking ribs ... As the Japanese were moving off, the man next to me groaned. One of the Japanese soldiers came running back and stabbed him once more. By this time I could hold my breath no longer. When I drew a deep breath the soldier heard me and inflicted four more bayonet wounds. The last thrust went through my ear into my mouth, severing an artery on the way. Seeing the blood gushing out of my mouth, he assumed that I was at last dead, he covered the three of us with coconut fronds and vine leaves and left.'

So terrible were the details of the massacre at Tol, and similar ones at nearby Waitavolo and Karlai, the Australian government suppressed the details for decades.

•

Eric Feldt – in Townsville during this time – had become increasingly concerned about the fate of his Coastwatchers, and indeed the entire Rabaul garrison, having heard nothing from them since the Japanese invasion on 23 January. Two days later, a signal was sent to Keith McCarthy, Coastwatcher and assistant district officer at Talasea on the island's central north coast, asking whether he might be able to travel to Rabaul and assess the situation. McCarthy had recently been brought into ANGAU, the Australian New Guinea Administrative Unit, formed in virtual panic to fill the vacuum left by the collapse of New Guinea's civilian authority in the face of the Japanese invasion. ANGAU operated under the direct control of the General Officer Commanding, 8th Military District, Major-General Basil Morris, a staff officer who the Deputy Chief of the General Staff General Vasey described as 'brave and stout-hearted' but essentially 'brainless'. Morris himself freely admitted to being out of his depth with a field command, particularly one as desperate as the Kokoda campaign, and from which he was eventually and thankfully relieved. But he at least had the good sense to urgently employ the talents of other individuals such as Keith McCarthy, who had previously been sworn in by Feldt as a Coastwatcher.

Frustrated by the lack of orders emanating from Australia, McCarthy too had been in the dark as to the fate of Rabaul. Suspecting the worst, he had taken it upon himself to deprive the Japanese of some local infrastructure. As Rabaul fell silent, he had set off with local planter George 'Rod' Marsland and a small party of native police, including a particularly gifted fourteen-year-old radio operator named Nelson, onboard a crowded 36-foot government launch, the *Aussi*, to 'decommission' various airstrips along the northern coast by carving deep ditches across their runways. When McCarthy received Feldt's request, he had just returned from tearing up the island's far western airstrip at Cape Gloucester. Between him and Rabaul was over 300 miles of mountains, jungles, dangerous tribes, and hostile Japanese. He agreed to set forth again immediately.

'McCarthy was a civilian, and I had no right to give him orders,' wrote Feldt. The two men knew each other well, McCarthy having worked as Feldt's assistant district officer in Medang. 'A tall, red-headed man of Irish descent, with the nature of a tall red-headed man of Irish descent', was Feldt's typically colourful description. 'McCarthy was no cold, calculating brain. His affections and emotions often governed him, but when his fine free carelessness had landed him in trouble, he could extricate himself, cold logic guiding his Celtic fervour, until the danger was past.' Several years earlier in the New Guinea highlands, McCarthy had displayed extreme coolness when extricating himself from a group of hostile tribesmen, managing to escape with three arrows in him, one of which he complained, 'ruined the beautiful symmetry of his navel'. For the ordeal that now awaited him, Keith McCarthy would need every ounce of coolness – and courage – he could muster.

An urgency to discover what had taken place in Rabaul soon caught hold of the higher command in Melbourne and Townsville, who began sending feverish signals imploring Feldt for news of Rabaul.

'McCarthy is on his way,' Feldt responded.

'How long will that take?'

'A fortnight to three weeks.'

'That is too long!'

'It is quicker than anyone else could be.'

'He may not get there.'

'If McCarthy can't get there, no one can.'

And so on.

In the meantime, another incident occurred which illustrated the fragility and dangers faced by all Coastwatchers. Situated roughly halfway along New Britain's southern coast lay the small settlement of Gasmata, a low-lying island separated from the main island by a small channel. A true backwater, very little of note could be said of Gasmata, save it being the site of a long-term native prison, a rough airstrip which had been beaten out of its firm coral base, and its claim for possessing the highest rainfall in New Guinea, precipitating nine months of the year, turning the surrounding areas into a permanent malarial marsh. This dismal spot also happened to lie under the most direct air route between Rabaul and Port Moresby, and so was an ideal position for a Coastwatcher station, a role filled by the local assistant district officer Jack Daymond, along with patrol officer Eric Mitchell and a medical assistant,

'Dickie' Squires. Following the fall of Rabaul, the Gasmata group had relocated from the island into the bush and soon began reporting on Japanese activity.

In one of his first transmissions, Daymond gave warning to Port Moresby that a large number of Japanese bombers were passing overhead and heading their way, allowing people in Port Moresby time to prepare and take shelter, and keep casualties to a minimum.

In an extraordinary lapse of security, the Australian Broadcasting Commission in Sydney allowed the story of the foiled air raid to be broadcast, recklessly including the detail that Japanese bombers had been sighted at Gasmata. A shocked Jack Daymond heard the bulletin himself and immediately protested that his safety had been compromised. Sure enough, the very next day, a Japanese aircraft conducted a bombing and strafing attack which Daymond managed to avoid. The Japanese then sent a landing party, and on 9 February, two weeks after the fall of Rabaul, a detachment of Japanese soldiers came ashore at Gasmata and asked the locals the location of the 'Kepi', the Pidgin word for local leader. Daymond and Squires were caught and taken away. Mitchell had managed to get off a signal raising the alarm, and was advised to head to the northern coast and meet up with a party of fleeing Lark Force men there. The warning was never acknowledged, and neither Mitchell, Squires nor Daymond were ever heard from again.

During this time, Keith McCarthy was proceeding along the northern coast of New Britain in the little *Aussi*, still 250 miles from Rabaul. When he heard that the large plantation at Pondo, 50 miles west of Rabaul, had been occupied by the Japanese, he decided that sailing blithely into Simpson Harbour might not be the wisest course of action, so he moored the little boat up a river named the Toriu, and took a 'back door' native track to where he might overlook the town from a distance. Coastwatcher and planter Rod Marsland would reconnoitre the coast.

With his bearers faithfully trudging along with the various components of the Teleradio, McCarthy had not travelled far when various groups of alarmed natives travelling the other way informed him of the rout of the Australian forces, and that Rabaul was now very firmly in Japanese hands. He was also made to listen to another example of Australian government short-sightedness from a number of dismayed native police who had had their weapons seized, and actually buried, by the Australian authorities prior to the Japanese invasion. All had professed their willingness to fight alongside Australian soldiers and were bitter at the insult and lack of trust at where their loyalties lay. Somewhat chagrined, McCarthy assured them that he could supply them with weapons, and invited them to join his party. 'They joined me willingly,' McCarthy would say later, 'and served to the end.'

Rod Marsland then returned, with the good news that Pondo Plantation had been visited only briefly by the Japanese who had issued a warning to owner Albert Evenson and his white staff before disabling then sinking a small motor launch, the *Malahuka*, and departing.

Gradually, the scale of the debacle at Rabaul dawned on the commanders at Port Moresby. After failing to prepare the men of Lark Force for the battle, then abandoning them following the defeat they long knew to be inevitable, the Australian Army higher command now turned to an essentially civilian Coastwatcher to show the leadership they had so spectacularly failed to provide. Being one of the only people on the ground with a grasp of the true situation, McCarthy was blandly asked to 'assist' any AIF personnel he encountered who had escaped captivity. From his original brief to reconnoitre the situation at

Rabaul, he would now be required – Feldt's words – 'to trek through practically unknown jungle, to find people whose whereabouts he did not know, and then, probably, to lead them out and transport them to New Guinea by means which were not apparent'.

McCarthy was, however, up to the task, and had already begun to formulate a daring plan of rescue, the hub of which would be the plantation at Pondo.

Arriving on 14 February, McCarthy noticed two prominent white flags and small groups of soldiers who had already found their way to the Pondo plantation in dribs and drabs. One small party of infantry was led by the ranking officer present, Captain Allan Cameron, who confirmed to McCarthy that the Rabaul garrison had indeed collapsed, and that hundreds of men were currently scattered all across the eastern end of the island, defeated, desperate and marooned.

Setting up his radio, McCarthy signalled Port Moresby, finally piercing the silence that had enveloped Rabaul for three weeks, with the grim news that, for the first time in its history, Australian territory was now under occupation by an enemy force.

That night, he outlined to Rod Marsland his plan to extricate as many of the scattered remnants of Lark Force as he could. From what McCarthy could glean, the battalion had split roughly north or south from Rabaul, with about 400 on the northern coast and slightly fewer on the southern side. The men would need to be contacted, rounded up and shepherded back to Pondo, from where they would be marched west to Cape Gloucester, from which point they would hopefully be rescued and taken back to the New Guinea mainland. Staging camps would need to be organised along the route for the men to rest, and food would be supplied by local villages, paid for by ANGAU, via the authority invested in McCarthy. The men would move off in stages so as not to overwhelm the staging camps, and an NCO would be put in charge of each group. Where possible, boats would be used to transport the men from stage to stage and, if this was not possible, they would have to walk.

On paper, McCarthy's plan sounded simple enough, but the reality involved a 350-mile trek to the opposite end of the island for men who were already exhausted, malnourished and largely sick with malaria. As for what would happen once they reached distant Cape Gloucester, McCarthy had no idea.

Captain Cameron objected to the plan, insisting that he and his men should be flown out, and directing McCarthy to request a flying boat be dispatched immediately for the purpose. McCarthy refused, setting up a battle of wills between the two men which was never settled. Taking objection to being under the orders of a civilian, Cameron declared himself to be the ranking officer. McCarthy insisted that as the highest ANGAU officer present, it was he who was in charge, and he was backed up by higher command in Port Moresby who had insisted that he be given 'full authority over all officers of rank'. This infuriated Cameron further, who then threatened to evoke the loyalty of his 'eleven armed men'.

'Why, you stupid arse!' responded McCarthy, finally losing his patience. 'Are we going to have a private war or are you going to help out in the jam we're in?' Cameron begrudgingly pledged his cooperation. As a gesture of goodwill, McCarthy put Cameron in charge of the *Dulcy*, a motor launch acquired from a plantation owner, requesting he proceed along the coast to set up one of the proposed staging posts further along the track at Talasea with the help of his 'eleven armed men'. Cameron obliged.

McCarthy's dealings with Cameron may well have influenced his decision to refuse the field commission of captain which was now offered to him by the army in Port Moresby who, unlike the navy, were finally starting to give the protection of rank to a few individual Coastwatchers. Later in his remarkable career, when working with the commandos of the highly secretive M Special Unit, McCarthy would accept the appointment, but for now he was happy not to have to answer to the likes of Cameron. He shrewdly declined.

At Pondo, Keith McCarthy had managed to gain one vessel and lose another. It transpired the Japanese had done a poor job of wrecking the *Malahuka*, and McCarthy employed Rod Marsland and Frank Holland to repair her. Accounts differ as to whether the Japanese actually sank the boat offshore or took to it on the slipway, but the damage to the hull was easily repaired. Fixing the engine proved more difficult but after several days she was running again. Rod Marsland proudly showed McCarthy the pieces of scrap metal from which he had fashioned new parts for the diesel motor.

Holland then proposed to McCarthy that he head south and scour neighbouring plantations for more soldiers and round them into the camp. Fit and knowing the area extremely well, Feldt described Holland as 'tall, thin and dour, whose speech was pure Hemingway'. Before departing on his mission, McCarthy gave him six of his best native police and a Webley service revolver, the only weapon he carried. Despite the dual mountain ranges that lay before him, and the territory of the dangerous Mokolkol tribe through which he would have to cross, McCarthy records that Holland set off along the jungle track whistling.

On 20 February, like a latter-day Pied Piper, Holland trekked south and soon came across groups of men scattered listlessly among mission stations and plantations, living off whatever food they could find from stores. They were broken, dispirited and simply waiting for the Japanese to arrive and either capture them or put an end to their misery. His news of McCarthy's escape plan was like a tonic.

McCarthy, meanwhile, headed further north to discover more men, equally desperate. 'Most had only what they stood up in; some had arms, some had not. They were suffering from malaria and sores, and were feeling hopeless, helpless and dispirited. Their ignorance of the country was their worst enemy.' At a plantation near Cape Lambert, a group of around thirty were camped in a desperate state of near-starvation. 'Christ, have you brought anything to eat?' one of them asked, barely able to stand from hunger. McCarthy pointed out the ripe and untouched cassava crop beside them. 'There's your food,' he said. 'The men were actually starving in a native food garden because nobody had taught them how to recognise tapioca.' A few roots were dug up, and soon the men were eating and cursing the army for abandoning them to such ignorance.

At another plantation, a group of about sixty, their clothes in tatters, lay about outside a storeroom filled with meat and rice, but were forbidden access to it by the plantation manager who insisted it was company property and would have to be paid for. McCarthy couldn't decide what astonished him most: the manager's attitude or the men having not simply smashed the lock off the storeroom and helped themselves. He soon realised they lacked the energy even for that. Signing a military requisition slip, McCarthy demanded the supplies be handed over, then suggested the manager might wish to take care of his health by evacuating from McCarthy's line of sight with all haste.

Further north, word went around the groups of isolated Australian soldiers that, despite being abandoned by their own army and government, help was at hand in the form of a Coastwatcher with a plan. The news was welcome indeed for

Captain Pip Appel, who had been mustering ever larger, yet ever more desperate, groups of men in the vicinity of Lassul Bay. Hearing of McCarthy's arrival, he emerged from the shelter of a plantation to meet McCarthy face to face, and inform him that he could have 145 men in Pondo in seven days by walking them overland, avoiding the Japanese who were now patrolling the waters. When McCarthy asked what shape the men were in, Appel recited a list of ravaging ailments including 'acute tinea, tropical ulcers, ringworm, dysentery, swollen glands, infected sores', and four out of five were suffering malaria. Despite this, Appel marched them across the mountains into Pondo, achieving the feat in five days.

The little *Dulcy*, however, was gone, courtesy of the embittered Captain Cameron, who had been given the task of establishing one of the staging camps. With his eleven men, accompanied by a planter friend of McCarthy's, Bert Olander, they had arrived at the allotted campsite where Olander disembarked and began making preparations. After remaining in the area for a short time, Cameron and his men simply took off again and sailed away to the west.

A few days later, Olander managed to return to Pondo, where he informed a furious McCarthy that one of his precious boats was gone. With far more pressing matters to attend to, McCarthy let the matter go. A week later, Cameron reached Salamaua, just in time for it to be invaded by the Japanese, managing to be airlifted out shortly before it fell. Later in the war, he would go on to prove himself as a fine soldier, winning the Distinguished Service Order twice, but his behaviour on New Britain permanently tarnished his reputation.

On the south coast, Frank Holland had managed to contact Hugh Mackenzie's naval party, which had grown in number and were still stuck in the southern part of the island. When news came through of McCarthy's escape plan, they pledged to join him, though time, they were told, was of the essence. McCarthy could afford to wait only a little longer, and the track up to Pondo, even for fit men, was hard. Every day that McCarthy and his men waited in their camp at Pondo for more men to arrive, food stocks dwindled and the chances of discovery by the Japanese rose. The fact they had not already been annihilated seemed a minor miracle in itself.

Mackenzie ordered that all but a handful of his men proceed north under the guidance of his subordinate officer, Connal Gill, while he would stay in the south and attempt to round up more men. Gill's party, which now numbered twenty-five, included two survivors of the Tol massacre, Alf Robinson and ambulance driver Private Bill Collins. Robinson, a government officer who had worked in Rabaul since 1926, was almost unique in being the only man to escape Tol unscathed. One of a group of nine men, he took his chance by ducking into a bush when the Japanese soldier leading them to their deaths along a track glanced the other way. 'Lower, Sport,' mumbled an unknown digger as he passed.

Collins had been shot twice in the slaughter, one bullet passing through his shoulder and another his wrists, which at least managed to cut his bindings. Playing dead, he controlled his breathing as much as possible as Japanese soldiers kicked and prodded the corpses around him. When their footsteps finally receded, he opened his eyes to find himself partially buried among the dead. Struggling to his feet, he wandered the jungle aimlessly until he was picked up by one of the island's European police and deposited with Mackenzie.

Proceeding over the mountains, Gill's men staged camp near Kalai Mission where, the following morning, two naval ratings, Yeoman of Signals G. T. Knight and Writer (a naval rank for clerk), T. J. Douglas, fell suddenly ill with dysentery. Mackenzie's orders had been clear: the party could not wait for any man who fell sick and they would be left to fend for themselves. Gill was torn, reluctant to abandon a sick man. 'Don't you worry about us,' Knight gallantly assured him. 'Mr Mackenzie is depending on you.' Preparing to depart, Irish Coastwatcher Stephen Lamont, who had previously been stationed on the tiny island of Anir, demurred, informing Gill that he would remain with the sick men. 'Those two sods can't be left to die on their own,' he said. 'I'll stay with them if you like, and you get on with the job of getting Mackenzie and the swaddies rescued.'

Gill later recalled, 'We had always jokingly referred to Lamont as the "heart of oak". It was the old story of many-a-true word being spoken in jest.' Gill gave Lamont 25 pounds in cash, a rifle and 200 rounds of ammunition and told him to use it to get anything for his men that he needed. Shaking his hand, Gill turned and, sick at heart, led the remainder of his party away.

They would never see any of the three men again. In just a few days, on 5 March, a Japanese patrol came across the trio. Douglas and Knight – still ill – were executed immediately, while Lamont was imprisoned at a camp at Malaguna, where he perished from either disease or at the hands of the Japanese, the exact cause never being determined.

On the New Guinea mainland, another rescue operation was getting underway in the form of an unlikely armada of small boats. Gwynne Caleb Harris, though born in Wales, found his calling as a patrol officer at Lae, which had been his station since 1937. In March 1942, he had just managed to stay ahead of the Japanese as they invaded Lae, having the foresight to empty the administration safe of all its cash before making a quick escape along the coast to Finschhafen, where he again had to hide to avoid a Japanese raid. Becoming heartily sick of running before the enemy, Harris determined to take his revenge by joining the Coastwatchers, and Eric Feldt was happy to have him. Feldt described Harris as 'a contradiction of a man ... big, fleshy with a bald head surrounded by a fringe of fiery red hair. He had a hard face and a soft, lisping voice, a truculent disposition and a courteous manner. Being red-haired, he was, following the Australian custom, called Blue.'

Harris did not have to wait long for his first assignment. Informed by Port Moresby via his Teleradio of the situation in New Britain, he was told that an unknown number of men were gathering on the north coast under McCarthy, on the run and in need of evacuation, and becoming more desperate every hour. A call had gone out to the operators of any small craft capable of carrying a man or two to prepare to assemble at Finschhafen harbour then make the crossing to New Britain. Harris was asked to lead the entire operation, and accepted immediately.

Perhaps curious as to why the rescue was being left to the likes of himself and not the Royal Australian Navy, Harris contacted everyone he knew in the vicinity who had a boat and quickly signed them up as members of ANGAU, then directed them to assemble at Rooke Island in the Vitiaz Strait between New Britain and the New Guinea mainland.

Four vessels made up the bulk of the flotilla, the 45-ton schooner *Bavaria*; the 15-ton government launch *Gnair*; the 35-ton *Totol* belonging to the Lutheran Mission in Medang; and the 23-ton motor vessel *Umboi*, which, with its twin diesel motors, became the unofficial flagship of what would be dubbed 'The Harris Navy'. None could exceed 8 knots or were larger than about 20 metres. They were joined by several even smaller government runabouts, *Thetis*, *Nereus* and *Winnon*. 'It would have been hard to find a more pathetic task force than this haphazard little group of launches,' recalled Feldt.

When each skipper reached Finschhafen on 5 March, they mulled over the official wording of the order sending them into the unknown:

You will proceed to the north coast of New Britain, contact Captain J. K. McCarthey [sic], and operate under his instructions. You will travel only by night with no lights showing anywhere, and hide your vessels by day. You will use the radio only in extreme emergencies.

Precisely how, thought Harold Freud as he steered the darkened *Umboi*, was he supposed to hide a 23-metre schooner with 12-metre masts in open anchorage in broad daylight?

On 9 March, Frank Holland returned to Pondo, appearing as fresh as when he had left a week or so earlier, unlike the group of twenty-nine men he had collected from around the south coast, many of whom appeared as walking ghosts in tattered clothes and near delirious with malaria, sunburn and sores. They would now join the several hundred similarly emaciated men from all points of the eastern end of New Britain following the rout of Rabaul. Exhausted, this pathetic remnant of a once proud army lay about the plantation at Pondo, eating what meagre provisions could be provided, gathering strength for the ordeal to come. As exhausting as the trek to Pondo had been, each man knew their trials were only beginning. At least now there was the glimmer of hope.

# Chapter 8

# McCARTHY'S ODYSSEY

'Brainless lot of buggers!' exploded Keith McCarthy to a now skeletal-thin and shoeless Rod Marsland, throwing down the headphones of his Teleradio. By mid-March, he had succeeded in moving most of the 200 men from Pondo to a plantation at Iboki, a little over 200 miles along the New Britain coast. It had been a predictably gruelling ordeal, driven by the strength and resourcefulness of McCarthy himself and his handful of unfailing assistants. Like a slow, shuffling train the men moved west along the coast, thinking of nothing but the placing of one usually shoeless foot in front of another. Up and down the line, McCarthy would travel, encouraging, cajoling, even threatening – anything to keep the men moving. Seventy-five of the most sick men were placed onboard the recently refloated *Malahuka*, but its resurrection proved a false dawn. Strewn with rocks and coral reefs, the coast was in some parts barely navigable and, at more than one point, the boat's already exhausted passengers had to get out and push her off the reef. The hasty repairs began to come undone and eventually the men had to be offloaded to join the land party, the *Malahuka* being finally scuttled not far offshore.

McCarthy was constantly busy: bartering for food with native people and the few plantation owners who had elected to stay on; organising canoes to take the most sick to the next stage of the journey; urging the men onwards. The few officers still capable of authority were directed to encourage the men to have faith and not give up. McCarthy knew, however, that it was a race against time. Lack of food was beating down even the most enthusiastic believers in the plan, and their condition was deteriorating daily. 'All were sick,' he observed. 'Debilitated by poor and insufficient food, weakened by malaria and exposure. Most had sores, the beginning of tropical ulcers, covered by dirty bandages. Their faces were the dirty grey of malaria victims, their clothes in rags and stinking of stale sweat.'

Each man was allotted a few pounds of rice and the lucky ones a can of tinned meat, all of which had to be carried. It was nowhere near enough. Much of the food that could be provided or gathered on the journey lacked protein, or was barely palatable, and even the fitter men could manage nothing faster than an ever-slowing shuffle. The rear parties were in even worse shape, constantly being urged to keep up and not spread too far back from the main group. The men's strength, McCarthy could see, was failing, and all the while, he was beset with the constant terror of a Japanese patrol bursting upon them with rifle and bayonet.

McCarthy also had his own health to consider. 'You'll never get out of New Britain,' the Pondo manager Albert Evenson had grimly predicted as they set off. 'Have you seen yourself lately? You must be due to crack!' Standing on a set of scales, McCarthy discovered he had lost 50 pounds in just a few weeks, and he was constantly dreaming of sweet sustenance such as cake and chocolate.

Other parties joined him along the track, further swelling the ranks. From an officer attached to one of these, McCarthy learned that Lae and Salamaua had recently fallen, removing his most direct line of retreat to the New Guinea mainland. McCarthy had no idea of an alternative plan, but every step west at least took him further from the Japanese.

As Feldt described the ordeal, 'There were, for most, days of sun, sweat and sand, with nothing ahead but the end of the day, with its surcease of sleep, then another day after that, and then another, and another.'

Another officer described the men as '... almost naked, the sun had raised great blisters on their bodies and their lips were cracked with open sores. The mosquitoes and insects drove them mad at night, for we had no nets and the smudge fires affected their eyes. Boots had begun to give out so that some wore hessian and cloth wound around their feet to protect them from the coral and rocks.'

With native bearers carrying the weighty components of the Teleradio, communication with Port Moresby was possible if sporadic. With the Japanese now having captured an unknown swathe of New Britain, and perhaps being in possession of Coastwatcher code books and even radios, as well as the chance that the enemy was listening in, the possibility of Feldt's coding system having been compromised was real. The only way of securing the essential identifying keywords for each operator was to have them constantly change. Feldt and McCarthy fell back on their mutual history. 'Use as keyword the Christian and surname of tall thin officer formerly chief of police,' Feldt would signal, to which McCarthy would reply 'John Walstab'. 'Fat officer who lived on fowls and ice cream,' signalled Feldt a little later, prompting McCarthy to identify another name from their past as patrol officers. Eventually, they all but exhausted their list of mutual acquaintances.

Soon after McCarthy and the men had made it as far as the plantation of Walindi near Talasea, along the centre of the island's north coast, Blue Harris and his little flotilla showed up. Coming ashore, Londoner Bill Money managed to eke some dark humour from the situation, and the exceedingly German heritage of the skippers of the little boats, by greeting McCarthy with a click of the heels and a Nazi salute. 'Herr Erik Feldt has sent Herr Obst, Herr Neumann, Herr Radke und Herr Freund to New Pommern. Heil Hitler!' he proclaimed, evoking the old Imperial title for the former German territory.

The smiles fell from the skippers' faces when they saw the state of the men they were expected to deliver to safety. Now the little boats began the vital work of shuttling small groups of the increasing number of men unable to walk from one staging post to another. The initial order had instructed them to travel along the coast only by night, but the large number of treacherous and unmarked reefs made this impossible. Even by day, the boats came aground and had to be hauled off by the men or forced to wait for a rising tide.

Far above, a daily procession of Japanese bombers made their way south in perfect formation as the Japanese began their air assault on Port Moresby. It was, McCarthy noted, always the same number – nine aircraft – flying out and later returning, a depressing indicator that Moresby was currently defenceless, with no way to strike at the enemy. The men further reflected with irony that it was their former base at Rabaul, along with its airstrips, which the Japanese were now using in their assault against New Guinea and, perhaps, Australia herself.

Onwards the flotilla of the Harris Navy sailed. On one occasion, the largest boat, the *Bavaria*, was stuck fast on a reef for eight hours. Skippers Adolph Obst and Dave Rohrlach could only wait for the sea to rise, but when the throb of aircraft engines could be heard approaching from the north, they were convinced their final moments had arrived. Luckily the Japanese bombers failed to notice the helpless target, or had other priorities, and passed over without incident.

With the Willaumez Peninsula still having to be crossed, and the western end of New Britain still hundreds of miles away, even with the most valiant efforts of the twenty-man-strong Harris Navy, McCarthy realised that the men were simply in no condition to complete the journey, and that many had reached their limits of human endurance. Holed up for a few days at Iboki, the men had their best feed in weeks, even tasting meat from a butchered resident water buffalo, but as McCarthy observed, 'Many simply wanted to sleep and not be awakened again.'

Their only hope, he felt, was immediate evacuation to the New Guinea mainland. But where? Moresby was beyond the range of the boats of the Harris Navy and the ports of Lae and Salamaua had already fallen to the Japanese. Contacting Moresby, McCarthy also learned that Finschhafen and the lower reaches of the Markham River were now in Japanese hands. McCarthy requested that flying boats be dispatched to collect the men of Lark Force. It would take several trips, and would be perilous for all concerned, but it was, he stressed, the only hope the men had of returning to Australia alive.

'Out of the question,' responded the 8th Military District staff officers at Port Moresby, under whose aegis he officially operated. Catalina flying boats, they explained, were still in short supply and could not be risked on a mere rescue effort for a group of probably already doomed soldiers. Instead, they suggested the small ships deposit the men south of Madang, from where they would need to march 75 miles over the more than 10 000-foot Owen Stanley Ranges to Chimbu in the central highlands, before they would presumably be collected in the Upper Ramu Valley by means yet undetermined, then forwarded to Port Moresby, provided it had not fallen to the Japanese.

McCarthy could not believe what he was hearing and, in disgust, turned off the Teleradio. Rod Marsland likewise had no answers, and McCarthy, for the first time, felt checkmated, not only by the Japanese but by the cold indifference of Australian military command at Port Moresby, as well as this primordial and unforgiving island, which seemed bent on punishing them as an unwelcome intruder. The fate of several hundred men, whom up till now he had been able to bluff, cajole and beg into moving forward, now seemed an unbearable weight which would pull him into the abyss.

Whether or not McCarthy at this point prayed for – or even believed in – miracles will never be known, but at the plantation at Iboki, deliverance arrived in the most unlikely of forms: a white, middle-aged woman.

When Mrs Gladys Henrietta Loveday Baker stepped off her single-masted pinnace, the *Langu the Second* (which she had just sailed herself), even the most exhausted and sick of the men looked up in slack-jawed wonder at the picture of grace and confidence striding up the beach at Iboki, convinced it must be a dream. Dressed in an immaculate white blouse and tailored trousers – still perfectly creased – Baker smiled at the silent men in front of her, then naturally gravitated to their leader, McCarthy, who she greeted with an extended hand. Tall, elegant and beautiful, she appeared as a vision from another world.

McCarthy had to blink several times himself and, for the first time in months, bent his mind to his own dishevelled state. But if her appearance was not remarkable enough, what she had to say was simply extraordinary, and would change the course of McCarthy's rescue of the men of Lark Force.

'The *Lakatoi*,' said Mrs Baker, 'is currently anchored at Witu, fully seaworthy and awaiting your departure.' McCarthy could not believe his ears.

•

Gladys Baker had arrived in the islands twenty years earlier when her husband, William Baker, took up the offer of one of the many former German coconut plantations being distributed to veterans of World War I. The two of them went on to make a huge success of their property, *Langu*, on the island of Witu, just under 40 miles north of the New Britain shoreline. In a few years, they had built a bungalow of seven bedrooms, each with its own bath, and could even afford the occasional European holiday where Gladys would indulge her taste for haute couture, returning home to fill her her wardrobes with 100-guinea gowns from Jean Patou and Norman Hartnell, which she insisted on wearing every night for dinner. Other luxuries included the finest silverware from London, Irish crystal and imported European furniture upon which her many guests took tea, followed, later in the day, by the obligatory gin and tonic, served by one of her dozens of staff.

Baker was also immensely practical, having worked as a nurse during World War I (she and William met while he was in a rehabilitation hospital), she'd acquired an excellent medical knowledge, particularly of tropical diseases, which she would use to treat anyone who needed it, including her native workers. She could, and frequently did, deliver native babies; became an expert yachtswoman; could hunt, fish and shoot; and communicate with the locals in perfect Pidgin. When William died suddenly in 1936, Gladys carried on the plantation alone, just as successfully. Even in her grief, she continued to dress for dinner, which she usually took alone.

A few weeks after the attack on Pearl Harbor, the first Japanese aircraft appeared overhead Witu, often circling close to take a good look at the house and the harbour below. Then the occasional Zero turned up – Gladys would recall the red glint of the rising sun on its wings.

Though the Christmas of 1941 was conducted with the same vigour and ceremony as in previous years, Gladys sensed that her comfortable colonial world was about to change drastically, and forever.

She owned a Teleradio and declined the messages to evacuate but received permission to remain on her island to use her medical knowledge for any troops who may need it. Then in January 1942, all communication from Rabaul, 200 miles away, ceased. Instead, looking west along the New Britain coastline, she saw smoke signals, and at night heard the reverberation of the garamut drums across the water, passing the news along that the capital had fallen.

Anticipating the desperate plight of the soldiers, Gladys conducted a series of supply trips across the water to New Britain, giving freely of her own extensive stores to create supply dumps of rice, flour and tinned food along riverbanks and coves through which she suspected Australian soldiers would be retreating.

A trip from Witu to New Britain could never be conducted in less than eight hours, and in rough weather it could be several times longer. Undaunted, Baker undertook several such trips, risking her life each time. On one such occasion, a Japanese floatplane began circling her little 27-foot craft. Aware of the consequences if discovered, she instructed her native crew on what to say if boarded, then hid under the deck boards in the filth of the bilge. A few minutes later, Gladys heard the sound of floats cutting the water, a gunning engine, then footsteps above her head. The crew played their part perfectly, explaining in polite Pidgin that their master had long left for Sydney and they were simply picking up a native work crew. The Japanese were convinced, even offering the sailors a cigarette and biscuit before departing.

Gladys emerged, covered in oil and filth. She shrugged her shoulders, resumed her place at the tiller, and carried on the voyage.

She had sent out other native parties in various smaller craft to scout for Australian soldiers, with strict instructions to return immediately and inform her if any were discovered.

A short time after the fall of Rabaul, the *Lakatoi* pulled in to the little harbour below her property, followed shortly by a native boat crew reporting groups of extremely sick-looking Australian soldiers gathering in groups at Iboki. Baker immediately exhorted the ship's captain to load up with supplies and head over to assist, but the man refused.

Later, in a brief – and absurdly modest – account, Baker recalled the incident: 'He [the captain] refused to move, saying that he and his officers were married men and could not chance their lives. With sheer disgust on my part, I loaded my own boat and set out at midnight for New Britain.'

When Gladys Baker told McCarthy that the *Lakatoi* was barely a day's sailing from their camp, he realised his plan of rescue may yet be snatched from the jaws of defeat.

Barely three years old, the 350-ton steel-hulled *Lakatoi* had been built in Hong Kong for Burns, Philp & Co. as an inter-island trader, running copra and other cargo between the company's extensive interests in New Guinea and the Solomons. As it happened, the last person to contact the *Lakatoi* had been McCarthy himself, who had been ordered by Port Moresby to direct her to the nearest friendly port as the Japanese closed in on Rabaul. After the initial contact, nothing more had been heard from her.

McCarthy now signalled Port Moresby that the *Lakatoi* had been rediscovered. Suddenly, the army was interested, demanding to know the exact location and state of the vessel, which they had presumed to have been either sunk or captured by the Japanese. McCarthy, pretending to know slightly less than he did, innocently requested that if he was able to reach her, might he be granted legal authority over her? This time, the army replied with an emphatic *yes*.

Events now moved with speed. On 19 March, McCarthy dispatched Connal Gill, Rod Marsland and another Coastwatcher, Mr Lincoln Bell, from a plantation near Talasea. Handing Bell a Thompson submachine gun, McCarthy instructed him that the *Lakatoi* needed to be secured at all costs but to use the weapon only if absolutely necessary.

The little party headed for Witu aboard one of the Harris Navy boats, the *Gnair*, sailing all night and arriving at the *Lakatoi* at dawn. Feeling very much like modern-day pirates, they boarded the ship and surprised the captain and first mate, explaining that they were taking her over in the name of the Australian armed forces. As Connal Gill recalled, 'The master and mate demurred. Bell waggled the "Tommy gun" around and suggested it might be advisable for them to cooperate. They decided to cooperate.'

Bell did not need the weapon as it was with relief that Captain Farrar handed over command of the *Lakatoi* to the Coastwatchers. Having spent the last weeks not daring to venture into the open sea for fear of being attacked by the Japanese, he was happy to be relieved of the responsibility.

The men made a quick inspection: her decks were covered in a matting of coconut branches and other jungle litter to hide her from the prying eyes of Japanese aircraft, and the men found her to be in fine condition and full of fuel.

Back at Iboki more men continued to dribble in from various parts of the island, sick, exhausted and with more tales of horror. McCarthy realised that a few more days were needed to organise the evacuation and put the capable Gladys Baker in charge of the Iboki camp. Over the next week, she worked small miracles, treating tropical ulcers, giving advice on native food, and distributing many of the stores she had brought over from her property at Witu. She even organised extended card games, at which, the men soon found, she was an expert who rarely lost.

Finally, on the night of 20 March, the little ships of the Harris Navy did their finest work, shuttling every man over to Witu, where the *Lakatoi* awaited. When they caught sight of the unexpectedly large ship, a tonic of renewed hope coursed through the men's veins. Inspecting the ship for the first time, McCarthy was well pleased and believed that she might indeed be able to carry off the entire contingent in one hit. Connal Gill, however, issued a note of caution. In the *Lakatoi*'s holds were nearly a thousand bags of copra. He had recently watched the *Horstein* burn like a torch in Rabaul harbour with just such a load, and one lucky bomb or shell would set the *Lakatoi* alight. McCarthy considered, then ordered the entire lot to be thrown overboard. Captain Farrar, who had apparently managed to find some courage after all, was aghast, pointing out that the load was worth over a thousand pounds. 'Who would be paying for it?' he asked.

'Put it on my personal account,' muttered McCarthy as the men went to work hurling the sacks over the side. When the load was emptied, the ship was now too light, and over 300 of the sacks had to be retrieved and filled with sand for ballast. For some men like Kevin Walls, who had been retreating for weeks, it was almost too much: 'This was the last straw to us, we were absolutely on our toes expecting to get away … it was a very slow job. The rest of the troops were on the shore loading the sand. Several of them fainted from the exertion.'

Those men not on sand-filling duty went to work on the hull with every spare tin of paint which could be found in her holds or on the island, transforming her beautiful – but far too prominent – gleaming white sides into a hideous hotch-potch of blue, grey, yellow and brown camouflage.

Five backbreaking hours later, the *Lakatoi* was ready to depart, her food lockers bursting with what provisions she could hold, much of it courtesy of the largesse of Gladys Baker. The men now filed onboard, quickly taking up every piece of space the ship could offer. There was barely an inch to spare.

McCarthy then made another momentous decision. Gill and Marsland had assumed they would all be heading to the New Guinea mainland to begin the trek over the mountains, as directed by Port Moresby. But McCarthy had little remaining faith in his superiors, and ordered the captain to set a course straight for Cairns.

Gill and Marsland were stunned, and pointed out that this would entail a 1200-mile journey through largely Japanese-dominated waters, bringing them dangerously close to enemy strongholds along the Papuan coast. It was also noted that no charts of the area around the reef-strewn Dampier Strait – and beyond – could be located (why Captain Farrar was not in possession of such mandatory items was never established) and that no one with any experience of these waters would be onboard to pilot them through. McCarthy put forward his case as the lesser of two extremely hazardous options. As Connal Gill remembered it, 'The men would probably nearly all die if they had to walk to the Upper Ramu, so the odds would not be much longer if we tried to get them out in the *Lakatoi* through at least 400 miles of Japanese-dominated waters.'

McCarthy also pointed out there was someone onboard with intimate knowledge of the local reefs, who was also an excellent mariner and could guide them through without the aid of a chart. As to who this might be, McCarthy nodded towards the stately figure of Mrs Gladys Baker.

Explaining the plan to the men, Gill encountered more opposition. 'But when they found the alternative was to walk to the Upper Ramu they decided the *Lakatoi* offered a sudden end, one way or the other, to the situation. I think everyone had developed a sort of fatalism by this time.'

On 21 March, McCarthy and Baker decided the time had come to take their chances. A final coded signal was sent to Port Moresby informing them of their imminent departure, then radio silence was observed. At 4 p.m., the *Lakatoi* discarded her disguise of branches and coconut fronds, fired up her engines and slipped out of the little harbour at Witu. Onboard were over 200 men and two women, Gladys Baker and her personal native maid, and everyone now held their breath for the days and nights to come. As a last link to her former life, Gladys had even managed to bring aboard her beloved little dog. Her personal papers, banking details and accounts were left behind.

Accompanying the *Lakatoi* were some of the ships of the Harris Navy. Onboard the *Gnair*, Lincoln Bell, Bert Olander and several other Papuan Coastwatchers turned around to head back to New Britain, believing they would be of better use in the jungle, continuing to spy on the Japanese over the coming months, possibly even years. In his hand, Lincoln Bell still clutched the Tommy gun McCarthy had handed to him. Calling out over the water, McCarthy reminded him that the weapon was still his property. 'Come over and get it yourself then!' replied Bell as the two men grinned, silently wishing the other the best of luck.

As the dusk came on and the outline of the small boats became fainter, McCarthy considered all those who had helped him to this point, the fellow Coastwatchers

who had risked their all trawling across the island through
the jungle, rounding up as many of the men as possible; he
thought of the plantation men such as Rod Marsland and Bill
Mason; those drawn from ranks of the army, navy and native
constabulary; and the natives themselves who had no option
to evacuate anywhere should the Japanese turn their cruelty
on them. 'Nothing is hopeless when there are men like these,'
reflected McCarthy later.

With Gladys Baker acting as pilot, the still jittery Captain
Farrar steered the *Lakatoi* through the reefs and shallows
surrounding the Witu Islands, then turned west. Just to be
certain he did not lose his nerve, an armed Gill and McCarthy
maintained vigil on the bridge, making sure the course was
kept. In the engine room, Rod Marsland held the watch,
relieving the engineer when required and keeping the *Lakatoi*
to a steady 10 knots.

When they were in open water, Gladys Baker went to work
setting up a sick bay for the most desperate of the men, tending
their wounds, doling out the daily ration of a pint and a half
of water per man per day (for all purposes), and keeping them
amused with endless rounds of card games, allowing herself
to lose to the extent of 11 pounds. Charmed by her dedication
and easy manner, many of the men assumed Mrs Baker to have
been born into a world of privilege, but in that they would
be quite mistaken. Baker, in contrast to her expensive style,
revealed that she hailed from the humblest of backgrounds
in the working-class Melbourne suburbs of Carlton and
Brunswick.

As the dawn came up the next day, the skies and seas were
mercifully empty of the enemy. It was far from safe though
as they would be required to run the gauntlet of the Vitiaz
Strait, between the two Japanese strongholds of Gasmata on
New Britain to the east and Finschhafen to the west, which

they were forced to pass by in broad daylight. With lookouts posted, they managed to slip by undetected. At one stage, all the men on the open deck were ordered below when the daily fleet of Japanese bombers passing overhead on their way to Port Moresby were seen, but they too seemed uninterested in the progress of the *Lakatoi*. That night, off Lae, the outline of a vessel could be detected in the gloom, crossing their bow. McCarthy was certain it was a Japanese destroyer making for Lae. They prepared for the worst, but carried on, unchallenged.

The next day, they came close to the Japanese air base of Salamaua and were again ignored, the possible reason for this being made clear by an ABC news bulletin they heard, describing a surprise dawn attack by the newly arrived fighter pilots of 75 Squadron RAAF, whose Kittyhawks wrought carnage on the unsuspecting Japanese airmen who, until this point, had had no idea of the Australians' presence in Port Moresby.

Onboard the *Lakatoi*, it was, as Patrick Lindsay describes, 'wall to wall people'. Soldier Kevin Walls describes sleeping on the steel matting of the deck, near the galley where the meals were prepared. 'There was hardly enough room for any of us to have more than six feet or whatever length we measured to lie down.' In such conditions, the tempers of the exhausted men became frayed. 'Our nerves were all keyed up. We were very hungry and the meals usually left us wanting more.'

A day later, the men felt the swells of the deep ocean as the *Lakatoi* finally departed the shelter of the Trobriand Islands, rounding the eastern tip of Papua into the Coral Sea. Then, to tears of joy, the radio came within range of Radio 4BQ Brisbane.

On 28 March, the *Lakatoi* received pratique to enter Cairns Harbour, her overcrowded decks filled with emaciated men and her hurriedly painted hull making a peculiar and unnerving spectacle.

'Where are you men from?' asked a stunned garrison officer from the bottom of the gangplank. 'Victoria Barracks, Melbourne,' replied a bootless soldier.

Placing his worn feet onto Australian soil again, Kevin Walls recalled that 'Our joy was unspeakable. It is rather useless to try to attempt to say what we thought as we landed.' The men were formed up in threes and marched away from the wharf up the main street of Cairns. It was a quiet Saturday afternoon, and the few onlookers who were present stared, blank faced, at these ragged, bearded soldiers, who looked like a ghost army, marching in loose formation, tears streaming down their faces. 'We were wrecks,' recounted Walls. 'People stared at us and wondered where we'd come from.'

Mick Smith, one of the junior officers, directed many of his men into the nearby Blue Bird Cafe for a feed. The astonished owner handed out menus which the men could only hold in their skeletal hands while staring blankly.

For McCarthy, the homecoming was overwhelming. As Feldt himself recounts:

As the ship touched the wharf, McCarthy, who had carried the burden for so long, drooped and wilted in complete mental and nervous exhaustion. With never a quip or a joke, he found nothing now of interest or value. Ashore, he sat at a table, a dead cigarette between his lips, an untasted beer before him, and answered questions in grunts and monosyllables.

Keith McCarthy and his team of Coastwatchers, plus a remarkably capable woman, had managed to pull off one of the most daring escapes in Australian military history. The men of Lark Force, who should never have been sent to Rabaul in the first place, were left there – undertrained and undersupplied –

to face the full fury of a vastly superior Japanese force they had not a hope of even slowing up, let alone defeating. Then, following their inevitable defeat, they were abandoned by their government and senior command, and left to rot.

Rabaul was a catastrophe entirely of Australia's own making. There were no extenuating circumstances in the form of foreign commands softening the culpability of a cold and uncaring Australian government who knowingly left its own people for dead.

McCarthy's exhausted spirits may have been lifted somewhat when news of another spectacular escape, that of a group of men under the command of Hugh Mackenzie, who had last been heard of heading for Rabaul's southern coast. On another vessel, the *Laurabada*, he and 145 men had been lifted off to safety, having suffered even more privations than McCarthy and his group.

Upon arrival in Cairns, Gladys Baker had lost 4 stone in weight and, like the men, was suffering from malnutrition. Her worst moment, however, was having her beloved dog taken away and shot by Australian Customs officials, as it was considered a threat to local health.

Sources differ as to how many men were eventually rescued by the *Lakatoi*, figures ranging between 190 and 250 individuals. Only six would be classified 'fit' and return to the war. The rest, says Lindsay, 'were shattered men – mental and physical wrecks, fearfully ravaged by malaria, tropical ulcers, malnutrition, exposure and stress. For most, the war was over, and scars of Rabaul would last a lifetime.'

Amazingly, McCarthy recovered and in just a few months was back in action with the Commando Z and M Special Units behind enemy lines in New Britain and other islands, earning himself an MBE. After the war, he would return to Rabaul, where he would be given the new rank of district commissioner.

Gladys Baker would also return to the islands, determined at war's end to rebuild the life she had fled in 1942. Having spent the remainder of the war assisting Allied intelligence with her knowledge of the islands, she joined the AAMWS (Australian Army Medical Women's Service), was awarded the rank of lieutenant, and was so determined to return and fight the Japanese she asked to train as a commando. The time for a woman – even of her ability – to play such a role had unfortunately yet to arrive. 'It will be a sad day for the British Empire when the Army has to fight with women,' scoffed a commanding officer with whom she raised the idea.

Despite RAAF intelligence informing her that her house and property had been utterly destroyed by Japanese bombs, Baker determined to return and rebuild, claiming in a newspaper article that she would be prepared to live in a tent if she had to. 'My friends all say I'm too old to start again, but I intend to try.'

One of the first civilians to return to Rabaul, Baker survived the trials of the evacuation, only to be struck down by the dreaded blackwater fever in 1947 and die at age fifty. A truly unsung hero, Baker was also awarded the MBE for her valiant work but was quickly forgotten to history.

# Chapter 9
# THE GOLDEN VOICE

In the pre-dawn of 2 February, just a week after the fall of Rabaul, the few remaining civilians of Port Moresby, and the men of the growing army garrison, were woken to the unfamiliar 'krump' of explosions as a formation of four-engine 'Mavis' flying boats passed overhead in the gloom and discharged their bombs. Although their aim was haphazard, the Japanese encountered almost no effective anti-aircraft fire, and with no defending fighter aircraft, returned to their bases at Rabaul unscathed. Emboldened by the ease of this first mission, the Japanese dispensed with the cover of darkness and would now begin attacks on Moresby in broad daylight, the pilots indulging in practice runs over their target before releasing their load at leisure, and the nimble Zeros giving arrogant displays of aerobatics over the town and harbour.

The pattern was set. Port Moresby, having revealed itself to be pitifully undefended, would be pummelled into surrender as a prelude to invasion.

The Japanese were not, however, operating unobserved. Almost as soon as Japan's air campaign began, Port Moresby would be given vital advance radio warning of almost every attack sent against it, allowing its soldiers and civilians to take cover while also denying the enemy, at the very least, the element of complete surprise. Weeks later, when the Kittyhawks of the RAAF arrived and the Japanese were finally met with opposition, these warnings would be a gift to the young Australian fighter pilots as they climbed into the humid skies to meet the Japanese head-on, giving them something of a fighting chance against the superior might of the enemy.

All of them would be provided by one man operating alone in the jungle, who never faltered in his calm, quiet delivery: the Coastwatcher they dubbed 'Golden Voice'.

•

What exactly inspired 24-year-old Leigh Grant Vial to turn away from his comfortable middle-class upbringing in the leafy Melbourne suburb of Camberwell, to walk away from his uncompleted commerce degree at the prestigious University of Melbourne and head north to become a patrol officer will perhaps never be known. Outwardly, Vial could hardly have been mistaken for the adventurous type: short in stature and quiet of voice, he was bookish, thoughtful and intelligent. Yet, in 1932, he applied for the lowly position of cadet patrol officer in the Mandated Territory of New Guinea, and was chosen, one of just ten from a field of more than 1600 applicants. His first posting was to the Morobe District on New Guinea's north coast, encompassing Lae, Salamaua and Finschhafen, which in 1942 would become the epicentre of the Japanese occupation.

While many people from cooler climates unaccustomed to the tropics would find the experience almost intolerable, Leigh Vial was one of those rarest of individuals who immediately thrived in this most challenging of environments. In Morobe, for months on end, Vial would vanish into the jungle on long patrols for months on end, learning to survive in its rugged wilderness, discovering its peaks and rivers, its peoples and their customs and languages. In a short time he was assessed as 'solid and dependable' by the administration hierarchy. In 1937, he became the first European to climb Mount Wilhelm, the territory's highest peak, and wrote long and instructive articles on New Guinea and its wonders for the armchair-travelling readers of *Walkabout* and *Oceania* magazines. Sometimes, he would deposit the handwritten sheaves in the villages through which he passed, relying on the native runner network to eventually see them posted back to Australia.

In August 1940, he was promoted to assistant district officer and given a new posting: Rabaul. Here, he began to sense the looming threat from Japan, and was under no illusions that the small number of barely trained soldiers arriving as Lark Force would be capable of holding them back.

On 23 January, the day before the Japanese invasion, he spirited away nearly 150 ground crew and staff of 24 Squadron along a track he had purposely reconnoitred to Put Put on the island's east coast. Here, two Catalina flying boats gathered up the men, lifting them and Vial to the safety of Townsville. It was one of the last air evacuations before the town's fall the following day.

In Townsville, Vial made a direct line to the office of Eric Feldt, and all but demanded to be signed up as a Coastwatcher and sent back into action. Feldt was more than happy to grant his request. He had known Vial in New Guinea, and was suitably impressed not only with his enthusiasm but his demonstrable knowledge of the region. Feldt believed he would make the ideal Coastwatcher.

The wheels of the defence bureaucracy had finally turned by the time Vial joined Feldt's organisation. Having previously refused to bring the Coastwatchers into the military, they now insisted upon all civilian operatives being given an officer's rank. Officer status, it was believed, would offer more protection if they were captured by the Japanese. Although it was soon discovered that the Japanese cared as little for captured officers as any other individual – soldier or civilian – who fell into their grasp, treating them with equal barbarity.

Being a navy man, Feldt naturally wished Vial to join his old service, with a commission in the Royal Australian Navy. But the navy was an old institution, set in its ways and not prepared to rush anyone into its venerable ranks, no matter the level of urgency. Feldt believed he could pull some strings to expedite the process but was shocked to find that Vial would need to go before a selection board, sit various exams and medicals, fill out reams of forms, and spend several months waiting for the machinery of naval process to turn, very much at its own unhurried pace.

In his book, Feldt wrote of his despair:

The Red Tape Plant is, of course, one of the wonders of biology. It flourishes in offices; the larger and older the office, the heavier the infestation. It grows apace, strangling and paralysing, its seed proliferated by letters from an already infected office, invisible seed which falls as the envelope is opened, and grows at once.

Vial enquired whether perhaps the air force – a considerably newer organisation less bound by tradition – might offer a speedier passage into their ranks. Feldt thought for a moment, picked up the phone, and in two days, Leigh Vial was commissioned as a pilot officer in the Royal Australian Air Force.

A little over a fortnight later, on 20 February, having been issued with a Teleradio, codes and various supplies, Vial was on a plane heading to Salamaua on the north coast of New Guinea, tasked with warning of Japanese air activity, particularly attacks against Port Moresby. He would also report on any Japanese landings, which were expected to take place along the north coast. For this he would not have to wait long.

At Salamaua, Vial organised a team of bearers, adhering strictly to the Coastwatchers' policy of paying for all native labour in cash. It was essential the native people had no reason to question their loyalty to the Australians as the cooperation of the villagers was vital.

On a trek lasting several days, Vial led the way, hauling not only the heavy components of the Teleradio, but food, supplies and even some token weaponry and ammunition, high up into the hills overlooking Salamaua.

He had selected the position carefully, a place from which he could both scan the skies above and the approaches to the port settlement of Salamaua below, including its vital airstrip. He chose it also for its jagged rocky terrain to confuse radio-direction-finding equipment, as well as its access to fresh water and lines of withdrawal to positions deeper into the jungle, amid native people he knew he could trust.

High in a self-designed jungle treehouse invisible from the forest floor, Coastwatcher Leigh Vial switched on his Teleradio for the first time and began broadcasting.

From the middle of February to May 1942, arguably some of the most critical months in Australia's history, he would report up to nine times a day, providing Port Moresby with vital 'eyes' on Papua's distant northern shore. He would always speak into the Teleradio's microphone in a calm and clear voice, giving no indication of the harshness of the situation in which he had placed himself.

In detail, he would announce the arrival of Japanese bombers from the north, then count them as they assembled in the humid sky before turning to strike Port Moresby across the other side of the Owen Stanley Ranges. He would provide the enemy's direction, numbers, formations and altitudes, allowing the intelligence officers a twenty- to forty-minute window in which to act before the raiders appeared over the town and its airfields.

The pattern was always the same: the Japanese took off in the early morning from Rabaul, and occasionally as far away as Truk, to arrive over Port Moresby around 10 a.m., then the impotent banging away of the anti-aircraft batteries would begin, lacking even the correct fuses and ammunition to reach the Japanese bombers' altitudes. The weary soldiers below could almost set their watches by it.

At dawn on 8 March, Vial watched as a fleet of Japanese ships arrived off Salamaua and began battering the shore. The long-expected invasion of the northern shore of New Guinea had begun. Undefended, the town fell after a single skirmish, and for the cost of a single Japanese casualty. From now on, Vial would be broadcasting under the nose of the enemy. In a few days, Japanese aircraft began operating from the airstrip at Salamaua, reducing their flying distance to Moresby and increasing their time over the target. The town and its harbour, the Japanese believed with supreme confidence, would soon be on the verge of capitulation. Then the amphibious invasion would simply arrive and sweep it up.

Soon the Japanese radio operators at Salamaua began to detect a lone and persistent voice broadcasting on a rare frequency, reporting their every move in open speech to the enemy. They could also hear that it was close.

•

The RAAF's 75 Squadron was formed by a rushed stroke of a pen on 4 March 1942, when a consignment of P-40 Kittyhawk fighters happened to fall into Australian hands after their intended recipients, the Dutch, capitulated in Borneo almost without resistance. Less than three weeks later, the first of 75 Squadron's fighters touched down on Port Moresby's Seven Mile Airstrip. Barely had their propellers ceased turning when the daily Japanese reconnaissance patrol – a single twin-engine bomber – appeared overhead to leisurely photograph the results of the morning's raid. This afternoon, however, two 75 Squadron Kittyhawks were sent up to meet it, their guns tearing open the raider's engines and sending it spiralling into the sea in front of an oily black plume of smoke. It was a seminal moment in the Pacific War, and the Japanese were taken completely by surprise.

For the next six weeks, the battle for the skies of New Guinea raged, with daily encounters between the young, green pilots of 75 Squadron and the hardened Japanese veteran airmen, some with years of combat experience in China behind them. In addition, the Kittyhawk, a powerful but heavy aircraft, was no match for the ballerina-like manoeuvrability of Japan's famed Zero. It had long been acknowledged that the only effective hope of victory for a Kittyhawk pilot over a Zero was to attack from above. Any attempt to engage it in a dogfight was usually lethal. Leigh Vial's role in this epic David and Goliath struggle would be monumental, particularly as Port Moresby even lacked effective radar, although this was no fault of the dedicated operators.

The RAAF's number 29 Radar Station was the first such unit deployed outside Australia, arriving at Port Moresby the same day Darwin was bombed by the Japanese on 19 February. Struggling to set up their heavy equipment atop a precipice known as King's Spur, 2 miles east of the town, the operating team found that so many parts were missing from the shipment from Sydney that the unit's power could only be sourced by simply hooking up to the town's overhead power lines. Nor was the motor to turn the radar dish to be found, requiring this vital element to be cranked by hand. Despite these setbacks, the operators managed to be up and running by 18 March. Yet what they were able to see was of almost no use to anyone. The vital northern direction from Port Moresby, from which quarter the town's attackers inevitably appeared, was completely blocked by the massive spurs of the Owen Stanley Ranges. It would be months before another station could be relocated higher in the hills with unobstructed lines of sight.

As the Japanese air attacks on Moresby intensified throughout April, and without assistance from radar, Vial's reports became ever more essential in allowing the defenders to climb into the skies and meet the Japanese on something approaching equal terms. In reality, even a headstart of twenty minutes was insufficient to allow 75 Squadron's powerful but heavy Kittyhawks to achieve their ideal position of being above the Japanese 'Betty' bombers and their escort of nimble Zeros, but without Vial's alerts, the Australians would have been caught on the ground and destroyed many times over.

At one stage, a newspaper reporter visited Port Moresby's Seven Mile Airstrip to report on the daily action, and heard for himself the calm steady tones of Vial broadcasting from somewhere 'out there' in the jungle. Without naming him, nor even reporting his location, he mentioned the man's 'clear, golden voice' and the name instantly stuck. Later, when informed of the moniker, the intensely modest Vial was considerably embarrassed.

The Japanese became obsessed with Vial and determined to locate and destroy him. Patrols were sent out high into the precipices above Salamaua and the tracks winding through the surrounding hills. Heavy radio-direction-finding sets were hauled up and switched on. Sometimes they caught a snippet of him, but Vial was canny enough never to stay on the air for a moment longer than necessary, and the rock formations which he had selected as his backdrop obfuscated his location further.

At least twice, Japanese patrols passed directly under his tree hideout. Vial watched them but had been meticulous in not leaving any clue on the jungle floor. As the weeks went by, the increasingly furious Japanese attempted to bribe local villagers to betray him, all of whom feigned ignorance of his existence. Afterwards, Vial estimated the Japanese gave him a 'scare about once a week'. He was constantly wet, beset by leeches and mosquitoes, and at times so badly affected by tinea that he could only crawl to his set to warm it up and broadcast. After his initial supply of rations ran out, Vial lived almost entirely on yams, taro and nuts from the okari tree, occasionally snaring for himself a cuscus or tree kangaroo, augmented from time to time with food from friendly villagers who risked their all in aiding him.

In mid-April, without warning, Vial's voice went silent. Without his information, 75 Squadron reverted to flying standing patrols, draining the energy of pilots and wearing out already overworked aircraft. The intelligence officers at Port Moresby feared the worst. Then, a few days later, an exhausted local villager appeared, brandishing a letter from Vial requesting a delivery of a number of radio valves which had failed in the humidity. A dawn parachute drop was arranged, and within a few days, Golden Voice was back on the air.

After a six-week struggle over Port Moresby, the exhausted 75 Squadron was withdrawn, and the air defence of New Guinea became a largely American operation. Now Vial came to be appreciated by the American pilots, among whom he began to acquire an almost mystical status, as a man, entirely alone, enduring the harshest of sacrifices and privations for the benefit of others. Though none of them had met nor even knew his name, one airman recalled, 'We all felt close to him'.

In June, Vial made the decision to relocate his observation post. No one would have resented him had he decided to remove himself from danger, but Vial instead moved even closer to the enemy. Frustrated at his hilltop view of Salamaua being regularly obscured by cloud, Vial packed up his Teleradio and, with the help of some devoted locals, moved down the hill to a new post under the cloud base, now barely a mile and a quarter from the edge of the Japanese airstrip. From here, he could accurately report on the Japanese aircraft being deployed to Salamaua, as well as the effectiveness of the growing Allied air efforts to knock them out of action.

A fortnight later, Vial came to suspect that a circling Japanese aircraft had spotted his hideout and so relocated a third time, and he resumed his broadcasts. In July, he was promoted to flying officer but eventually the conditions began to overwhelm him. Increasing bouts of malaria, dengue fever, isolation and an inadequate diet took their toll. Added to this was the months of straining for hours a day through binoculars, causing his eyesight to begin to fail, and excruciating eczema, brought on by the permanent tropical damp. In August 1942, after receiving the signal finally relieving him, Vial packed away the Teleradio for the next Coastwatcher to report on the comings and goings at Salamaua, then headed off into the jungle. For two days, he made his way on foot to the Australian base of Wau, from where he was flown to Port Moresby. After his debriefing, his intelligence officer reported that 'not on any single occasion did he neglect to get his messages through'.

Even while undergoing an extended recuperation, Vial continued to serve, compiling a manual on jungle survival, all the while making it clear that he intended to return to the jungle to resume his Coastwatching duties. His superiors thought otherwise, believing every ounce of luck Vial had needed to survive as long as he did was all now expended. Instead, he was placed in charge of the Port Moresby office of the Far Eastern Liaison Office, FELO, a propaganda and field intelligence outfit established by General Thomas Blamey. From the unfamiliar surroundings of an office, Vial wrote and organised the dropping of propaganda leaflets, supply drops and patrols into enemy-controlled territory.

Promoted to flight lieutenant in early 1943, Vial began flying with American Liberator aircraft, overseeing jungle supply drops. It was on one of these, on the last day of April, that his pilot miscalculated a turn and crashed near Bena Bena in the central New Guinea highlands, killing all twelve onboard. The bodies were eventually recovered, and Leigh Vial, the quiet Coastwatcher warrior, the Golden Voice, who contributed so much to the Allied cause in New Guinea, was buried in the Lae war cemetery, survived by his wife and three children in Melbourne.

Vial's death sent a pall of grief through New Guinea, particularly among the Americans, who saw fit to bestow on Vial their second highest award for bravery, the Distinguished Service Cross. No such honour – nor any official recognition at all – would ever be forthcoming from the Australian armed forces he so gallantly served.

# Chapter 10

# THE WAR COMES TO BOUGAINVILLE

From his tiny, heart-shaped island of Sohana, District Officer Jack Read gazed eastwards along the waters of Buka Passage, and – not for the first time – wondered if the eye of man could possibly behold a more idyllic view. To his left, the southern shore of Buka Island, with its gleaming white ribbon of perfect beach, bordered by palm and fragrant beauty leaf trees stretching out from the jungle boundary to offer a little shade.

Behind this stretched the 30-mile expanse of Buka Island itself – home to 10 000 natives and several dozen Europeans – a largely flat landmass, save for a line of gently rising hills on its western shore. To his right, his eye could follow the mangrove shoreline of the northern edge of Bougainville, with its population of about 70 000 natives and 150 European settlers and missionaries. One hundred and twenty miles long and 40 miles wide, Bougainville was an island of breathtaking beauty: a primordial landscape of rugged mountains, deep rivers and mysterious jungles receding away to a bluish backdrop of jagged hills, shimmering in the tropical heat, 'rising like flexed muscle from the serene sea'. Separating the two islands, Buka Passage, half a mile long and 300 yards wide, flowed like a drowsy palette of aqua and Prussian blue.

Along the Buka shoreline, a row of thatched huts – perfectly straight – formed a village where peaceful, dark-skinned Melanesians lived, cultivating taro and banana, or drying copra, for cash to spend at the stores of the Cantonese traders who formed their own community around a hundred strong further along the coast. Occasionally, a government launch or native canoe made its way past the reefs, its dozen paddlers stroking in time to a six-note chant of harmonised voices ranging from mature bass to a young boy's soprano. It was, as Feldt described it, 'a lotus land, where a man might live a large part of his life away, peacefully going about his daily tasks, and find with surprise, years later, that so much of his mortal span had gone'.

Despite having lived and worked in New Guinea for twelve years, Read had never once visited this part of the territory until tasked by Feldt to establish a Coastwatching network in November 1941. Soon, Japanese floatplanes began to appear, flying low and lazily over Buka Passage, a grim harbinger of what was to come.

Read's wonderment at the sheer beauty of the islands would never leave him. When compiling his Coastwatcher reports, he would frequently become diverted in detailed descriptions of his surroundings, even when the enemy was closing in. And yet, standing on the little jetty on the tiny island of Sohana, watching the sea flow through the passage, Read sensed his patch of paradise would soon be engulfed by the tide of war.

By October 1941, in anticipation of the coming conflict, the RAAF had established an intermediary refuelling base for their Catalina flying boats at Soraken, 10 miles away. As Read recalled later, 'Usually a couple of these craft would drop down in the late afternoon, spend the night, and then take off at dawn on reconnaissance patrol.' On Buka, an as-yet incomplete 1400-foot airstrip – initially levelled with the picks and shovels of local Bougainvilleans in 1940 for civilian use – was being guarded by twenty-five soldiers of 3 Section, 2/1st Independent Company under the command of Lieutenant John H. Mackie. Mackie's men had shipped north in July 1941 and enjoyed 'an idyllic life [which] drifted along' on Buka, camped behind the small local Chinatown where they could buy a beer and get a meal at Chin Yung's or Laurie Chan's cafe. Only one aircraft had bothered to visit the airstrip, a lone Wirraway which had dropped in from Rabaul.

Aware that this lotus-eating existence was doing his men no good whatsoever, Mackie relocated to the airstrip and, demonstrating a level of foresight sadly lacking at Rabaul, insisted his men conduct familiarisation patrols into the jungle as well as prepare lines of withdrawal and supply dumps further inland.

At the time, the 2/1st was the only unit in New Guinea trained in jungle guerrilla warfare and, in the event of attack, Mackie was under orders to blow up the strip along with its stores of bombs and fuel. In reality, there would be little he could do with the token amount of explosives he had been given for the task, and he was under no illusions about his ability to prevent the Buka airstrip falling to the Japanese.

When the first of the Japanese reconnaissance flying boats appeared overhead, the soldiers had opened fire with every weapon they could get their hands on, including a Webley revolver and even an old Vickers machine gun from World War I. A cheer had gone up when one Japanese aircraft appeared to turn away, but Mackie knew this was simply the beginning, and ordered the runway and storehouses be prepared for demolition.

Jack Read likewise sensed the Japanese to be just days away.

•

Born in Hobart in 1905, Read had felt the lure of the islands early in life, and had been accepted into the New Guinea territorial service aged twenty-three, arriving at Rabaul on the SS *Montoro* in 1929. The day before he embarked, he married his childhood sweetheart. There is no record of his bride's reaction to the hasty departure, but the fact the nuptials took place raised the ire of the New Guinea Administrator, Walter McNicoll, who had just instigated a policy of accepting only unmarried men as cadets, and Read was told his appointment was to be terminated. Due to the fact McNicoll's stipulation had not been indicated previously, the decision was overturned by the Commonwealth Public Service Board, and Read was permitted to continue, even succeeding in arranging for his wife to join him. Infuriated, McNicoll proceeded to saddle Read with the worst, most difficult jobs in the territory, determined to force his resignation. Instead, Jack Read thrived.

By the beginning of World War II, Read had served across New Guinea at Sepik River, Ambunti, Madang, Wau, Lae and Rabaul. He had also become a close colleague of Eric Feldt. In 1940, Read proved his mettle further when he had taken Italian and German gold miners into custody prior to their internment in Australia then, in early 1941, withdrew his wife and young daughter to Melbourne for some overdue leave, this time returning to New Guinea alone.

As always, Feldt offers a colourful description of his friend: 'He was a wiry fellow, with dark hair, clear grey eyes, and a thin straight gash of a mouth above a long, firm chin. His voice was deep and a little harsh, his laugh explosive. His manner was blunt and straightforward, rather firm than tactful.'

Feldt had marked the capable Read as a potential lynchpin in his Bougainville Coastwatcher network, and stood in front of him as he read the oath after willingly agreeing to join. Given charge of the Buka Passage subdistrict, Read, like many civilian Coastwatchers, carried out his twin duties of administration as well as supplying regular reports via his Teleradio. Early on 21 January 1942, the Catalinas at Soraken took off without their usual goodbyes and headed towards the Australian mainland, having removed much of their records and permanent equipment. 'We regarded their sudden departure as rather ominous,' recalled Read, who suspected they would not be returning anytime soon. Two days later, the news reached him of the fall of Rabaul, just 200 miles to the northwest. Japanese reconnaissance aircraft appeared overhead and began making long, slow circles over his post at Sohana. 'My intuition warned me that the Passage was next on the Emperor's list,' recalled Read.

Swearing he would not be taken into captivity by the Japanese, Read sought local knowledge of the area and was told that the tiny mountain village of Aravia, across the passage on Bougainville, would be a suitable place to establish a new camp.

At dawn the following morning, he sent off a party of native workers with his supplies, while he left a few hours later on a government launch, the *Nugget*, with the vital Teleradio. Only a mile or so into his trip, a Japanese floatplane appeared to be passing overhead. Suddenly, it banked, dived and made straight for the *Nugget*, almost skimming the water. Then, the hammer of its machine guns could be heard, and white splashes tore into the sea around the little boat. But after a half-hearted single pass, the pilot chose not to pursue his quarry. 'I have often thought,' wrote Read years later, 'that the Japanese pilots might not have been so easy on us if they had guessed the part our Teleradio was destined to play in their defeat at Guadalcanal.'

Disappearing over the strait, the floatplane returned a short time later, now leading a formation of five aircraft, which proceeded to bomb Jack Read's former station and other buildings on Sohano Island. Watching from the boat, Read looked on as his few worldly possessions vanished under a pall of flame and thick oily smoke. Then the airmen turned their attention to the village, vindictively strafing the perfect line of native huts along Buka Beach, sending bewildered Melanesians scattering in confusion, the harmony of their village life shattered forever.

Read's journey to his new post was a difficult one. 'In order to reach Aravia from the Passage,' he recalled, 'it was necessary to take a road down the east coast of Bougainville for about 20 miles to the Banui Plantation, then travel inland and climb for nearly two hours to reach the settlement – more than a thousand feet above sea level.' The effort, however, was worth it. Aravia was elevated, gave commanding views of Buka Passage and the north Bougainville coast, and was all but isolated.

Panic meanwhile gripped the European population of Bougainville. At the local administrative capital of Kieta, roughly halfway down the island's eastern coast, a local boy had reported that a Japanese seaplane had alighted just outside the harbour. Although the sighting turned out to be a mistake, another two Japanese aircraft then flew low over the town. It was enough to convince the local district officer at Kieta, J. I. Merrylees, that the town was under attack and to issue a directive that the government was fleeing, and any remaining Europeans who wished to do the same should head to the dock and jump on a ship. 'If you wish to join the party,' the notice added, 'proceed with all speed to Kieta, bringing clothing and bedding. Rations will be provided.' The panicky missive not only provided a nightmare to the shipping organisers, but sent Kieta spinning into chaos.

Jack Read had previously been organising evacuations of his own. At his own district in late December, he had rounded up thirteen women and children who assembled at his headquarters and were then lifted off from the little jetty at Sohano. Then, at plantations along the Bougainville coast, he had urged planters and missionaries to leave ahead of the expected Japanese invasion, and he collected any who wished to be brought down to Kieta, from where they could take a larger vessel to safety.

As early as 12 December, just days after Pearl Harbor, the Australian government had ordered the evacuation of European women and children from all its New Guinea territories, but unlike at Rabaul, the Solomon Islanders showed more reluctance to comply. Read found many, who believed themselves to be sufficiently removed from the course of battle, simply refused to consider abandoning their well-established properties and lifestyles, concerned their authority would be diminished in the eyes of the natives.

On Buka, he had argued in vain with Mrs Huson, who had resided at her and her husband's Hanahan Plantation since 1917, but she insisted on staying put to take her chances. At Teop on Bougainville, his pleas to Mrs Falkner to leave her impressive Tearouki Plantation likewise fell on deaf ears and Mrs Campbell at the large and wealthy Raua Plantation on the north coast refused to leave without her sick husband, Claude, even though the government had promised to evacuate them both. Read would later state, 'The women were advised that if they remained on the island they would be doing so at their own risk. I later regretted that I had not taken the initiative and forcibly moved them aboard ship.'

Some of those evacuations were themselves flawed, with many people being taken not to Australia but north to Rabaul, from where they would need to be removed a second time when the invasion of New Britain was imminent. And to Read's considerable disgust, forty Japanese civilians were put onboard

the steamer *Malaita* and taken to be interned in Australia 'with
the luxury of a cabin and bunk, and waited upon by stewards
in the dining salon'.

Further complicating matters, the government had
given nurses, missionaries and clergy an out, leaving it up to
themselves to decide to stay or remain. Many believed the
tenets of the Church would protect them from such worldly
matters as wars and foreign invasions in any case. At their
mission at Hanahan, Read had tried to convince the Sisters
of St Joseph of Orange that this would not be the case, but
they were immovable. He listened but simply shook his head.
'Those few words of the proviso,' he later said, 'eventually
created one of the biggest problems that the Coastwatchers
were faced with on Bougainville.'

With Merrylees's alarming directive at Kieta any
complacency vanished, and Bougainville's remaining European
population scrambled to board anything that could float
heading to the southern Solomons, or west to Australia itself.
Merrylees and his staff, to Read's disgust, were one of the first
groups to flee, having commandeered the *Herald*, a small ketch
owned by a local Chinese trader. 'Varied and vivid,' Read later
stated, 'were the stories told by reliable eyewitnesses of the
arguing and jockeying for a place on the vessel.' Some of those
who remained stranded on the dock after the *Herald* pulled
away jumped on bicycles and vainly attempted to chase it down
the coast.

Incredibly, Merrylees also took away the precious Teleradio
assigned to a Coastwatcher in the south. The local natives –
amazed to see their white masters fleeing like terrified birds –
moved into the vacuum and helped themselves in a frenzy of
looting and destruction.

•

One man Read would not attempt to persuade to leave was the manager of the Inus plantation on Bougainville's east coast, fellow Coastwatcher Paul Mason. Mason was pleased to see Read when he called at Inus, not least because he had recently received a message addressed to both of them from Eric Feldt in Townsville.

'You will be of great value,' Feldt stated, 'if you can remain and keep contact for over six months. Suggest you prepare a base two days inland and retire to it when necessary. Make a garden and stock up with pigs and fowls. If you want essential spares and stores, advise your requirements and we may be able to drop them.'

The two men read the words again, struck by the gravity of their meaning. Feldt was requesting – though not ordering – his Bougainville Coastwatchers to insert themselves into what was soon to become enemy-occupied territory as spies, fully aware of their fate should they be captured. They looked at each other, nodded, and immediately sent a reply stating they would accept the challenge. As Read later said, 'My attitude was that I thought it a little too early to abandon the show altogether as was apparently being done in Kieta.'

Paul Mason concurred. 'I now realised I had a chance to do something. Even if I had not been a civilian Coastwatcher, I should have stayed on with my transmitter making the best of an opportunity I had long dreamed of.'

Feldt later admitted six months was 'a pure guess on my part – I felt that something should have happened by that time, for us or against us, which would resolve the whole question of Coastwatching'.

Born in Sydney to a Danish seafarer and an Australian widow, Paul Edward Mason had been too young to fight in World War I, but to ease his family's financial burden, at fifteen he'd followed his older brother Tom to the Solomons to help establish an island trading business in the little island group known as the Shortlands. Adapting surprisingly quickly to islander life, Mason accepted a role managing the Associated Plantation Company's large holding at Inus when he was twenty-four. On his first day on the job, he enquired as to what had become of the previous manager, and then was casually told that they had been hacked to death by angry plantation workers. This seemed not to bother Mason in the slightest, and he busied himself criss-crossing the Solomons recruiting labour, learning both the country and local village traditions. He also developed a deep regard for the native people who, for their part, became intrigued with this unusual young white man who seemed quite devoid of the typical arrogance of the European settler and displayed a genuine interest in their culture.

To his fellow islanders, however, Mason became something of an eccentric. Although warm and genial, he was gauche and shy, ill-kept, bespectacled and bookish. He was also short in stature, somewhat buck-toothed, a little deaf and spoke with a slight speech impediment, induced by continued bouts of malaria. When World War II arrived, he applied for military service, but was scoffed at by the military authorities, not least for simply being too old.

Eric Feldt, on the other hand, was more than happy to have 41-year-old Mason join his ranks, describing him as being 'less like a "tough guy" than any other man on Bougainville … he gazed benignly through his spectacles and spoke slowly, generally pausing thoughtfully before replying even to a casual remark'.

If, with his film star good looks, Jack Read appeared born for the role of a hero, Paul Mason was cut from a different cloth. Yet it would be Mason who 'represented the upper limits of continuous bravery', according to some of the RAAF's most intrepid Catalina pilots, and who would literally change the course of one of the great battles of World War II. Working in tandem, Read and Mason would become two of the greatest Coastwatchers of the war.

Soon after reading Feldt's message to remain in Bougainville, Read received word that Kieta had not actually fallen to the Japanese, nor had it even been attacked. Desperate for information as to what was happening in the town, he resolved to go there and, if necessary, do his best to assert his authority. A day later, after sailing overnight, he pulled up into the town's little harbour in the early morning to be met by the gigantic, bearded figure of Sergeant Yauwika, and Corporal Sali, two reliable men from the native police. He had worked with both of them in other parts of the New Guinea territory, and they would later be decorated for their services to the Allied cause. They were overjoyed to see him.

Despite their best efforts, both men had struggled to maintain order in Kieta, explaining that a Doctor Kroenig, a former district officer during the old German administration, had placed himself in charge following the departure of Merrylees and the local government. Read listened, thanked the men for their efforts, walked over to the flagpole, atop which was a large white flag of surrender, pulled it down and ran up the Union Jack.

An incensed Doctor Kroenig arrived, bristling at Read's appearance. Glancing contemptuously up the flagpole, he declared loudly that he had been forced to take over Kieta after the undignified exit of the British and their failure to keep order. Read took in the man – well known for his openly Nazi affiliations – and informed him that, as district officer, he was assuming control of the town. Kroenig began to remonstrate, and Read's two native police took a small step forward. Kroenig backed down. Later, he withdrew to his plantation where he was compelled to return a swathe of government equipment he had acquired during his brief, self-appointed reign. Kept under a close watch, Kroenig was later apprehended by Mackie and deposited onto a ship to Australia to spend the rest of the war interned as an enemy alien.

Read restored a semblance of order at Kieta, giving Sergeant Yauwika and Corporal Sali plenipotentiary powers, and even managed to retrieve most of the food, fuel and other items which had been carried off by the villagers. Knowing he would soon be depending on their loyalty, Read took care to exact no retribution.

Several weeks later, Read's Teleradio caught the ABC bulletin from Townsville describing the heroic exploits of district officer Merrylees: how he had successfully evacuated scores of Europeans, then sailed the tropical waters to the safety of Port Moresby entirely without navigational instruments. And Merrylees even had the gall to recount how he had had the foresight to secure the administration records and destroy the office prior to his departure. For Read this was too much, as he had been the one left to carry out the task himself. And Read had indeed shown foresight when he blew open the door of the office safe and retrieved the administration cash reserves of nearly a thousand pounds which, along with tradeable goods such as calico and tobacco, would be vital in securing the cooperation of native helpers in the dangerous months ahead.

But Kieta's fate, he knew, had merely been forestalled.

'Despite the pandemonium created by Merrylees,' recalled Read, 'I realised that the fall of Kieta was only a matter of time. I immediately began to establish hidden supply dumps and cleared the town of anything that might prove valuable to the enemy.'

Read's responsibility now was to establish a Coastwatcher network with the handful of men remaining on Bougainville he believed up to the task. He also had the help of Lieutenant Mackie, who had agreed to lend Read some of his men for Coastwatching duties. Read would need every one of them, as the formerly peaceful island of Bougainville would soon be a war zone. Then, instead of the passive Fernandos Eric Feldt envisaged, the Coastwatchers would become spies playing the deadliest of games behind enemy lines.

Not all were up to the task. Drummond Thomson at Numa Numa Plantation cited poor health and took the opportunity to evacuate. Feldt was understanding, knowing full well that 'only a fit man could endure what was ahead'. Thomson did prove some use in persuading a number – but by no means all – of the more recalcitrant European civilians to leave with him. This was welcome news for Read. Aside from their own safety, every European remaining under Japanese occupation was a potential source of information for the enemy.

In Drummond's place, Read assigned one of Mackie's men, Corporal Dolby, to Numa Numa. Other stations were established in a pattern designed to cover all of Bougainville, with the exception of the undeveloped west coast, which Read believed unlikely to be visited by the enemy. At Kessa, on the northwest tip of Buka Island, the strategically important Queen Carola Harbour was under observation by Coastwatcher Percy Good, but at over fifty years of age, Read decided he was simply now too old for the job. In his place two more men from Mackie's detachment, Signalman D. L. Sly and Corporal Harry Cameron, were appointed, and three native police. While not doubting their enthusiasm, Read was aware that Sly and Cameron knew little of the country and were completely inexperienced in Coastwatching. To assist them, Read was more than happy for them to be joined by the Reverend Usaia Sotutu, a 41-year-old Fijian missionary who had previously requested to join the Coastwatchers, even removing his wife and children to safety in anticipation of being accepted. Sotutu brought with him twenty years' experience in Bougainville with the Methodist Mission Society; he knew the country and its people, and had built up a large personal following. Jack Read was delighted to sign him up.

Read was operating from the little hamlet of Aravia in the central north of the island, from where he could view both the east and west coasts, each 7 miles distant. From his plantation at Inus over on the east coast, Paul Mason would observe the central approaches to the island, though soon he would relocate to cover the south.

By 6 March, the Bougainville Coastwatcher network was in place, manned by a mixture of soldiers and civilians who, between them, covered a large proportion of the island. For the foreseeable future, they would place themselves in harm's way as the primary source of Allied intelligence regarding the Japanese on Bougainville.

For his part, Percy Good was initially aggrieved to be relieved of his Coastwatching duties and replaced by Sly and Cameron, but he eventually accepted Read's argument that his health was probably not up to the rigours of operating in the midst of the enemy.

Good had lived and worked as a planter at Kessa Point for years and had become an expert in the use and construction of radios; he was known for even making his own coils by hand-winding hundreds of yards of fine copper wire.

No sooner had Good's Teleradio been dismantled, removed, and hidden further into the jungle than the Japanese decided to pay him a visit. Humble and suitably deferential, Good assured them that while radios were indeed his hobby, he was no longer in possession of one. This was in spite of his house resembling, in Read's words, a radio repair shop, with valves and other wireless detritus scattered across the floor.

One of the Japanese officers paused in front of a patch of wall above a bench, where a faded outline indicated where an AWA Teleradio set had been placed. Good felt his pulse quicken, but gave nothing away. Inexplicably, the officer walked on. Good was placed on 'parole', warned not to leave the island, and told he would be watched carefully. He bowed low as the Japanese left.

On 9 March, Read picked up a curious message from Signalman Sly's station situated a few days' trek from Good's plantation at Kessa Point. The prefix indicated that it was urgent, but nothing more was heard. Read suspected a technical fault in the Teleradio, so travelled the 40 or so miles from Aravia up to Kessa to deal with the problem himself, only to discover the poorly trained Sly was simply not using the set correctly. Despite this, the news Sly had been endeavouring to convey was significant.

A few days earlier, Sly and his men had observed six Japanese cruisers and two destroyers patrolling Queen Carola Harbour and laying marine marker buoys, indicating their intention to return. Sly had then observed the first elements of the Japanese occupation of Buka and Bougainville but had been unable to broadcast it, and now precious days had been lost informing the Allies. One of Sly's team, Lance-Corporal Jack Matthews, later recalled the incident:

At 0900 hours on 9 March, we noticed a number of ships on the horizon, which appeared to be approaching. This proved to be so, and later we could identify them as Japanese naval vessels ... Sig Sly immediately tried to contact WJ Read on the radio for half an hour but with no success. During this time the ships were getting very close, so I decided to dismantle and hide the radio in case they should land in our vicinity.

Read immediately forwarded news of the Japanese ships' appearance. A day or so later, while conducting an impromptu class in elementary wireless operation for the benefit of Sly and his team, he picked up an ABC news bulletin from faraway Australia which shocked him to the core.

Eight Japanese warships, announced the bulletin, including cruisers and destroyers, were reported to have recently anchored in Queen Carola Harbour on Papua's Buka Island.

The Japanese, of course, heard it too. And with no Allied aircraft operating anywhere nearby, they deduced their movements were being watched and reported, with the obvious candidate being Good, the deferential planter whose house indicated the recent presence of a powerful radio set. Jack Read realised it too, and although he was the one who had sent the signal, it was Percy Good who was now in danger. Once again, in a rerun of the tragedy of Gasmata on New Britain, a careless news broadcast placed Coastwatchers' lives in peril.

Read quickly organised a small armed party to hurry to Good's plantation and extract him to the safety of Bougainville. As they prepared to depart in a small ketch, a native scout brought news that the Japanese had beaten them to it, and had returned to Kessa the previous day. Read could only pray that Percy Good had been able to talk his way out of trouble once again.

It was two days before Read arrived at Good's plantation. Instantly, they knew that disaster had preceded them: doors wide open, windows and furniture smashed, and the floor stained with bloodied footprints made by the unique twin-toed boot used by Japanese Marines. And there, close to the house, a fresh shallow grave. In tears, some of Good's native boys confirmed the story. The Japanese had arrived, looted the place, then shot Good in cold blood, leaving him a crumpled heap in his own passageway. His staff had done their best to inter him in his beloved garden, even decorating the humble grave with shells and coral. To make certain, Read and his men exhumed the body. It was evident Good had been badly abused and shot through the head.

The moment stayed with Read the rest of his life:

> We stood trancelike – shocked and angered. There was a strained silence: not a word was spoken as the body was reburied in its shallow grave. Only the roar of the Pacific as it crashed violently against the coral, reef-bound shore behind us broke the quiet. Suddenly a flying boat droned low over the tall palms of Kessa, and I noticed the dull red disk on its fuselage. My only thought at that moment was that Percy Good, the first of our number to fall victim to Japanese barbarism, would someday be avenged.

When news of Good's murder reached Eric Feldt, he was enraged, though not merely at the clumsiness of the ABC's censors. For months, he had been agitating for his Coastwatchers to be given the protection of military rank. Even if this would have no effect on their treatment at the hands of the Japanese, it would at least ensure their widows and families received a pension and other compensations in the advent of their death. His old friend and boss, Rupert Long, had been sympathetic, but the long entrails of red tape still clogged the passages of the defence establishment. All Feldt wanted was for his Coastwatchers to be recognised for what they were: unseen soldiers, engaged in a desperate, clandestine war, demonstrating immeasurable bravery against a brutal enemy. To achieve this, a little less deference would be required.

'I knew that Long, a personal friend, would not mind if I fired a delayed-action shell at him in the hope that it would explode somewhere beyond him and blow the red tape away.'

In a letter to Long, Feldt broke protocol by including, verbatim, the report given him by Read, and used it to devastating effect:

> Read Reports, 'Good murdered in his house by brutal handling. Strong presumption this due to broadcast news plus refusal to give information ...' As Good was Coast Watcher, performing his duty, what is the position of Mrs. Good and others regarding pension rights? Is any progress being made to appoint Read, Mason and Page to naval forces or are they expected to give their lives as Good had done without recompense or protection?

The rocket had the desired effect. Within fourteen days, on 2 April, Jack Read, Paul Mason and Coastwatcher Con Page on New Ireland were all either petty officers or lieutenants in the Royal Australian Navy Volunteer Reserve. And from this point onwards, all subsequent Coastwatchers would be brought into the ranks of the Australian military.

A lull followed Sly's sighting of the warships in Buka while the Japanese consolidated their gains further north. The Coastwatchers quickly used the momentary break to their advantage. Departing at dusk on 29 March, aboard a small government motor launch, the *Nugget*, Jack Read headed back with a crew of two native police to his old turf at Buka Passage where he'd conduct reconnaissance around some of the tiny islands off Soraken. Mackie meanwhile would set off with a handful of his men to finish the job of demolishing the Buka airstrip before the Japanese took it for themselves. Once completed, he was to withdraw to Buka's east coast where he would establish a new Coastwatching station and carry on his war from there.

Read and Mackie's timing was exquisite. Read later remembered noticing, in the fading light, the smoke of ships on the western horizon but thought little of it. Then, at around nine at night as he approached his old base of Sohana Island at the mouth of the passage, his alert companion, Corporal Sali, detected the outline of a ship in the darkness ahead. Read and his second native crewman could see nothing, but Sali insisted a ship ahead was hugging the coast. Read cut the engine and allowed the launch to drift for a little in the silence but detected nothing but the gentle swishing of the current against the boat. Then, as he was about to restart, the sudden roar of a high-speed boat engine – apparently heading towards them – shattered the silent gloom. Spinning the launch around, Read threw open the throttle and sped away, keeping a desperate watch on their stern and thankful that the *Nugget* was 'a silent running job'. Eventually the sound receded. Low on fuel, they hid the boat in mangroves on the Bougainville side of the passage a mile or so down the coast, and with the assistance of some local villagers, sought refuge in a local Catholic mission.

•

It is unclear whether Mackie had time to complete his demolition before the Japanese arrived. No sooner had he landed at the airstrip than groups of what looked like soldiers were seen approaching. Hastily withdrawing to a nearby ridge, Mackie and his men observed more Japanese arriving with each hour and beginning to fan out. In need of information, he risked reporting in via a secreted Teleradio, and learned that large warships flying the rising sun pennant had earlier been sighted off Buka's northernmost tip, Cape Hanpan. This was no mere raid, thought Mackie. He and Read had all but stumbled into the Japanese landings on Buka Island.

As Mackie and Read would learn, the soldiers' existence on Buka had been betrayed to the Japanese by a local native corporal – either sympathetic to or simply terrified into talking by their new conquerors ('He was a dead man if ever I caught up with him,' said Read at the time) – and now Mackie and his unit were being personally pursued. Trapped, with avenues of escape blocked by the enemy, and unable to access supplies they had previously hidden in the bush, the position of Mackie and his men on Buka looked dire.

Salvation, however, was at hand, from the unlikely figure of Reverend Usaia Sotutu. Hearing of Mackie's plight via his own Teleradio, the Fijian Coastwatcher took it upon himself to travel by canoe to Buka, where he not only evaded the Japanese but tracked down Mackie's party and announced he was leading them to safety. Sotutu led the men to friendly villagers he knew, who hid and fed them for a day. That night they were transported by canoe across the passage to the relative safety of Bougainville. Private Andy McNab, a member of Mackie's group, later recalled:

> The villagers hid us in their huts, cooked up a feed of chicken and kau kau [sweet potato] and made a present of the meal to us. It was delicious. Finally at dusk, we decided to take the bit in our teeth and go. There was a light breeze so we hoisted a sail and Usaia, Jack, Harry, Snow and I all paddled with our hearts in our mouths and our eyes swivelling in all directions. I thought we were travelling at our maximum speed, but as we passed Sohano we saw a light flashing around where the guns and searchlights were situated. At that point, the speed of the canoe doubled in a very quick time.

Read would later recommend Sotutu for a decoration, with the words 'Each individual member of that party stated without reserve that only the presence and ingenuity of this Fijian enabled their inexperience of local conditions to win through.'

Read and Mackie would survive their close shave on Buka as the Japanese slowly pushed south into Bougainville. Soon, their attention would be directed on the great chain of the Solomon Islands, beginning the campaign that would define the course of the war in the Pacific.

# Chapter 11
# THE FALL OF TULAGI

Like a twin-stranded necklace, the Solomon Islands stretch nearly a thousand miles across the Pacific, a bejewelled archipelago of over 900 islands which rise like majestic green walls from the sparkling ocean. At the top of the chain, just below the equator, the New Guinea territories Buka and Bougainville reach down to touch the Solomons proper. Here, exotically named places such as Choiseul, Vella Lavella and Santa Isabel stretch further into the Pacific. Forming the bottom of the necklace are the larger and more populous islands of Malaita, San Cristobal, and one which would resonate through history, Guadalcanal.

In between, the protected waters form a deep but largely calm lagoon marked on the old charts as New Georgia Sound, but which is more commonly referred to by the name given to it by weary American Marines in 1942, 'The Slot'.

Approaching the Solomons from any direction, one is met by a truly primordial landscape: largely empty green jungles ringed by white beaches, steep slopes reaching up to impossibly angled mountain peaks, half obscured by cloud or wisps of smoke from the Solomons' two active volcanoes. Crowning the dramatic tableau, daily towers of cumulus reach to infinity in an otherwise azure sky.

Remote and beautiful, the Solomons were unknown to Europeans until they were stumbled upon by the Spanish in the mid-sixteenth century. Due to lack of proximity to the world's great trade routes, however, they were of little interest to the great European powers and forgotten about for another two centuries, until British and French explorers began to name some of its innumerable features and promontories. In 1886 Germany claimed great swathes of the northern Solomons as part of their New Guinea territories but expressed so little interest in the place that several years elapsed before they felt sufficiently motivated to pay it a visit. Only in 1893 when copra and coconut oil emerged as lucrative commodities did Britain step in, declaring the islands to be the British Solomon Islands Protectorate. Germany issued a token protest, politely asking if they could keep Bougainville and Buka, and let the British take the rest. Meanwhile, the estimated 100 000 Melanesian natives simply carried on with their remote and tribal lives, largely oblivious of the handful of white planters and missionaries who fancifully claimed this wild land as their own.

Tulagi – barely 2 miles long and half a mile wide, little more than a dot in the subset of the Florida group – served as the administrative capital, occupied by a few Europeans, and a modest Chinatown of corrugated iron shacks, cheap cafes and hotels clustered around the harbour. Down the centre of the island ran a forest-covered ridge, below which could be found the Solomons' few paved roads – quiet streets lined with decorative shrubs and bungalows with wide verandas and hinged shutters to keep out the ubiquitous heat and tropical downpours. Even so, mould and mildew were a constant enemy.

Atop the highest point of the ridge, noted Feldt, the resident commissioner had his own, slightly larger home, from which he gazed down upon his underlings, 'like a chairman at a board meeting'. Since 1939, it had been William Sydney Marchant, a career colonial administrator who had previously 'run the show' in patches of Britain's far-flung empire such as Zanzibar and Tanganyika. From his balcony, he would watch the busy traffic of small boats and launches flitting back and forth between the causeway-linked islands of Gavutu and Tanambogo, which were run by the commercial giant Levers Pacific Plantations Limited, and nearby Makambo, whose occupants worked almost exclusively for Burns, Philp & Co. Aside from his administrative duties, Marchant was also in charge of the nascent Solomons Coastwatcher network established by Feldt before the war. While Feldt's opinion of Marchant is not recorded, he insisted on sending Australian planter and now naval lieutenant Don MacFarland to Tulagi to quietly keep an eye on the network.

In early 1939 the Australian government leased part of Tanambogo from the British as an RAAF advanced operating and meteorological base. Before the Pacific War began, it had been a leisurely posting for the crews of the Catalina flying boats from 20 and 11 Squadrons as they conducted reconnaissance and meteorological flights across the Pacific. On their days off, the men would drop down into perfect isolated beaches for a swim or a fish, and look forward to a meal of fresh seafood, or perhaps being entertained in the mess or the town.

The Solomons' time-warped collection of around 500 under-stimulated imperialists, capitalists and eccentrics lived remote lives, largely removed from the flow of European concerns, which they nevertheless steadfastly emulated. They were reluctant to properly explore the interior of their own colonial world with its whispered legends of bottomless swamps, crocodiles and headhunters. Every evening they put on silk, and donned white helmets and malacca canes for an evening promenade along the causeway, comforting themselves as best they could with the requisite colonial trappings of a cricket pitch, tennis court and small social circles revolving around boredom, gossip and gin.

'A pleasant place,' noted Martin Clemens of his time in Tulagi before the war, 'but life there seemed so artificial, and I was impatient to get my teeth into something real.' He would not have long to wait. By 1942, the Solomons' bucolic paradise would be shattered by the spectre of war.

Having swept south through northern New Guinea, the Japanese were established at Buka and Bougainville by March 1942, with the Solomons virtually undefended and ripe for the taking. From here, as well as Port Moresby – which Japan soon intended to be theirs – they would expand further east into the territories of Fiji and New Caledonia and, more importantly, dominate the supply lines between the United States' west coast and Australia's eastern seaboard cities of Brisbane and Sydney. From Moresby, they would be capable of hitting the Australian mainland, playing into the populace's most morbid fears of an actual physical invasion. And yet, as March turned to April, the Japanese juggernaut, inexplicably, appeared to stall.

Air attacks on Tulagi had begun soon after the fall of Rabaul. First single aircraft – large Kawanishi flying boats – flew low, dropping their bombs with the same haphazardness they had demonstrated in Port Moresby. Soon larger formations appeared, targeting the elaborate steel lattice of the radio station tower above Tulagi Harbour. In this, the Japanese were deceived. The Tulagi station was outdated and practically decommissioned; the real transmitter was situated across the water at the RAAF base at Tanambogo. This remained cleverly concealed, undiscovered by the Japanese for months.

Born in Aberdeen, Scotland, in 1915, Warwick Frederick Martin Clemens had no intention of joining the British Colonial Service. As a bright and engaging Cambridge undergraduate dreaming of 'a life with some kind of adventure', he learned that the natural sciences degree for which he toiled would see him inside a laboratory, so when the opportunity to apply for the Colonial Service arose soon after his graduation, he jumped at it.

At the selection board, the administrators looked him up and down. 'Now, Clemens, you like sailing, don't you?' Martin was quick to answer, 'Oh, rather, sir!' even though he had never stepped foot on a boat. 'Excellent,' they responded. 'How would you like to go to the Solomon Islands?' Clemens brightly replied that he would be absolutely delighted to do so, shook hands, then dashed into the nearest library to find out where the Solomon Islands were, and was shocked to learn that they were on the other side of the world, one of the farthest possible points on the globe from the British Isles.

Although charming and personable 'with somewhat aristocratic tastes', Clemens's background was actually one of 'high expectations but little means'. The son of a Scots musician, Clemens won scholarships to various schools, then found his way to Cambridge where he only just missed out on earning a rowing blue in the early 1930s. By 1938, aged twenty-two, he was on his way to Tulagi as a cadet to begin a life that would eventually entail more 'adventure' than he could possibly have imagined.

'I spent my time walking up hills and down dells and going to various villages and learning the customs of people and passing more exams, and that sort of thing,' wrote Clemens years later. 'That was my start.'

Once in the islands, Clemens spent his early years in road and development projects in the most populous settlements on Malaita and San Cristobal. When the war in Europe began, he and the younger members of the administration longed to escape what he described as the 'fretting inactivity of the Solomons and do something more active, preferably in a military capacity'. Eric Feldt knew Clemens and was quick to bring him into his Coastwatchers, but what Clemens really wanted was to put on a uniform. This would require being released by the colonial establishment, a prospect he was told would be in no way forthcoming.

As the war overseas raged on, Clemens reached his three-year probation and graduated as a full district officer, earning himself a month's leave in Sydney. In a moment of truly exquisite timing, he arrived in the harbour city on 8 December 1941, just as news of the Pearl Harbor attack was breaking. This simply made Clemens more determined to join up than ever. The whole city, he recalled, 'was in a complete panic. No one appeared to know anything, with one exception: all the armed forces recruiting agencies had been informed that cadets and officers of the Western Pacific administrations were NOT to be taken on.' In interview after interview, Clemens presented brilliantly to the recruiting officers of the various armed forces, but when the subject of his current position in the Colonial Service was raised, a curious look crossed their brow, a finger was run down the list of 'reserved occupations', and yet another door was closed, albeit politely, in Clemens's face.

Though dejected, Clemens would soon have no need to find his way to the war. The war was coming to him.

Resigning himself to returning to his Pacific backwater on the expiration of his leave, and after a desultory send-off from some of his friends, Clemens boarded the Burns, Philp coal steamer *Morinda* for the 1700-mile run up to the Solomons as news of Japan's unstoppable advance into the Pacific dominated the headlines. Pulling out of the harbour, Clemens symbolically tore up a one-pound note and let the pieces fall into the water.

This, he soon became aware, was far from a conventional trip. The only other passengers on the usually crowded steamer seemed to be a replacement policeman and an island tax collector, as apparently not even a world war could be permitted to stand between a government and the collection of its revenue. More ominously, the crew confessed to Clemens the holds were filled with fuel and bombs for the RAAF station at Tanambogo, and a machine gun had been mounted on the stern, albeit a single antique Vickers from World War I.

As the ship glided for several days through the waters of the Coral Sea, the notion of war receded until it seemed remote, even surreal. Everything changed when the *Morinda* entered the Mboli Passage near Tulagi, and a Japanese flying boat approached the little ship, dropping its six bombs, all of which fell wide. It was Clemens's first vision of real war. A short time later, pulling up at the Tulagi wharf, the town was unrecognisable: thick with smoke from bombing and looting, and a crowd of Europeans desperate to get onboard. Tulagi's normally ordered streets were in chaos. Clemens walked down the gangway, the single disembarking passenger amid a sea of European islanders desperate to evacuate.

Later, he reflected on the chaos. 'To this day, the memory of the scene on the wharf has remained with me – drawn faces, no islanders in sight, and piles of luggage and unpacked belongings ... I found the place in a state of hysteria. The police force had been discharged ... now everyone was looking out for himself, and looting appeared imminent.' More alarmingly, the resident commissioner himself, 48-year-old William Sydney Marchant, seemed simultaneously ignorant of and overwhelmed by the situation.

Entering the administration office, Clemens found Marchant and his staff packing up the office and preparing to evacuate to Auki, on the larger island of Malaita. Marchant was red-faced and perspiring with stress. Clemens cleared his throat noisily and announced that he had just returned from leave and was reporting for duty. Marchant looked at him as if he were a madman. After an awkward pause, Clemens then suggested he might return to his former post at San Cristobal, whereupon Marchant waved to a map on the wall and insisted he travel north to take over the office on the island of Gizo. Clemens then pointed out that Gizo was already occupied by the Japanese, and to go there would be suicide. Scratching his head, Marchant told Clemens that he could tag along with him to Malaita.

Reluctant to be fleeing so soon after his arrival, Clemens instead enquired about another large island 20 miles to the south, Guadalcanal. Recalling that his Guadalcanal District Officer Dick Horton and his assistant Henry Josselyn had both just quit to join the navy, Marchant approved the appointment with a flustered wave of the hand. 'Yes, all right, Guadalcanal,' he said as he continued to dismantle his office. Then, as an afterthought, 'Oh, and they need an intelligence officer there. That can be you!'

Marchant also tried to take Don MacFarland and his Teleradio to distant Malaita with him, but the single-minded young Scot was reluctant to remove himself from the Coastwatchers' Solomons network. Marchant barely took in what he was saying and left the room in haste. Later, MacFarland and Clemens would work as a formidable team.

Although far from Resident Commissioner William Marchant's finest hour, he would prove himself useful on Malaita by relaying much of the Coastwatchers' signals to Port Moresby and beyond.

Clemens later reflected that, other than being vaguely told to 'act as an intelligence officer', he was 'given no instructions, policy, or plan'. In a couple of days, he was on his way to take up the role of district officer and Coastwatcher on the island of Guadalcanal. Travelling down to the dock, Clemens noted that 'Tulagi looked ghastly – every place littered with smashed crockery and furniture.' He tried to stop some natives loading up a canoe with stolen booty, but soon gave up. Seeing the very concerned-looking local bishop, Walter Baddeley, who had bravely decided to remain, Clemens handed him a fine pair of near-new shoes. 'I felt I might not need them much longer.'

As the small government motor schooner pulled away from the Tulagi wharf, the reverberation of explosions could be heard throughout the town as the few remaining soldiers began blowing up what was left of the government stores, and the looters found their way into Chinatown. It appeared to Clemens as the collapse of civilisation itself, and he was glad to be leaving it.

•

Over the following weeks, from his initial position at Aola on Guadalcanal's northern shoreline, Clemens could see the Japanese aircraft attacking Tulagi 20 miles away with increasing intensity, but as the town had now been evacuated, there was nothing left to bomb. And as the weeks went by, the expected physical invasion failed to materialise. The Japanese appeared to have halted their advance.

Historians have often cited this lull in Japan's initial advance in the early months of 1942 as one of the primary reasons for their eventual defeat, but for the Coastwatchers of the Solomons, it came as a blessing. As the all-conquering Japanese – dizzy with the unexpected scale of their initial victories – expanded their plans, regrouped, and sought ways to feed their now ever-lengthening supply lines, those in their expected path also consolidated, preparing for what was to come.

For Martin Clemens, the pause gave him time to attend to his other duties as district officer in Guadalcanal. One of his first roles was to organise the repatriation of hundreds of plantation workers who had, overnight, been abandoned – mostly without pay or provisions – by their European masters, many of whom Clemens had observed weeks earlier at Tulagi Harbour, jostling in an unedifying manner for a spot onboard a ship to take them away. Clemens had been sickened by the whole business, and he could hardly blame the native people for being shocked at the spectacle of their bosses bolting like rats before the enemy had even arrived. Most of the workers had come over from villages on the island of Malaita, and within hours of his arrival, Clemens began organising any vessels he could find to take them home.

To Clemens's greater amazement, some of the European islanders on Guadalcanal decided to remain in their plantations, convinced their world of commerce would continue, aloof from the tide of war. With orders to deny the enemy any resources, Clemens found this particularly galling, and was more than once forced to listen to the boasts of plantation managers waxing about their latest copra crop which they fully expected to ship out, with or without the cooperation of the Japanese. Jack Read observed the same phenomena, commenting, 'they steadfastly refused to take the future seriously'. Lacking the power to physically expel them, Clemens simply shook his head in disbelief.

Three days after taking over Guadalcanal, a crowd of native headmen crammed into his office at Aola, hoping he could assuage their fears. 'What could I say to them?' recalled Clemens. 'Terrified of what the Japanese might do to them and their families, they wanted to know that I would not desert them.' The Japanese were a people for whom the Solomon Islanders traditionally had little respect: scruffy sailors who robbed their reefs of their pearls and trochus shells, and who abused women and spread venereal disease. How could the British be defeated by such people? they asked. Clemens sympathised with them completely. Sucking on his pipe, he spoke slowly in perfect Pidgin, pledging that if they stuck with him, someday, somehow, relief would come and the Japanese would be thrown out. 'It was a flimsy promise, and it was with a sinking heart that I made it,' said Clemens, 'but it was the basis for the tremendous show put up by the people of Guadalcanal during the dark days that followed.'

The pause in the Japanese advance also gave Clemens time to establish a network with others who had signed up for Eric Feldt's organisation. Despite naming his wartime memoir *Alone on Guadalcanal*, Clemens, at least initially, was accompanied by two other men, both Australians. Don MacFarland also chose to relocate to Guadalcanal, and Ashton 'Snowy' Rhoades, a tough World War I veteran with a face, according to Feldt, which 'resembled a prize fighter', was also keen to remain on the island and operate from his copra plantation at Lavoro on the island's far western tip. Initially he was without a radio, until Clemens acquired one for him via the RAAF.

Clemens then asked MacFarland to set up a station at Berande on the island's mid north coast to cover that quarter. Having only recently received his commission, MacFarland adored his newly issued naval whites and wore them – perfectly pressed – at every opportunity, even when deep in the jungle.

With the new stations on Guadalcanal, eight Coastwatcher teams now operated across the Solomons and Bougainville and Buka. Clemens covered the centre of Guadalcanal as well as the crucial eastern coastal plain from Aola.

In the lull before the Japanese arrived, the Coastwatchers consolidated their crucial teams of native bearers, suppliers and runners, without which none of them would survive a week. Feldt's directive of paying regularly, and in cash, was adhered to. Bags of coins and bundles of banknotes became an integral part of any aerial supply drop. Throughout April, Japanese air attacks on Tulagi ramped up, but there remained no sign of any advance further south into the Solomons. Clemens used this time to explore other potential observation positions, and was advised that the village of Paripao, 8 miles away atop a thousand-foot ridge, gave a commanding view over the northern coast of the island.

On 1 May, as he was setting off to investigate, he was surprised by the arrival of a Catalina flying boat on the beach below him – complete with its crew of a dozen airmen. It had been towed by a launch 20 miles from Tanambogo, where it had been damaged in a recent Japanese air raid. The pilot, Flight Lieutenant Ekins, jumped onto the sand from the ship's bow hatch and introduced himself to a bewildered Clemens, enquiring if Clemens might be able to 'hide' the plane for him. Unsure how a large flying boat could be hidden from anyone, Clemens nevertheless directed his team of native labourers to drag the crippled aircraft onto the beach and conceal it among the mangroves.

The next evening, as Clemens supervised the work, an urgent message came in from Don Kennedy, Coastwatcher on New Georgia, that a large formation of Japanese ships was currently steaming by him at 15 knots, heading in the direction of Tulagi. At their current speed, they would reach Tulagi within twenty-four hours. The Japanese, finally, were on their way.

That night, as Clemens burned as many unnecessary government papers as he could in preparation for the now urgent move to Paripao, he was surprised by the boom of explosions reaching him from across the water. That same day, permission had been given for the RAAF to commence destroying the base at Tanambogo to prevent – or at least forestall – its use by the Japanese. Sticks of gelignite were strapped to 44-gallon drums of aviation fuel in an attempt to level every existing structure. The noise of the explosions could be heard clearly and the glow of the fires were visible from Malaita and Guadalcanal. Tulagi, the colonial capital of the Solomons, was being abandoned to its fate.

Although officially classified a 'Light Task Force', the Japanese Solomon Islands invasion fleet comprised two destroyers and two mine-layer transports as well as eight other vessels including transports. The fleet had split off from a much larger force named Operation MO, which had left Rabaul on 30 April bound for Port Moresby. Soon, with both Port Moresby and the Solomons secure, the Japanese would be able to expand their empire further east into the New Hebrides, New Caledonia and Fiji, isolating Australia and New Zealand, and dominating their Pacific lifeline to America. As history tells us, however, the larger force would be turned back by the airmen of the United States Navy in the Battle of the Coral Sea, forever scuttling Japan's best chance to take their prize of New Guinea's capital. The invasion of the Solomons, at least initially, met with far greater success.

On 3 May, the forty or so remaining RAAF personnel on Tanambogo, having destroyed what they could of the base, boarded the *Balus*, a fast launch which had been hidden in the mangroves. Under the cover of a misty squall, they dashed out of Tulagi Harbour just as four Japanese warships sailed in. Four hundred Japanese 'Marines' of the 3rd Kure Special Naval Landing Force – some of Japan's most experienced and brutal soldiers – landed unopposed at Tulagi and immediately began setting up facilities. Soon, sixteen Japanese ships were anchored in the harbour. Then the signal was given for six Kawanishi flying boats – which for weeks had been daily delivering their bombs on Tulagi and its harbour – to land. At almost no cost, the Solomons capital had fallen.

The next morning, 4 March, aircraft from the US carrier *Yorktown* struck back, surprising the Japanese, sinking the destroyer *Kikutsuki* lying at anchor in the harbour, as well as two of the minesweepers, and causing many casualties among the soldiers on shore. There would be more such raids on Tulagi, but it would take much more than that to dislodge the Japanese.

With the enemy now at Tulagi, Martin Clemens and his Guadalcanal Coastwatchers suddenly had a good deal more to report. They now put into action the network of native runners and scouts they had been preparing for weeks. One of Clemens's most trusted and reliable scouts was a young man by the name of Bingiti. He had recently completed training as a native agricultural instructor, and hated the Japanese with a passion. Not only would Bingiti report on them with remarkable accuracy, but he organised spy sub-networks of his own.

Working among the Japanese with the cover of being a simple labourer, Bingiti gave one of the first accounts of the Allied air raids on Tulagi, luridly describing sharks feasting in a bloodstained sea on the bodies of hundreds of drowned Japanese sailors and troops killed when the destroyers were caught in the harbour. A short time later, he would lead a party of natives from Malaita who had been working as cooks and staff at RAAF Tanambogo back to the recently evacuated base to spirit away a cache of rifles and 25 000 rounds of priceless .303 ammunition, virtually under the noses of the Japanese. Even more important than the weapons was the Teleradio Bingiti brought, which had likewise been left behind in the stampede to evacuate. This brought an end to several sleepless nights for Clemens. Had this been discovered by the Japanese, every Coastwatcher broadcast would be open to them to hear. Nor was Bingiti's work finished. For many months, he would think nothing of paddling miles across the open sea in a canoe to deliver intelligence for Clemens and the Coastwatchers.

As the Japanese settled into their new base at Tulagi, they methodically planned their next step. They quickly discovered life would be made as difficult as possible by Allied airmen, whose turn it was to attack the port which had for so long been the target of the Japanese. The results of the continuing air raids were reported back to Clemens via his increasing numbers of scouts, all risking their lives by spying on the enemy. One indentured native worker at Tulagi reported that one raid had caught a large number of soldiers out of their slit trenches and 250 had been killed or wounded. The hospitals were reportedly overflowing with Japanese casualties.

Some villages, particularly in the north of the Solomons, threw in their lot early with their new Japanese conquerors, proudly displaying the rising sun armbands they had been issued, and even attending special schools set up by the Japanese to educate them on the glories of the Chrysanthemum Throne and its divine Emperor. Little was actually taught except the correct depth of bow with which one was supposed to greet an Imperial Japanese officer.

The vast majority of Solomon Islanders remained loyal to the British administration, with many taking extraordinary personal risks to scout, deliver information, and later conduct fierce guerrilla campaigns against the enemy. It was a loyalty, said Clemens after the war, secured in no small part by the Coastwatchers themselves. They, after all, were the only visible remnant of the British administration to have remained on the islands to face the invader. As the war progressed, and the increasingly desperate Japanese began to exercise their cruelty on the native populations, whatever loyalty the Coastwatchers had enjoyed eventually evaporated.

Clemens finally relocated to the panoramic village of Paripao, establishing himself in his dual role of Coastwatcher and district officer. The move to the mountain from the coast at Aola had involved the toil of more than a hundred native labourers, who hauled everything from the Teleradio, supplies of tinned food and even administration stationery up the steep mountain paths. The district officer's safe was buried, hopefully to be exhumed in less perilous times.

Upon his arrival at Paripao, Clemens found that the village had already been prepared: a main hut for himself combining a home and office, where his desk – also hauled up from the coast – was already in place. A radio aerial mast, camouflaged with palm fronds, gave a clear signal, and there was even a 50-foot tree at the edge of the village, in which a platform had been built overlooking Tulagi. Here, a series of native watchers would be on permanent duty, reporting any sign of enemy activity with a loud blow into a conch shell.

Further along the coast, Don MacFarland relocated to a new position nearly 3000 feet up in the very centre of the island at a former gold mining village called Gold Ridge. Here he was joined by Coastwatcher Ken Hay, a former planter and one of the true characters of the Coastwatcher ranks. Gold Ridge suited Hay – known for his love of the fine life – perfectly. Instead of a native shack, the Coastwatchers in Gold Ridge enjoyed a palatial, five-bedroom house, formerly the home of the mine manager before it was realised the mine contained almost no gold and was abandoned. Hay even insisted an Electrolux kerosene refrigerator be hauled up the mountain so he could enjoy his butter served in ice.

Gold Ridge came with an on-site Fijian caretaker, the highly capable Kelemende Nabunobuno, who became a proxy host to the Coastwatchers and their party and evolved into something of a master spy in his own right.

For a few weeks, there was little to see as the Japanese seemed content to remain in Tulagi. Then, in late May, one of Clemens's scouts burst – breathless – into the camp at Paripao, reporting that the Japanese had begun landing patrols at various places along the Guadalcanal coast, the closest being Tenaru, just 15 miles away. A week later, a neat row of tents was reported on the central grassy plain around the mouth of the River Lunga, not far from the town (and future capital) of Honiara. A destroyer was also seen ferrying men and equipment ashore, and smoke appeared as the Japanese began burning off the tall kunai grass which covered the coastal plain. The beginnings of a small wharf seemed to be being built. As to what the Japanese were up to, the Coastwatchers had no idea.

From their height at Gold Ridge, far closer to the new Japanese activity at Lunga Plain, Don MacFarland had a perfect view. His initial assessment was that the Japanese were clearing land to access timber for the rebuilding of Tulagi. Far away, Clemens's and MacFarland's reports were absorbed, and they were told to keep watching and reporting.

On 6 July, a twelve-ship convoy anchored off Lunga and began to disgorge tractors, rollers and other heavy construction equipment, including two miniature locomotives and a dozen hopper cars.

'Looks as if the Nips are going to stay,' noted Clemens in his diary. Any doubt about the Japanese laying down foundations was now clearly dispelled.

## Chapter 12
# ENTER ISHIMOTO

One early July morning, a handsome young Japanese man, impeccably dressed in a finely tailored civilian suit, stepped off the transport *Kinryu Maru* and surveyed the beach in front of him. Taking out a silver cigarette case that he had bought in London, he tapped a cigarette on its gleaming cover and lit it up. It was an American cigarette, of course. Far better than those ghastly things issued by the army. The young man was pleased with what he saw. Already, the earth-moving machinery was in place, and some of the Korean labourers had begun to arrive. Some soldiers from the arriving Base Guard Unit passed him, momentarily confused at the sight of a well-dressed civilian in a war zone, and bowed, unsure whether or not to offer a salute. The man glanced at them momentarily, then looked away. Terushige Ishimoto drew again on his cigarette and smiled, glad to be back in the Solomon Islands.

At twenty-nine years old, Ishimoto had seen much more of the world than the average Japanese person growing up in the insular and deeply militaristic Japan of the 1920s and 1930s. A brilliant student, he had graduated from the esteemed Yamaguchi Commercial College with honours, before being snapped up by the giant Marubeni Shoten trading company, who selected him as their European representative for five years. He travelled to the United States, studied in England, and learned English and French to fluency, and also acquired the tastes and demeanour of a typical English gentleman. He wore Savile Row suits, adored the music of Mozart and Haydn, and bathed and changed his clothes twice a day.

In 1939, Ishimoto returned to Tokyo to be put in charge of the Pacific operations of the South Seas Trading Company Ltd, based in Rabaul. For two years, he became a regular figure there, with a ready excuse to be constantly on the move exploring the islands of New Guinea and the Solomons. Not only did he acquire an excellent sense of the geography of the region, but he learned Pidgin, again to a high standard. Then, in November 1941, he mysteriously disappeared, only to return with Japan's South Sea Islands invasion force in January with the honorary rank of a naval lieutenant. His role was as interpreter and guide, communicating Japanese intentions to the native people as well as any remaining Europeans and, most important, making it clear to everyone that the British were gone and Japan was now the new master. Such was the esteem in which he was held by the local military that, after the initial invasion, he was given a quick trip back home – by air – to see his parents.

Now, on the beach at Lunga, Ishimoto would begin his new role, one that would usher in the most desperate period for the Coastwatchers of Guadalcanal.

Gazing up into the towering central peaks of Guadalcanal, Ishimoto knew that, somewhere up there, Allied spies were reporting on his army's every move. Hoping to hunt them down with foot patrols would be akin to finding a needle in a haystack, he thought. Instead, Ishimoto knew he would need to outsmart them. But first there was an airstrip to build.

In a few days, two construction battalions had arrived, made up largely of indentured Koreans, along with 400 soldiers to guard them. Hundreds of crates of cider labelled *Mitsubichampagne* also came ashore, along with an ice-making plant to keep them cool. Many more men would be needed to make the airstrip operational so local villagers were to be encouraged – coerced if need be – into volunteering as a ready source of labour for their new masters. Ishimoto would be kept very busy. The Japanese occupation force's Order No. 1 was drafted and distributed:

Men only over 14 years old or less than 50 years have to work for Japanese troops at some places on this island. After a month's labour they will be given the identity as civilians on this island. During work for the Japanese troops, they will be supplied with meals, etc.

When the people in the surrounding area heard the decree, delivered by Ishimoto standing in front of a squad of armed soldiers, they glanced at each other, understanding they had no choice, and nor were they to be paid – something the British would never dare to instigate. As for what being given 'identity as a civilian' on their own island meant, none of them could guess. Nevertheless, with a shrug of their shoulders, a stream of men began to make their way down to the beach at Lunga to place themselves at the disposal of the Japanese and accept whatever fate awaited them.

For the Japanese, it was a fatal mistake. The scouts and agents of the Coastwatchers inserted themselves among the workforce and almost immediately began to filter back their close-up observations of the Japanese. Some of these local men had even been clerks who had worked with Clemens and MacFarland in Tulagi, and who needed to hide their soft hands, obviously unused to hard labour, from the Japanese.

One of those was Martin Clemens's most devoted aide, Daniel Pule, who had in a previous life spent endless hours meticulously restoring order to Clemens's famously errant filing system. The Japanese had given him a job unloading vessels and barges on the beach, unaware that he was quietly taking note of everything brought ashore. One morning, Pule felt the gaze of a tall Japanese officer a short distance away. He kept on working, although his blood ran cold. He had recognised the officer instantly, having even exchanged a few words with him inside a Tulagi office two years previously. Suddenly the man was beside him. 'My friend,' said Ishimoto in almost accent-less English. 'I have known you before, have I not? In Tulagi?' Pule did not miss a beat. Feigning not to understand English, he instead indicated by dumb show that he was hungry. Ishimoto paused, snapped his fingers at a passing sentry, and had some rice brought over. Ishimoto watched Pule eat, then leaned in close, giving the faintest of smiles. 'You're a liar,' he said coldly. Again, Pule acted the simple villager, now indicating he wanted some betel nut. Ishimoto gestured towards a nearby tent where some of the ubiquitous local delicacy was being doled out and watched him go carefully, before continuing on along the beach. Pule took his chance, went behind the tent and through the perimeter, disappearing into the jungle. He hoped the encounter would be forgotten.

As work on the runway progressed, the Coastwatchers began to receive more reports that the Japanese were closing in. Worse, Clemens's best scout, Bingiti, arrived via canoe from Tulagi with the disturbing news that the Japanese had occupied Savo Island, a small volcanic peak guarding the western approaches to Tulagi. Here they planned to establish an observation post, but in the process had captured an educated native medical assistant, George Bogese, who was assisting the elderly and somewhat frail resident European store owner, Lafe Schroder. While not an official Coastwatcher, Schroder had been given a Teleradio patched together from bits and pieces by the RAAF at Tanambogo, and had been putting it to good use. While Schroder managed to evade the Japanese by hiding in the jungle, Bogese – who knew all about the Coastwatching network – was captured, taken to Tulagi and, under threat of execution, was soon talking freely. When the news reached Feldt, Bogese was immediately classified, perhaps unfairly, as a 'defector', and the situation was flashed to all Solomons Coastwatchers, many of whom began making preparations to move camp.

Soon, other reports came in of a tall Japanese officer questioning villagers about the Europeans up in the hills. 'Tell us about Mr Snowy,' he would ask in a tone of apparent concern, or 'Would you happen to know the whereabouts of Mr Mac?' Other reports indicated the Japanese were aware of the exact number of Teleradio sets in use among the Coastwatchers, their approximate locations, and the names of most of their users.

At one stage, Clemens was particularly concerned at rumours of bloodhounds being brought in to track him and his men across the jungle paths and peaks, but nothing more came of it. Leaflets were distributed among the native villagers claiming that British rule had now ended and the Japanese were in charge, and the direst consequences were outlined for anyone harbouring an Allied soldier, or even failing to report their whereabouts.

Then a Japanese patrol came ashore at the closest coastal point to Clemens, precipitating him to make a third move inland to Vungana, a village he had picked as a fallback. He paid off many of his native workers so only a small party of a dozen or so scouts and carriers made their tortuous way high into the central mountains to this new camp further from the Japanese. For two days, Clemens struggled through mud and debilitating heat, shepherding his precious equipment, particularly the batteries being carried on poles by the porters up the vertiginous tracks. One slip of the carriers' footing and the batteries would smash against the rocks or at best spill their precious acid, rendering them, as well as Clemens himself, utterly useless.

Finally, the trek brought Clemens to a 4-foot-wide, knife-edged track scaling a toothy peak which connected to a 'miserable-looking' village. It was not much to look at, but at least offered a clear – though more distant – view of the coast. In his new camp, Clemens occupied a one-room, former headman's hut with an uneven, split-palm floor. His living conditions were reduced to the most basic. His body, already underweight from a starchy diet of taro and sweet potato, could look forward to the nourishment from the tins in the crate labelled 'mixed meat' the porters had hauled up to Vungana with them. Upon opening one, however, he found the contents did not resemble the description on the crate. He then opened a second, then a third to find the same. It soon transpired that every one of his 'mixed meat' tins had been mislabelled and were in fact 'Tasmanian Scallops in Curry'. For the next few weeks, Clemens consumed almost nothing but the oily and unappetising morsels, prepared every way he could think of to break the monotony. For the rest of his life, he could never go near scallops again.

Here Clemens encountered another unanticipated problem – cold. The weather at the higher altitude of Vungana was more turbulent and cloudy than nearer to the coast, and at night the village turned into an icebox. He had brought neither blankets nor adequate clothing, and the clothing he did have was becoming shredded. His shoes were likewise deteriorating, and he was soon reduced to getting about in 'John the Baptist' sandals, fashioned by a local native constable from a canvas mail bag and jungle vine. The frigid temperature also seemed to hasten the decline of the radio batteries, which could no longer hold a decent charge for any length of time. The valves and components had also been knocked about and some damaged seals made them subject to damp.

Water, which had to be drawn up from a stream far below, became harder to access, and washing was practically impossible. Nor could he any longer confidently vouch for the loyalty of the surrounding villagers, who dreaded incurring the wrath of the Japanese for harbouring a European spy.

The wireless signal from his high position was excellent though, and when the radio worked, he could communicate with Don MacFarland and Ken Hay over on Gold Ridge, who were facing trials of their own. With the Japanese probing closer, and his camp easier to access than Clemens's, MacFarland was also forced to consider another move. This prospect filled the substantial Ken Hay with dread, as he commented later, 'There's too much of me to run.'

One afternoon, as an exhausted Clemens was dozing in a patch of open ground trying to take advantage of the warmth from the infrequent bursts of sun, a Japanese aircraft roared overhead at low level. He dashed for cover but was certain the pilot had caught sight of him and his obviously European appearance. From then on, the Japanese made a regular daily flight, scouring the central ridge of the island at low level while Clemens continued to broadcast.

At the northern tip of the island, the tough war veteran Snowy Rhoades was likewise feeling under pressure. A scout reported that Ishimoto had visited Visale, the next village along, and knew exactly where 'Mr Snowy' was located. Ishimoto told the villagers that when he caught up with Snowy he would not execute him but cut off his hands and feet. That night, when the warning reached him, Rhoades was packed and on his way. Two dozen carriers transported him and his equipment 12 miles to the coast, where a launch had been hidden in the mangroves for just such a purpose. One night, at the mouth of a river, he slept on the beach by his equipment awaiting a relieving group of carriers who would arrive with the dawn and take him further on. In the darkness, he was awakened by the approaching sound of a boat's diesel engine, and, too late to run, slowly buried himself under a pile of coconut fronds. With one half-opened eye, he watched a boatload of Japanese, clear in the moonlight, come within 50 yards of the beach before moving further on.

On Gold Ridge, Don MacFarland and Ken Hay's camp was upended by the arrival of a dozen or so Europeans who had become terrified of the Japanese and their increasingly aggressive forays into the island. For weeks, they had carried on their plantation lifestyles but with ever more stories of Europeans being taken away or simply executed, they headed for Gold Ridge, imploring the Coastwatchers to get them away to safety. It was just the sort of attention Hay and MacFarland had sought to avoid, and when two Zero floatplanes appeared over the trees and commenced a strafing run down the length of the camp, they decided to evacuate.

Like Clemens, they moved to a new camp even further into the interior, in a gloomy valley of the Sutakiki River, closer to the southern shore where the mountains dropped in near vertical crags to the sea. Ken Hay had to be lowered down several levels by means of a rope tied around his large waist, like a piece of cargo unloaded from a ship. Food was running low, carriers were deserting, and the reception of some of the native villages on this side of the island was openly hostile. Reports came in of a 500-strong Japanese patrol making its way down the south coast to look for them. On 15 July, MacFarland radioed his plight to Feldt in Townsville. The reply was encouraging but vague: 'Good work. Bad luck. Position not as bad as appears. Stay in bush but do not repeat nor transmit from any position within 10 miles of your camp.

Stick it out for four more weeks and I will rescue you but do not move to beach until instructed.'

Clemens's signal to Feldt was similar: 'Cannot do very much good for very much longer. Have you instructions?'

The only response was a similar request to 'stay in bush' for a while longer.

Despite the worsening plight of the Guadalcanal Coastwatchers, the network of scouts continued to gather intelligence. Clemens could now clearly hear the rumbling of trucks moving about on the grassy plains of Lunga, the sound climbing up the slopes from the beach. Unbelievably, Daniel Pule risked discovery by returning to the Japanese construction site for work, and in early August produced a detailed report, including numbers and dispositions of troops, trucks and labourers, as well as a scaled map showing the locations of a radio shack, anti-aircraft gun positions and slit trenches.

The scouts organised by Gold Ridge's Fijian caretaker Kelemende also produced detailed information: 'Runway in position previously mentioned but is gravel and clay from nearby hills not cement stop ... as near as can be gauged from tent and hut accommodation for thousand troops of which half labour corps ...'

He also reported that the increasing US air attacks on Lunga were having an effect, with many native workers having already deserted, and casualties mounting among the Japanese.

Clemens and MacFarland continued to send everything back to the intelligence officers in Townsville, but headquarters' demand for yet more detail seemed insatiable. Over one thirty-hour period, Clemens transmitted eight separate messages, including numbers and dispositions of troop billets and mess facilities, bomb and fuel storage, and the siting of a new naval gun for defence from the sea. Still the demands came: 'Any reliable additional information as to number, type, location troops, positions, types and calibre of guns to be sent now.' Requests were made for tidal observations, weather patterns and descriptions of Japanese uniforms. Clemens continued to work furiously when his deteriorating equipment allowed.

Target suggestions were also sought, sometimes directly resulting in air attacks carried out over the following days. 'There's a stunt brewing,' MacFarland signalled to Clemens. Hungry, and increasingly fearful, the Guadalcanal Coastwatchers did their utmost, swallowing a rising resentment that senior commanders failed to appreciate the conditions under which they laboured while they demanded ever more. Then, a series of encouraging, if cryptic, messages began to trickle in: 'It won't be long now', and '... things are happening for the best', leading them to believe that relief was on the way, although when, and how, remained unclear.

By late July, MacFarland had had enough and decided to evacuate. 'We are all living on hope,' he signalled to Clemens. 'If nothing happens before the weekend, I intend to flit. I would suggest you do likewise. [Jap] patrols are approaching the Ridge, and I don't intend to wait here until I can't get out.'

Clemens adopted a similar tone. 'We had long gotten past the depression stage, but even so, the gloominess continued to increase ... the whole position looked very black, and to cap it all my miserable charging engine was out of action again.'

A few days later, MacFarland proved he was as good as his word. 'We are moving Monday morning and hope to see you. I don't think we will have any trouble for a few days but after that, well, who knows? Anyway, if I can get off the island I intend to. There are Jap cruisers, destroyers and floatplanes everywhere ...'

On 5 August, in a final desultory message to Townsville, he signalled: 'Cannot obtain anything reliable. Native reports very conflicting.'

The exhausted and demoralised Guadalcanal Coastwatchers were nearing the end of their tether.

•

On the Japanese airstrip itself, Captain Tei Monzen, the commander of the more than 2500 construction troops and the 400 soldiers guarding them, had good reason to be pleased. In barely a month, an almost complete airstrip had been hacked out of raw tropical wilderness. Only a small section of the runway now remained to be graded; repair shops and bomb shelters had been built, as well as finger wharves and workshops, and an air compressor plant for torpedoes was nearly up and running. The administration building had even been fashioned to represent a traditional pagoda. This would be bound to please his superiors.

Though not scheduled to arrive for several more days, he could almost hear the roar of the first Zero fighters coming in to land as he gazed across the hard-packed red clay surface of the runway. His team of workers had done well. A celebration, he decided, was called for, and on 6 August, he ordered an extra ration of sake to be distributed to all hands as a reward for their patriotism and industry, which would bring further glory to Japan and, naturally, himself.

By contrast, all Martin Clemens could taste that night, as he later wrote, was 'the bitterness of defeat. We were cut off. I would never see home again. I couldn't stand it. Turning face down on my bedroll, I lay there, listening to the water roaring down the river, till my ears hurt.'

In just a few hours, however, his entire world would be turned upside down.

# Chapter 13

# OPERATION WATCHTOWER BEGINS

After a fitful night on an empty stomach, Clemens was in a deep sleep when a terrified and panting native scout burst into his small hut at dawn. Pointing towards the coast, he explained he had just heard that the entire Japanese navy had arrived from Tulagi and was anchored along a vast line stretching in both directions from Lunga Beach.

Awake in a flash, Clemens said nothing but instinctively leaped up to his Teleradio. In the interminable minute spent waiting as the set warmed up, he heard a series of distant, rumbling vibrations from the north. Some were relatively close, but others – great deep boomings – appeared distant. Desperate for any news on what might be happening, he had already begun the mental preparations to evacuate.

As he searched for a frequency on the receiver, the dial caught a snippet of a voice. 'Orange Base to Blue Base … come in, Blue Base …' it said, in a distinctively American accent. Another voice mentioned the 'ammo dump', then the 'fuel dump', then, 'Whoa, did you guys see that?' Then another voice, rising in excitement: 'I see a truck, I see two trucks, I see a hell of a lot of trucks. Swoop in low and you'll get a good haul.' In a flash, he realised what he was listening to: US pilots being directed into attacks. Somewhere over the horizon there must be an American aircraft carrier dispatching its pilots. Then more explosions could be heard as a barrage opened up from ships – American ships – parked just off the beach at Lunga. Clemens could barely contain himself. At the very edge of despair, relief had come.

Further west, MacFarland and Hay knew exactly what they were seeing: an entire amphibious invasion force, their guns turned towards the Japanese positions at Lunga. Despite the grey dawn, they could clearly make out the dark blue dive-bombers swooping down like sea birds, disgorging their bombs before pulling up. Further out, the ships left a criss-crossing pattern of white wakes on the calm sea.

As the morning light strengthened, they could make out a fleet of more than eighty ships of all sizes: destroyers, cruisers and cargo vessels, and in the centre, a great battleship, its big guns flashing followed seconds later by a deep, rumbling report. Somewhere just over the horizon, three US aircraft carriers – *Saratoga*, *Wasp* and *Hornet* – were in feverish action, having steamed across the Pacific from their home ports in America, unleashing large numbers of fighters and dive-bombers in tight groups like swarms of bees. It was a spectacular sight. Some of the major vessels of the Royal Australian Navy – including the cruisers *Australia*, *Canberra* and *Hobart* – had joined the armada. *Australia*'s 8-inch guns were among the first to open fire upon the shore at Lunga. Had he known, naval officer MacFarland's pride would have swelled further.

Native villagers gathered around them to watch the spectacle. Through binoculars they could see as small, snub-nosed boats were lowered from larger ships then cut towards the beach and unloaded men before swinging around and heading back to the big ships to reload.

A message of warning was received, alerting the Coastwatchers to be vigilant for Japanese soldiers retreating inland from the beach. This, thought Clemens, was surely it. The long-awaited American invasion had arrived to throw the Japanese off their airstrip, take it for themselves and turn it against them. Operation Watchtower, the great campaign for Guadalcanal, had commenced.

That morning, in his diary, Clemens recorded the first words of optimism in weeks: 'Callooh-Callay, Oh, what a day!!'

•

A few weeks earlier, Major-General Alexander Vandegrift of the United States Marine Corps sat in stunned silence in an office in Auckland, New Zealand, as the commander of the US Navy South Pacific Area, Vice-Admiral Robert Ghormley, outlined the plan. Both Vandegrift and the three staff officers accompanying listened, gradually becoming convinced that what they were hearing was sheer madness.

Some of America's most senior commanders had wanted to hit the Japanese in the Solomons for some time, but had been thwarted, not by the Japanese, but by their own superiors in Washington. Although Admiral Ernest King, the colossus at the head of the US Navy, and Pacific commander General Douglas MacArthur detested one another in every way and on almost every level, they nevertheless united in their resolve that America's real fight was not in Europe but with those who had brought America into the war in the first place, the Japanese. And yet, even the combined power of their famously titanic egos and ruthless determination was not enough to shift the belief of President Roosevelt and his Washington General Staff that America's policy would, for the time being, be wedded to the notion of 'Europe first'. Japan, they decreed, would have to wait until Hitler was defeated, or at least contained. It was even rumoured that the rising star of General Eisenhower was prepared to let Australia fall to the Japanese rather than agree to shift anything more than token resources to the Pacific theatre.

In mid-1942, the massive – and wholly unexpected – Japanese defeats of the Coral Sea, and particularly Midway, where the bulk of Japan's carrier force was wiped out in a single morning, caused the mood to shift. While Hitler remained impregnable in his European fortress, a victory anywhere would serve the Allies well and offer relief to the success-starved populations at home. King and MacArthur seized their chance, arguing that a unique opportunity to launch an offensive in the South Pacific had opened up. Washington, with reservations noted, gave the green light.

It was here that the visions of King and MacArthur spiralled off in different directions. MacArthur's plan, of which he would be the primary driver, was for a direct assault on the Japanese stronghold of Rabaul, which since the January invasion had been transformed into a formidable fortress, its two runways expanded into six, thousands of troops embedded, and with a deep network of defences. Any frontal attack here would be a bloodbath, and the US Chiefs of Staff dismissed MacArthur's plan for the costly madness it was. The navy's idea to retake Japan's more recent conquests was looked on more favourably.

King's chief operational planner, Rear Admiral Richmond Turner, was given a free hand to hammer out the details, and immediately pursued the logic of dismantling the Japanese empire from its outer extremities and most recent conquests, like the Solomons. His plan involved sending in amphibious troops to take back the capital of the British protectorate, Tulagi, then establishing the first of a series of airstrips in the vicinity, thus removing the threat to the supply lines to the US, and thwarting Japan's attempts to expand further east. Consulting his map for the site of an airstrip, Turner decided the grassy plain running along the central north coast of Guadalcanal, beside the mouth of the Lunga River, seemed ideal. A date for the dual invasion – now christened 'Watchtower' – was set for 1 August, and the men chosen for the job were the 11 000 as yet untested Marines of Alexander Vandegrift's 1st Division, United States Marine Corps.

General Vandegrift's first thought was why, in God's name, had Admiral Chester Nimitz, the commander of the US Pacific fleet, given command of the entire enterprise to the wholly uninspiring man droning on in front of him, Robert Ghormley, an officer who hadn't held a sea command for years and had barely stepped foot onboard an aircraft carrier his whole life. His appointment in fact had been a compromise Nimitz would soon regret.

As usual, Ghormley was hesitant, vague on detail, and seemed to have no idea where Guadalcanal actually was. In this, at least, he was not alone, as neither did Vandegrift nor any of his staff. Yet, it was to the shores of this remote, probably heavily defended tropical beach that Vandegrift was being asked to land his completely green Marines for their first engagement of the war. And this was only one of his problems.

As Vandegrift attempted to explain to the admiral, the convoy containing the first elements of his division had only just arrived in New Zealand and much of the rest was still at sea. Furthermore, the availability of ships had been so limited, and space so tight, that much of their weapons, personnel and equipment had not even been loaded. While they might be equipped for a landing, they were totally unprepared to mount an amphibious assault on a defended position. In addition, an entire reinforced infantry regiment had been earlier sheared off the division to defend Samoa in case the Japanese decided to invade there (they never did), with the remainder untrained in large-scale manoeuvres.

Admiral Ghormley listened, gazed at the floor and shuffled some papers. In a tone utterly devoid of enthusiasm, he then informed Vandegrift that the invasion was set for five weeks' time, and that he should commence arrangements for the Guadalcanal operation as soon as possible.

Even greater than the ludicrously short preparation time was the problem of intelligence. In the words of author Walter Lord, 'Nobody seemed to know anything about the place.' Even today, there are large swathes of the Solomon Islands represented on the map by nothing more than the word 'uncharted'. Unsurprisingly, therefore, in mid-1942 when Vandegrift sent his chief intelligence officer to Melbourne to find out what he could about the Solomons and Guadalcanal, he reported that they were heading into *terra incognita*. Not a single decent map of the islands could be found, and the few former European islanders that could be interviewed appeared to know nothing outside their own patch.

More alarmingly, little was known about the extent of Japanese infiltration of the island, nor their numbers, strengths or disposition.

Then, the devastating news that the Japanese had begun construction of an airfield of their own at the very site decided upon by the Americans. With renewed urgency, a B-17 was dispatched to photographically survey the entire island. In a stroke of much-needed fortune, the photos were processed in Townsville, where they would be supplemented by the most recent information provided by Eric Feldt's Coastwatchers, an organisation of which the Americans were then barely aware.

Meeting with Feldt personally, Vandegrift's operations manager, Colonel Merrill Twining, listened as Feldt unlocked the features of the photographs, then handed him detailed sketch maps of Lunga, Tulagi and its neighbouring island of Gavutu, annotated with fortifications, gun emplacements and other supporting installations, all meticulously prepared from information supplied by the men of his Coastwatching organisation. Stunned, Twining was then informed about the extent of the network on Guadalcanal. Feldt gave him the name Martin Clemens, strongly suggesting he be contacted as soon as the Americans were ashore, and provided the correct codes with which to do so.

Only half expecting to be given an answer, an impressed Twining probed Feldt for his estimation of the number of Japanese currently on Guadalcanal. Feldt said nothing, then slid him a note he had prepared earlier, the most recent Coastwatcher estimate of Japanese troop numbers. Twining looked at it like a winning lottery ticket. Feldt believed the Americans had overestimated Japanese strength by nearly half. Instead of the 5000 Japanese the Americans believed they would be facing, Feldt estimated it would be closer to 3000, a vast difference.

In his memoir, Feldt casually noted the occasion: 'Thus it was that when officers of the US Marines came to Townsville from the South Pacific Area, they could be given complete information about their objective.'

The Marines were stunned. When they returned to New Zealand with the information, General Vandegrift was visibly relieved, and determined he would meet this remarkable Mr Clemens personally.

•

As often happens in war, the complete reverse of what had been foreshadowed became the reality. While it was expected Tulagi and its neighbouring islands of Tanambogo and Gavutu would fall easily, the Marines were told to expect the defences of the Japanese airfield at Lunga Beach on Guadalcanal would be significant. Instead, they walked ashore at Lunga in the face of almost no resistance and Vandegrift had safely landed almost all his men by 0930. The bombardment had shaken the spirit of the largely non-Japanese construction workers, who along with the 400 garrison troops took to the jungle. Some Marines reported that the breakfast being prepared in the outdoor mess was still warm.

It was a different story 20 miles away in Tulagi where the hard Japanese troops of the 3rd Special Naval Landing Force – men often compared to the US Marines themselves – put up fierce resistance for two days, including several night counter-attacks. These soldiers almost always fought to the death. On Tanambogo, some Japanese were armed with nothing but poles and sticks, yet they still refused to surrender.

On faraway Rabaul, the Japanese at their Pacific headquarters were stunned and affronted by the American assault. Immediately they began preparations to throw the Marines off their tiny foothold and back into the sea.

## Chapter 14

# PAUL MASON'S FINEST HOUR

Almost 350 miles to the north of Lunga Beach, high on a hill behind Buin at the southern tip of Bougainville, Paul Mason shielded his eyes from the sun's glare and peered upwards through his round, metal-framed spectacles. Somewhere from the north, a deep, throbbing sound was rising. Grabbing his binoculars, he scanned the horizon. In a few moments, the sound of aircraft engines seemed to fill the sky. Then he spotted them. Two formations of twin-engine bombers in two perfect V's sailing overhead, their pale underbellies and round red circles clearly visible. As he began counting, he knew it was the largest formation of aircraft he had ever seen. 'One … two … three …' – breaking off the count momentarily, he switched on his Teleradio and set a frequency before picking up the binoculars again – '… ten … eleven … twelve …'

Something, finally, was happening. Mason's Coastwatching on Bougainville had so far been a frustrating experience. Although reporting on the Japanese when he was able, he had been forced to move a number of times to avoid their patrols, been struck down with a particularly severe bout of malaria, and was dangerously undersupplied as a number of drops had gone awry. One from a Catalina was mistakenly unloaded more than 70 miles away from his position due to the general paucity of decent maps. He travelled the distance on a bicycle with a flat tyre to locate the supplies, but after two days' searching found nothing, only to be later informed that due to a mix-up in the orders at Port Moresby the supplies had been delivered to a completely different part of the island. Another drop was closer, but most of the valuable food and equipment came down in a swamp. One package at least survived, containing his new badges of naval rank and epaulettes, which he was unable to attach to his shredded clothing in any case.

He knew the Japanese were aware of his presence – even his name – and were after him. Raiding parties had visited his former position at Kieta, then later Buin, dispersing a group of Australian soldiers of Mackie's Independent Company who then decamped with Mason, causing some amount of friction as supplies were short. Nor did Mason's opinion of the men improve after they displayed, in his opinion, a lack of understanding of the island, the natives, and the Japanese. Frictions between civilian and military Coastwatchers would be an ongoing issue, as the former planters and administrators often found the army operatives both clumsy and ignorant of the islands and its people.

On Bougainville, as on Guadalcanal, a concerted and far more successful effort was being made by the Japanese to win the native population over to their side. Reports of another English- and Pidgin-speaking Japanese man, Tsunesuke Tashiro, began to emerge. Tashiro had lived for several years in Kieta before the war working for a Japanese trading firm and was apparently on friendly terms with most of the Bougainville Europeans including Mason, who came to the opinion that he was 'very crafty'. Tashiro had been interned by Australian authorities after Pearl Harbor and taken to Rabaul, where he managed to escape and board a ship to Truk. Now back in the Solomons, and addressing ever-larger groups of villagers, Tashiro repeated the standard line that the Japanese were in possession of the islands, and that the few Europeans remaining were of no consequence. Those who cooperated with the new masters would be rewarded; those who did not would be punished.

To counter Japanese intimidation of the natives, Mason used simple logic, explaining to those natives who were aware of his presence, 'We are here to let the US forces know where the Japanese are located, and where the friendly natives are situated. Unless we are allowed to remain, the US forces will not know friend from foe.' The majority of people around Buin, including those working for the Japanese, accepted Mason's reason and did not betray his position.

Some Japanese propaganda was repeated by a number of the remaining Bougainville missionaries, who were happy enough to accept the Japanese as their new masters in exchange for being left alone. Mason gradually sensed that support for the Coastwatchers and the Allies was eroding, and as well there was a shift in the natives' attitude towards him, with more and more people avoiding him or glancing at him askance.

One night, he was wakened by the sound of bombing coming from the direction of a new Japanese installation on Shortland Island, which they had occupied since March. With something approaching delight, Mason realised the sound must be American bombers in action. It was only then that he felt there actually were other people besides himself in this war opposing the Japanese. As Feldt reflected, the Coastwatchers could listen to the broadcast news, 'but it seemed to relate to far-off, impersonal matters – someone else's war'. Now, things were changing.

•

Four hundred miles to the north, at the other end of Bougainville, Jack Read maintained his Coastwatcher post at Aravia in the central north of the island. Though elevated and relatively secure, it was now considered too distant to closely observe the new Japanese air base 17 miles away at Buka Passage. Unlike at Lunga, there would be no Marines to storm ashore and wrest it from the enemy here, and while the Buka strip was still too small to take bombers, it could accommodate the formidable Zero fighters with ease. The ability to observe Buka was therefore critical. Reconnoitring the area via the network of jungle tracks with which he was familiar, Read decided that the mountain village of Porapora, 4000 feet above the water on the northwest coast, would offer a panoramic view of Matchin Bay and Queen Carola Harbour.

Like Mason, Read found supplies were an ever-present problem. Every item which could not be obtained locally – radio spare parts, clothing, ammunition and occasional letters from home – was to be dropped by parachute at a prearranged location. As the risk to pilot and aircraft flying deep into enemy territory was considerable, the drops were infrequent and top secret. At Read's first drop in June, he was standing on a beach at Kunua as a lone Hudson bomber appeared over a plantation from the seaside, barely clearing the palms. Over several runs, a crate could be seen being ejected from the side door, followed by a white parachute. The last chute, however, became caught on the aircraft's tail elevator, prompting the pilot to execute a series of dramatic manoeuvres to free it. Then the Hudson's turret gunner attempted to shoot it off, all to no avail. Finally, with a sympathetic hand waving from the cockpit, the aircraft turned away, still dragging the crate, towards the west, leaving Read feeling 'alone and isolated, standing on the sands of Kunua'.

Bizarrely, some of the remaining Europeans – including some of those who had refused earlier pleadings to leave – now demanded a share of the supply drops for themselves. 'When the news of my supply drop became known,' recalled Read, 'certain members of the European community demanded similar treatment.' Although many of the wealthy planters were 'definitely living better than we were', they sent a delegation to Read headed by planter Claude Campbell (who had apparently made a remarkable recovery from his illness) with a list of luxury items of which they were running low, and which they demanded be replenished by government airdrop. Gritting his teeth, Read smiled, took the list and dutifully promised to forward it. 'No reply was ever received,' he recalled, 'and nor did I ever feel justified in following it up.'

Like Mason too, Read also needed to keep abreast of the mood of the native population, upon which he likewise relied for his survival. Read was less concerned than Mason about Japanese influence in his sector of Bougainville, believing they had already committed serious errors of judgement. One report told him of a village chief who refused to attend a ceremony at the Japanese headquarters at which rising sun armbands and flags were handed out. The chief's absence was noted and he was later hunted down and publicly executed as a warning to others.

Other recalcitrant villagers and their leaders were flogged and humiliated. Read later reflected, 'the lasting effect on these simple people can well be imagined. Allegiance was being extorted by fear rather than by free will.' In the short term, however, the Japanese methods, particularly in the north of the island, were effective. Read was, to a certain extent, sympathetic. It was the native Melanesians who were forced to live under these new conquerors after all, and the Japanese were now appearing in force.

Apart from the natives, Read also had to contend with the loyalties of some of the remaining resident Europeans. To his alarm, he heard that the Austrian-born manager of the Hakau plantation, Fred Urban, already known for his Nazi sympathies, had made plain his willingness to cooperate with the Japanese, potentially undermining the entire Coastwatching system on the island. Read sought urgent advice from Feldt, who did not mince his words. 'Take any measures you consider necessary for your own safety,' he signalled in reply. 'There will be no inquest.'

Several weeks prior to the American landings on Guadalcanal in August, Mason had requested he be moved to Malabita Hill, overlooking Buin on Bougainville's southern tip, where the Japanese were beginning to build up a naval anchorage. No sooner had he started reporting from there than Feldt suddenly ordered both Read and Mason to lie low and, unless in the case of dire emergency, cease broadcasting altogether. At the same time, they were instructed to come up with a fresh callsign based only on personal knowledge. Mason was asked to be known by the first three letters of his sister's married name. This being Stokie, Mason's callsign became STO. Read was in turn asked to provide the initials of his daughter, Judith Eugenie Read: JER.

Although Feldt could not reveal the impending invasion of Guadalcanal to his Coastwatchers, he knew their role would become paramount, and any risk of their discovery had to be avoided. Radio silence, for the time being, would be maintained. In addition, they would need to be in excellent positions to observe the battle that was to come.

Mason and Read could do nothing but sit and wait.

•

In war, the advantage of surprise is short-lived. So completely had the Americans managed to conceal their intention to attack the Solomons that a formation of large Kawanishi floatplanes was destroyed at their docks at Tulagi, having not had a chance even to untie their moorings. For the disbelieving Japanese, such humiliation could not be allowed to stand.

Not surprisingly, barely hours after the first Marines stepped foot on the shore of Guadalcanal, a formation of twin-engine bombers roared off the runway at Rabaul, formed up and in perfect V formation turned towards the southeast. The Americans, they believed, would not have had time to establish a defensive perimeter and would be caught completely off guard by Japan's quick response, just as their big cargo ships were involved in the difficult job of unloading.

One might have assumed that the Japanese pilots would take a less direct route from Rabaul to the beaches at Lunga – flying in a more southerly direction, then swinging north to arrive over the Americans from the sea. Japanese airmen, however, were notoriously poor navigators, and a long detour over the sea could make them miss their target as well as eat into their limited fuel capacity. The formation therefore flew the most direct line between Rabaul and Guadalcanal, taking them, as it happened, almost directly over Paul Mason's Coastwatching station on Bougainville.

'… Sixteen … seventeen … eighteen …' Mason now knew why Feldt had ordered him to stay silent. Something had indeed been brewing, and the evidence of it was currently passing over his head. Reports of enemy shipping, it had been established, could be broadcast by Morse, but Japanese aircraft were to be announced in plain voice. While this posed far more of a risk of being detected by the Japanese, when it came to air attack, time was of the absolute essence.

So it was that Coastwatcher Paul Mason, at around 11.30 a.m. on the morning of 7 August 1942, broadcast what would be one of the most important signals of the entire Pacific War. Picking up the Teleradio's microphone, he switched to the secret Frequency X and announced in a clear calm voice, 'From STO. Twenty-four bombers heading yours.' It was short, but it was enough. The signal was picked up initially by Marchant's station on Malaita, then relayed to Port Moresby, who in turn passed it to Townsville, and then to Canberra. In a flash, it had been picked up over shortwave by the American listening station at Honolulu, then sent across the Pacific by the giant transmitters at Pearl Harbor. Within fifteen minutes, the Americans disembarking at Lunga Beach had firm knowledge that the Japanese were on their way. Armed with the codes to identify the source of the broadcast, they calculated that it emanated from Mason near Buin, around 300 miles away. With the cruising speed of the Japanese aircraft roughly 160 knots, this allowed the Marines nearly two full hours before they arrived. Not a second was to be wasted.

Klaxons rang out and men ran to their stations on the ships. Landing procedures were immediately suspended, and those personnel already on shore were told to remain there. In moments, the ships had begun to weigh anchor, make steam, and begin to disperse, with every gun manned and ready. On the carriers further out to sea, the Grumman Wildcat fighters currently conducting combat air patrols were ordered to come in and refuel, and others were made ready. The Wildcat, a tough and well-armed little aeroplane, could not match Japan's Zero in climb or manoeuvrability; its sole chance for advantage relied on gaining height and attacking from above. Accordingly, they were ordered to fly west and stack up ready at 20 000 feet. Then they would come in and pounce.

The atmosphere onboard one of the Australian warships, HMAS *Canberra*, was somewhat less hurried, with the bosun's mate taking his time to inform the crew over the loudspeaker that 'The ship will be attacked at noon by twenty-four torpedo bombers. All hands will pipe to dinner at eleven o'clock.'

The bosun's mate was an hour out with his timing. It was not until 1315 that a patrolling navy pilot gave a 'Tally-ho' and the Japanese appeared, right on cue, west of Savo Island. It would not, however, be the surprise the Japanese had anticipated. Not only would they be met with a wall of defensive fire from sea and sky, but they would find hardly a target to attack.

Paul Mason was likewise slightly mistaken. It was twenty-seven Japanese aircraft, primarily torpedo bombers, which attacked Lunga on the first day of the battle. How many were shot down remains a matter of conjecture. Some sources say only one made it back to Rabaul, others that seven or eight limped home, some trailing smoke.

An hour after the attack, the Allied ships came back in and the landings resumed. By nightfall, the American Marines, still having encountered almost no resistance, fanned out south and west from the beach, bedding down and amusing themselves by cracking coconuts.

•

The next morning, 8 August, the Bougainville jungle again reverberated to the sound of aircraft engines. Stunned by the previous day's reception, but still determined to wipe out the American position on the beach, the Japanese now directed forty-four aircraft – a mixture of bombers, torpedo bombers and fighters – to take off from Kavieng, the new Japanese base 100 miles further north of Rabaul, on New Ireland. Taking only a slightly altered route from the first attack, the pilots flew south, this time passing directly over Jack Read's position at Aravia.

Read had spent the morning struggling with his batteries then sent off his daily weather and observation report.

Before him and his bearers lay an arduous trek followed by a 4000-foot climb into the mountains, so they could reach their new location 8 miles to the north at Porapora, and Read was anxious to get moving. Before dismantling the Teleradio for transport, he decided to make a quick scan of the frequencies, as he later wrote, 'for any interesting transmissions. I suddenly picked up a broadcast that made me forget for a moment my departure for Porapora.'

Loud and clear in his headphones, American voices could be heard speaking of place names around Tulagi; and amid the unmistakable banter of pilots he could discern what sounded like aircraft identification names being called in and dispatched. Read sat mesmerised, quickly realising he was listening to the flight control tower of a nearby US aircraft carrier. He turned to inform his most capable native policeman, Sergeant Yauwika, but his focus was directed to the north. In a few seconds, they all heard the dull beat of many aircraft engines. From Read's height, the Japanese seemed to be flying at low level, and through a break in the jungle, he watched as two formations of different types flashed past. He would forever recall the dull red discs on their wings and the flashing of their propeller blades in the sun.

Thanking whatever it was that prevented him from dismantling the radio himself, by his callsign, Read radioed Malaita and took the risk of broadcasting in open voice. Infuriatingly, no one answered. Nor did anyone seem to be on duty at Port Moresby. Meanwhile, the sound of engines was already beginning to recede. Read swore, then the faint voice of another Coastwatcher, whose identity he never determined, came on the air. 'Relay following,' said Read urgently. 'FROM JER. FORTY-FIVE BOMBERS NOW GOING SOUTHEAST.'

Read could now only sit and wait. Returning to the radio, he kept the 7-megacycle frequency open to hear the American operators mentioning names like Tulagi and Guadalcanal. Something, he knew, was happening, but what?

Suddenly, the voice of the controller was heard recalling the aircraft to refuel and rearm before dispatching them once again to patrol at 20 000 feet.

Read and his native scouts and bearers listened in to the drama – in which they had played a significant part – unfolding 500 miles away.

On this second morning of the Guadalcanal Campaign, it would be the Americans initially caught off guard. Instead of retracing the previous day's route, the Japanese had the sense to swing around nearby Florida Island to attack Guadalcanal from the east. Right on noon, the lookouts on the *Australia* saw them first: twenty-three torpedo bombers skimming in just above the waves. Avoiding the warships for the moment, the Japanese went straight for the transports. Admiral Richmond Turner, however, had given his captains nearly ninety minutes in which to adopt evasive action and man their guns. As the ships were steaming at high speed in tight circles, the Japanese found them almost impossible to hit.

Then the American gunners found their aim, ushering in ten minutes of slaughter. Japanese aircraft exploded in mid-air, or caught a wingtip on the water, sending them spinning along the surface like a flaming Catherine wheel. Then the dive-bombers plunged, but they too missed their mark, failing to hit a single ship. The USS *Jarvis* was the only warship struck when the destroyer suffered a glancing blow from a torpedo which tore a 50-foot gash in her bow and left her dead in the water. Then, by accident or design, a Betty bomber flew straight into the side of one of the transports, the *George F. Elliott*, leaving her a blazing wreck but sparing her crew, who abandoned ship a few hours later. The *Jarvis* was not so lucky. After limping over to the newly retaken Tulagi Harbour, her captain either ignored or failed to receive an order to proceed to the New Hebrides for repairs. Instead, barely able to make cruising speed, the *Jarvis* inexplicably left during the night and attempted to sail all the way to Sydney. The following afternoon, a lame duck, she was spotted by a wave of Japanese aircraft and sunk with all 233 hands, one of only two major US Navy surface ships to suffer such a fate for the entire war.

Back at the Buka Passage, Jack Read was still tuned to the American pilots' frequency and was given a vivid account of battle by an excited but unknown young navy pilot. 'Boys, they're shooting 'em down like flies, one, two, three … I can see eight of them coming down in the sea now!' Another Coastwatcher who had also managed to tune in later commented to Clemens that although 'the Yanks seemed to conduct it more like a ball game than a battle', it was indeed 'sweet music'.

Two hours later, Read saw for himself the results of his timely warning, as the Japanese aircraft passed back over his position. This time, he had no trouble in counting them as a gaggle of just eight – all semblance of formation now gone – limped back to Kavieng. More would straggle back later, but the final tally was upwards of twelve aircraft destroyed for minimal damage to the unloading ships.

Now, and for the next six months, the pattern had been set. Almost every day, the Japanese would attempt to send formations of aircraft down The Slot towards Guadalcanal, and every day the Coastwatchers would sound the alert to their arrival. Read later wrote, 'Practically every day, we would watch the awe-inspiring, streamlined formations of Japanese planes heading southward over our position. Then five or six hours later, whatever was left of the attacking force straggled home in small groups for an hour or more. [Although] the reporting of these enemy flights soon became routine, I shall never forget the thrill and euphoria of that first morning.'

As the campaign progressed, Read's reports became more specific:

TWENTY-SEVEN BOMBERS, 12 FIGHTERS GOING YOURS. TOTAL 17 FIGHTERS GONE YOURS PAST HALF-HOUR.

Sometimes, due to cloud cover, the enemy formations could only be heard, but a report was issued nonetheless. On 18 August, Read took pleasure in relaying to his team a message sent by Paul Mason: 'Commander Task Forces Tulagi and Guadalcanal has expressed appreciation of air attack warnings given by you.'

Read's view was further enhanced upon moving to what he termed his 'grandstand view' at Porapora. 'It was rather an impressive sight to watch several squadrons of Japanese heavy bombers come out of the northwest in perfect order. They circled lazily over Buka, while the Zeros took off in pairs from the airfield below. As soon as the fighters trimmed into formation, the fleet of from 40 to 60 planes would head south – many of them never to return.'

Always aware that the Japanese might at any time discover his hideout, Read had prepared his native crew. 'I always had a picked team of ten boys standing by,' said Read after the war. 'Each was schooled to grab a particular piece of equipment. My party could be up and off within four minutes of an alarm.'

The Americans' early luck was not to last. Historians still debate furiously the justifications, or lack thereof, behind the fateful and enduringly controversial decision of Admiral Frank Fletcher, commanding the US aircraft carrier force at Guadalcanal, to pull up his anchors and abandon the area on the evening of the second day of the campaign, 8 August. His fighter force, admittedly, had taken significant losses, and he believed his fuel reserves, and that of his carriers, were running low. Moreover, the landings were taking longer than anticipated, and Fletcher believed it had only been luck that had prevented the Japanese land-based bombers from discovering his position just over the horizon from Guadalcanal. That luck, he believed, could not last forever, and the risk to the carrier force was simply too great. Explaining his reasons to Admiral Turner, who gave his assent, Fletcher left the Marines to their own devices.

Once the protection of airpower had been removed, the cargo vessels, still only partly unloaded, also departed for safety, despite vast amounts of the Marines' equipment – including huge stocks of food and ammunition – still deep in their holds.

General Vandegrift, the Marines' commander, was furious, and for the rest of his life loudly proclaimed his men at Guadalcanal had been betrayed by the navy. The already deep rift between the two services widened further.

Along with the materiel which sailed away with the cargo vessels, Vandegrift was also deprived of a good deal of his administration, including much of his intelligence. Two former district officers – as well as Coastwatchers – Dick Horton and his assistant Henry Josselyn had landed with the Marines as guides the morning of the invasion, but their knowledge of the interior was limited. More than ever, Vandegrift needed to know what lay in the jungle beyond the coastal screen, and how many of the enemy it was concealing.

Then, barely a day after the departure of Fletcher's carriers, Japan's Admiral Mikawa somehow managed to slide a force of eight warships, mainly heavy cruisers, right down The Slot and into the midst of the Allied fleet. Catching the Allies completely by surprise, and aided by the light of the still burning *George F. Elliott*, Mikawa sank four cruisers and a destroyer, including the Royal Australian Navy's HMAS *Canberra*, and damaged many more. Over a thousand men were killed with another

700 wounded for almost no loss to the Japanese. Little wonder the engagement, the worst day in the history of the US Navy, came to be known among the veterans as 'The Battle of the Five Sitting Ducks'.

The easy part of the fight for Guadalcanal, Vandegrift well knew, was over. From now on, he and his men would be locked into many months of hard and bloody slog – battling for the possession of a remote and muddy airstrip at the intersection of the furthest ranges of the two combatants' land-based airpower, and accessible only through dauntingly long lines of communication and supply.

One man, who was probably even now looking down from his mountain hideout, could help.

## Chapter 15

# DOWN FROM THE MOUNTAINS

From his post at Vungana, Martin Clemens climbed to the highest peak he could scale to watch the breathtaking spectacle of the Marines landing at Guadalcanal, and from that moment knew his war was about to change. In the first instance, it substantially increased his standing among the villagers, who could now see with their own eyes that their former rulers had not abandoned the Solomons after all, and were preparing to throw out the Japanese with considerable force. Clemens's earlier promise that, at some stage, the British would return could be kept. The Japanese, he could now tell them, had been pushed out of Tulagi and were on the run in Guadalcanal. The remainder of the Solomons, he assured them, would be next.

As Feldt reflected on this significant juncture in the Coastwatchers' war, 'To the Marines, it was the beginning of the campaign. To the Coastwatchers, who had waited in the jungle since the Japanese invasion, it was the passing over the crest of the hill. At last, they could feel that it was not a one-way war, with the Jap always pushing forward.'

As the days passed, Clemens waited for further instructions, but none were forthcoming. Even more perplexing was the sudden absence of most of the armada of cargo vessels, which had followed the departure of Fletcher's carriers. The airwaves had returned to silence, as the regular patrols by the navy Wildcats had also ceased. At least the dreaded Kawanishi flying boats had not reappeared in their place.

More ominous had been the terrible sound of battle the night of Savo Island – the booming reports and the display of explosions in the distant ocean, and the fireworks of every shade and colour which had accompanied it.

In the interim, Don MacFarland at Gold Ridge had taken pity on Clemens's complaint of being without proper footwear and, by runner, had sent over his best pair of navy dress shoes, still glistening black, though a full size too small. Clemens was suitably amused but vowed to wear them, just to show him.

Finally, late on 13 August, Clemens greeted an exhausted runner who handed him a printed yellow envelope marked 'U.S. Marine Corps Field Message' with 'Native runner' entered in the space reserved for the messenger's name. 'American Marines have landed successfully in force. Come in via Volanavua and along beach to Ilu during daylight – repeat – daylight. Ask outpost to direct you to me at 1st Reg. C. P. at Lunga. Congratulations and regards.'

Finally, Clemens's hour of liberation had come. 'I so longed to be away,' he said later, 'that had the scout flown with winged heels I would have cursed him for being late!'

By the next morning, Clemens had packed up and was ready to depart. As if in anticipation, his problematic Teleradio, now well and truly falling apart, suddenly revived and began to work perfectly, despite its rusted bearings and broken knobs. Gingerly, Clemens started to pack it up. 'I almost hugged that Teleradio,' he wrote. 'It had been my constant companion for over five months. In spite of its travels it had really worked jolly well, and I would miss the friendliness of the morning "sessions".'

He was likewise grateful to the people of Vungana, this unprepossessing village which had protected him over several months. As a sign of thanks, Clemens gave away all his non-vital possessions – coloured handkerchiefs to children, and an ageing pair of shorts to the chief, which he donned immediately with pride.

Following the directions outlined in the message, Clemens and his small party of native bearers finally began to descend the mountains, making 15 miles on the first day. Trudging through swamp, ravine and jungle, he was soon sweating in the familiar heat, hauling his equipment and praying not to run into a Japanese patrol. His only armament was a .32 calibre pistol of doubtful reliability, and a useless .22 rifle which he gave to one of the young men to swing jauntily over his shoulder. Lacking adequate footwear, Clemens was barefoot the entire way.

On the second day, reaching the lower plains, the party had strung out in a line and were passing through an area of open grassland when in the distance large-calibre gunfire was heard. Then, overhead, a trio of what he thought were American aircraft approached low from the northwest. Instinctively, Clemens waved and the others followed suit. The aircraft waggled their wings in recognition. To his horror, he noticed the dull red circles on the wings and tail. He ordered his men to stand their ground firmly where they were and, whatever they did, not to stop waving. Whether the Japanese were bluffed he never knew. But as soon as the planes had passed, he and his men scattered into the jungle before the Japanese could come back for a second look.

Finally, after months of tension, hardship and danger, and of barely speaking to another person in his own language, Clemens and his party emerged onto the beach at the designated point and began marching east. After a short time, they rounded a corner, and there stood a group of green-clad soldiers wrangling a small truck off the beach. They looked up at this ragtag bunch walking towards them in an odd military gait, led by a dishevelled and heavily bearded European with a tattered uniform, and immediately raised their rifles. Clemens waved. Then they noted the new-looking pair of patent leather shoes into which he had just prised his worn and blistered feet. Slowly, they lowered their guns.

As the Marines gathered around them, Clemens handed over the letter but, overwhelmed with emotion and exhaustion, found himself unable to utter a single word save for his own name, which he gave in a rasping whisper. A Marine handed him a cigarette. Another, a piece of chocolate. Soon, multiple hands were extended and, in burning curiosity, myriad questions asked. Taking him back through the perimeter in a jeep, every man paused to look at this wild-looking warrior who, the word soon spread, had been living *out there, beyond the perimeter*, right under the nose of the enemy.

Over several debriefings, Clemens disgorged everything he knew to a series of officers. Following a decent night's sleep in an army cot, he was taken to General Vandegrift. 'The general was clean shaven and had a pink complexion, but his jaw was set and he had an air of quiet determination,' Clemens observed.

The two men spoke at length, Clemens giving the general a crash course in the island's key features. In half an hour, Vandegrift learned more than he had over the previous five weeks.

Then, regarding him intently, Vandegrift's tone shifted and he revealed that, three days earlier, a party of twenty-five of his men had set out on a patrol under the leadership of the division's intelligence officer, Lieutenant-Colonel Frank Goettge. A captured Japanese warrant officer, taken on the first day and then plied with alcohol, had indicated that some Japanese troops – many of whom were sick and malnourished – would be willing to surrender to the Americans. In addition, a white flag was seen at the mouth of the Matanikau River 4 miles away. A party was organised, including an interpreter, to investigate and possibly bring back some vitally important prisoners.

Travelling by boat, the Americans made for the river mouth and disembarked. It was a trap. Well prepared, the Japanese greeted the Americans with a hail of fire from the cover of the jungle as soon as they set foot on the beach. For twelve hours the Marines were picked off one by one. Only three survived by swimming back through a shark-infested sea, one of them driven insane by the experience and immediately discharged. The other two reported the Japanese mutilating the dead and wounded bodies of the Marines as they lay on the sand.

Clemens listened soberly. As the general continued to explain, Clemens realised the mighty garrison which had looked so impressive from afar was in fact in the most vulnerable of situations, and things were only expected to worsen. Almost nothing was known of the island, nor the real strength and disposition of the Japanese who, although ejected from Lunga, still dominated everything beyond the perimeter, which was never more than two and a half miles from the centre of the airstrip, and at the southern end, just a few hundred yards. With the departure of the navy, the Marines were incapable of building up strength quickly enough to take the offensive and were already running short of every conceivable supply. Even with the excellent work being done by Coastwatchers like Clemens, Read and Mason, warnings of the daily Japanese air attacks were of limited use if there were no aircraft with which to retaliate.

Without information on the enemy, Vandegrift feared, there would be more – many more – massacres like that at

Matanikau River. He then asked if Clemens would be willing to take charge of all intelligence-related matters on the island, using his knowledge and network of scouts to report on the enemy and also supplying guides to assist patrols.

Martin Clemens's war now changed drastically. He swapped treetops and isolated mountain peaks for an old Japanese tent and a muddy dugout on the edge of an airstrip. He was clean-shaven, given a new uniform, fed three times a day, and in place of his lonely vigil, he was now surrounded by people. His fight against the Japanese continued, as he rallied his army of scouts and runners to keep hundreds of unseen eyes on the Japanese who, shocked by their initial defeat at Lunga, now visited unrestrained barbarity on any native or European they suspected of not actively supporting them. Even Europeans previously left alone by the Japanese were hunted down by Ishimoto and others. One of the first reports Clemens received in his new role was the discovery of the naked bodies of a priest and a nun, bayoneted to death by retreating Japanese soldiers on their mission station, just a few miles along the coast from Lunga.

With the Coastwatchers' role in the Japanese army's humiliation now suspected, if not fully appreciated, they came under renewed pressure, with the enemy swearing to redouble attempts to wipe them out without mercy.

On 19 August, sharp-eyed soldiers on night shore duty reported interruptions in the usually gentle wave action breaking along the beach, caused, they suspected, by the passing of large ships at high speed. They realised the Japanese had begun reinforcing their army by night, and there was nothing the Marines could do about it.

More than ever, Clemens's network would be needed to keep an eye on this new development, quickly dubbed Tokyo Express. Some of his most trusted scouts, such as Daniel Pule, were given roles directly with Marine patrols, guiding them through the maze of jungle tracks almost invisible to all but a native's eye.

•

Colonel Kiyono Ichiki was no stranger to ruthless and determined military assaults. A notoriously aggressive infantry commander even by the standards of Imperial Japan, Ichiki had, in 1937, commanded a 500-strong battalion stationed around the Marco Polo Bridge near Beijing, where he had helped fabricate the military provocation sparking the Second Sino-Japanese War. Now, the commanders at Rabaul selected him to lead 2000 men – dubbed (in the Japanese fashion of naming certain military units after their commander) the Ichiki Detachment – to drive the Americans on Guadalcanal back into the sea.

Landing his force in two stages directly from Truk, Ichiki was told to patrol up to the American lines and test their defences, then either attack or wait for the remainder of his detachment to arrive. Six destroyers – the washes of which were detected by the Americans on the beach – landed the men on the night of 19 August. Ichiki sent out several patrols, one of which happened to intercept a large native man near a village. He seemed friendly and cooperative and, naturally, knew nothing of the American positions around Lunga. Suspecting he was somewhat wiser than he made out, the Japanese officer decided to search him.

Forty-two-year-old Jacob Vouza was known across the islands as a colourful character. Tall and strongly built, he had joined the native constabulary in 1916, serving on many of the larger islands of the Solomons as a police constable and gaining a reputation for discipline, which occasionally involved taking the law into his own hands. Upon the outbreak of war, he was assigned back to his home island of Guadalcanal and immediately became a valuable part of Martin Clemens's Coastwatcher scouting network. At first Clemens was wary of including such a notorious firebrand among his ranks, but Vouza soon proved his worth, wrangling and encouraging some of the less confident scouts, and proclaiming his patriotism by draping himself in a large Union Jack and brazenly walking up to the disembarking Americans at Lunga, shaking their hands as they came up the beach. What the Marines themselves made of the exuberant Vouza can only be guessed at. A day later he returned to the interior to pluck a downed US Wildcat pilot from the jungle and lead him back to the American lines.

Two weeks later, with Japanese activity across the island increasing, Clemens requested Vouza lead an all-native patrol beyond the Lunga perimeter, to report on any Japanese activity. Whether from a momentary lapse of reason – or perhaps a fondness for flags in general – Vouza accepted the gift of a small Stars and Stripes flag proffered him by a well-meaning Marine as a souvenir. Reason should have told Vouza to discard it, but he thanked the soldier, folded it carefully, and hid it in his kit as he and his patrol departed the defensive perimeter.

Appearing simply as a group of local men travelling from one village to another, Vouza and his patrol struck south, but saw no sign of the enemy. He then turned inland to widen his search, before turning north to reach the coast on the other side of the garrison. At some stage, he seemed to have reflected on his souvenir and the consequences if it was discovered by the Japanese. On the point of dumping it in the jungle, he happened to pass close by his home village of Volonavua, to where he detoured, alone, to secure it before rejoining the patrol.

It was the very worst of timing. As Vouza approached his village, a fresh-looking squad of Colonel Ichiki's men suddenly appeared around a bend of the track directly in front of him, and began asking questions. Vouza played dumb, and believed he was close to fooling the soldiers into letting him go, when a junior officer insisted his pack be searched. In a few minutes, the carefully folded flag was unfurled.

•

Sources differ as to the identity of Vouza's interrogator. Some claim it was the calm but ruthless Ishimoto, others allude to another multilingual officer. Taken to the nearby village of Tanevatu, Vouza was astonished to see Japanese soldiers in their hundreds obviously preparing for an attack. The questioning at first was straightforward: How long have you been working for the Americans? How many of them are there? What are their plans? Vouza did nothing but shake his head. The atmosphere quickly darkened. They dragged him outside where he was tied to a nest of red ants. Despite the burning agony, he kept silent. His captors, now infuriated, hauled him against a tree, repeatedly slamming his face with rifle butts. Still, he said nothing, enraging his captors even further. With a scream, a sergeant pierced his arms with his bayonet. Multiple thrusts then followed, tearing into his torso and neck until finally an officer drew out his sword and slashed Vouza's throat. Bleeding profusely, he lapsed into unconsciousness and his tormentors left him for dead to prepare for the night attack on the American positions.

By 1.30 a.m., Vouza appeared as good as dead and the Japanese, more concerned with their impending attack on the Americans, departed the village. But Vouza refused to die. Finally alone, he managed to wriggle out of his bindings and collapse to the ground. Summoning whatever strength his large frame had left, he crawled and stumbled into the dark jungle. Step by step, hand over hand, he slowly made his way back towards the American lines. At one point, a green flare sizzled in the sky above his head. Inch by inch, Vouza pulled his broken and bleeding body forward, amazingly remaining unseen by the Japanese soldiers busily preparing their positions as he crawled past them in the dark. Finally, he headed into no-man's land and eventually saw the outline of a Marine foxhole in front of him. He prayed the soldiers would not mistake him for a Japanese soldier.

•

Several hours later, Martin Clemens received an urgent phone call from an officer at the front. A native man, the officer said, had appeared, having apparently crawled through the Japanese lines, and was asking for 'Mr Clemens' by name. He advised him to hurry, as the man was not expected to survive. Clemens and Daniel Pule flew to a Jeep immediately.

Vouza was too weak to even sit up. Clemens and Pule propped him behind the Jeep and, by the glow of a cigarette lighter, Clemens wrote down all that Vouza managed to relay, albeit in the barest of whispers. Clemens wrote as fast as he could with one hand, while holding Vouza's hand with the other. It was agony for Vouza to speak, but what he had to say was pure gold. The Japanese, he said through the pain, were gathering at Tanevatu for an attack from the east. He had observed their weapons and strength and had even passed through them as they made their way to the perimeter. A stray Japanese bullet then ricocheted off the other side of the Jeep. Clemens asked for a field telephone and relayed to the divisional commander all Vouza had said. Vouza, his job done, asked Clemens to take down a final message for his wife and son, then slumped into a complete collapse.

With Vouza's information, a detachment of Marines struck out towards the Ilu River to the south of the perimeter, then swung around and hit the Japanese flank and rear. Not expecting to encounter the Americans this far from their positions, the Japanese were taken completely by surprise. In what became known as the Battle of Tenaru River, the Japanese attempted a series of outflanking manoeuvres but were caught trying to advance across a wide sandbar at the river's mouth and were slaughtered. For a loss of forty-three Marines, the Ichiki Detachment was almost entirely wiped out in a storm of fire. Tenaru River was one of the first major victories the Americans had over the Japanese at Guadalcanal, and proved an important fillip to their fighting spirit and morale. Colonel Ichiki, who had been told the Americans numbered only a couple of thousand badly trained and demoralised men, burned his regimental colours, then killed himself.

Amazingly, Jacob Vouza lived. He was rushed to a field hospital for an infusion of nearly 8 litres of blood; the astounded Marine surgeons counted seven separate bayonet wounds, then patched up his broken body. He remained unconscious, coming to from time to time only to mutter his insistence that he had told the Japanese nothing. Then, after twelve days, Vouza suddenly sprang back to life, insisting he be returned to duty. Barely two months later, his wish was granted and Vouza joined another Marine patrol as guide.

After 20 August, the first US aircraft began to touch down on the newly completed runway, now named Henderson Field after Major Lofton Henderson who, at the age of thirty-nine, died while leading his squadron of Marine dive-bombers against a Japanese carrier at Midway back in June. Finally, some air protection could be given, at least by day. But it was under the cover of night that the Japanese toiled, sending their fast-moving destroyers charging down The Slot in high-speed thrusts from Rabaul and Truk. In the dead of night, they quickly offloaded men and supplies – building up for the next offensive – then vanished out to sea with the dawn, rendering any American air superiority redundant.

By day the Marines, often guided by one of Clemens's scouts, would patrol the alien jungle beyond the perimeter, traipsing through this surreal, leech-filled world of mud and putrid undergrowth; of tangled mazes of tree roots which – a hundred times a day – caught the ankles of cursing, stumbling men; of airless silences interrupted by the sudden shrieks of unseen creatures; of snakes and gargantuan spiders, and crocodile-infested swamps into which a man could disappear forever with one misplaced step. And all the time, a pounding, unrelenting humidity drenched men's bodies in enervating streams of sweat. Suffering from an unquenchable thirst, they lifted their heads imploringly towards the barest whiff of breeze.

And with every squelching step, there was the maddening knowledge that, somewhere, the Japanese were lurking, waiting, perhaps a mile away, perhaps behind the next wall of green. *Not here*, men prayed in a constant, murmuring supplication, *let me die anywhere, but not here.*

When the story of Jacob Vouza and his ordeal permeated through the ranks of the Marines, the Coastwatchers began to take on something of a mystical status: somewhere out in that wilderness toiled an unseen army of brave men, living in the jungle, fighting, outwitting and confounding the Japanese at every turn, risking their lives to keep the Allies one step ahead. As the campaign ground down to its long and bloody stalemate, the notion gave the weary Marines some sense of hope.

Clemens's army grew daily in daring and cunning. Ignorant of modern machinery their entire lives, they nevertheless learned fast, and soon began to recognise the various types of Japanese ships and aircraft, and distinguish the nuances of weapons and calibres.

In the patronising overtones of the era, the Marines initially dismissed the accuracy of some of the scouts' reports. Sergeant Andrew Langaebaea, one of Clemens's recruits from the Solomons' native police force, displayed considerable daring in observing the nightly build-up of Japanese east of the Lunga perimeter, landed by the nimble destroyers of the Tokyo Express. Four thousand men, he reported to the Marines, had been assembled over four successive nights between Taivu Point and Tasimboko village, with a path being cut by the engineers directly through the jungle to an area south of the perimeter at an assembly point from which an attack, presumably, was to be launched.

The Americans dismissed the level of detail in Langaebaea's report, considering it a confection born of over-enthusiasm. Then, after one battle, a large swathe of equipment and supplies was caught on the beach near Tasimboko. After examining the piles of food, ammunition and regimental diaries, the Marines estimated it to represent a formation of around 4000. The native scouts were completely correct. According to Coastwatcher Dick Horton, the incident 'did much to make the division staff treat them with more respect in the future'.

Another man, known as Alika, a native of nearby Santa Isabel Island, also demonstrated vast courage and a shrewd brain. When the Japanese first occupied his home village near Rekata Bay, he simply walked into their camp smiling beatifically, with a load of fresh fish and vegetables for sale, as his fellow villagers fled. Infuriated at his audacity, the Japanese arrested and interrogated him immediately, then lined him up as if preparing to shoot him. The Japanese commander asked if he was not afraid to be shot. 'Shoot me if you like,' replied Alika, 'but I am still a friend of Japan.' So impressed was the commander, he not only released Alika, but bought his produce regularly and befriended him, allowing him full access to the camp. He would even be given tours where new gun emplacements and defences were proudly shown off.

All of it was carefully noted by Alika then fed back to the Coastwatchers, who passed it to the Marines, who then mounted a particularly successful air raid on Rekata Bay. Alika, however, was not done. Re-entering the camp after the attack, he commiserated sincerely with the commander, who then pointed out the damage and the body count. This was likewise reported then compared to the combat observations of the pilots themselves. All of it was vital intelligence.

# Chapter 16
# MACKENZIE'S RETURN

Although working largely with the Americans after the initial landings at Lunga, the Coastwatchers on Guadalcanal nevertheless maintained their own streak of independence – touching occasionally on defiance – particularly after the arrival of Hugh Mackenzie, Feldt's old classmate and one of the heroic leaders of Rabaul. Like Keith McCarthy, Mackenzie had organised a daring boat rescue, spiriting 153 of his men to safety under the noses of the Japanese. Despite his ordeal, Mackenzie insisted on being put back into action barely a month after stepping off the *Laurabada* in Port Moresby. His request duly granted, he was sent to Guadalcanal to take over the running of the Coastwatchers there, as Martin Clemens became more subsumed in working directly with the US Marines, eventually joining their ranks entirely.

Immediately, Mackenzie's independent streak shone through. Although noted for getting on well with the Americans, he did not always share their values. In early October, as the Japanese on the island increased in numbers but continued to fail in successive efforts to break the Americans at Lunga, they spread out through the island, particularly towards the western end of Guadalcanal, endangering the position held by Coastwatchers Snowy Rhoades and Lafe Schroder at Lavoro. Their situation had become so precarious that they were now held up in a series of caves, with the Japanese closing in daily. They were also unable to report without grave risk of capture, rendering their Coastwatching abilities almost useless. Mackenzie decided the time was ripe for Schroder and Rhoades to be extracted to safety and requested General Vandegrift lay on a small team and a boat for the purpose. Vandegrift, while sympathetic, shook his head, telling Mackenzie the risk of a rescue so close to the Japanese was too great, and that his small boats were too precious and too few. Accepting the general's decision without complaint, Mackenzie nevertheless determined that his Coastwatchers were not expendable, and quietly organised a rescue anyway.

Risking Vandegrift's wrath, Mackenzie 'borrowed' the *Ramada*, a former district commissioner's vessel, currently requisitioned by the Americans. Dick Horton, patrol officer and Coastwatcher who had arrived with the Marines as a scout, was asked to quietly put together a native crew and make the roughly 60-mile round trip to pluck the two Coastwatchers from a prearranged spot on the beach near Tangarare Mission. Although 'small, slow and defenceless', Horton had sailed the *Ramada* in the past and regarded her low profile as a distinct advantage. Setting off at dusk, he glided through the glassy sea at 6 knots, praying not to meet any of the nightly Japanese supply runs. As difficult as the trip would be to make at night, Horton knew the dark would at least give him cover. The return trip, on the other hand, would need to be in broad daylight. 'If we're attacked, get into the water and hide under the boat' was the best advice he could give his crew of four. 'If we're near the shore and the boat goes down, swim for it and make your way back to Lunga over the mountains.'

The trip up to Tangarare was thankfully uneventful. Approaching the shore, Horton rode the little boat through the ocean swells and peered through his binoculars for signs of life on the beach. Instead of just two Coastwatchers, Horton was astonished to see a large group of figures frantically waving to him from the beach. Besides Rhoades and Schroder, an entire party of Europeans were apparently preparing to board, including most of the remaining nuns and priests of a local mission, plus two extremely relieved-looking American airmen who had been rescued and looked after by the sisters for several weeks. In all, twenty people proceeded to clamber aboard the *Ramada*, and as Horton headed back east, he prayed they'd avoid any Japanese, and that the overly laden boat wouldn't capsize.

All went well until Visale Point, when Horton noticed a series of black objects bobbing near the shoreline. Calling up Rhoades, he asked his opinion. 'Jap barges,' muttered the old war veteran grimly, peering through glasses. 'We watched them and thought they seemed to be moving,' wrote Horton years later. 'If they had caught us, we should have been blown out of the water.'

Rhoades had had the presence of mind to assemble the Teleradio, and decided to call for help. 'This is Rhoades calling HUG – calling HUG – come in please.' In an instant, the clear voice of Hugh Mackenzie at Lunga came on the air. The situation was explained, and a reassuring 'wilco – over and out' was heard. Turning their binoculars back to the shore, Horton and Rhoades now detected the ant-like movement of people and prayed they had not been seen. Within minutes, however, the drone of aircraft was heard overhead, and a formation of US Marine P-40 Kittyhawks arrived. Then the sound of machine guns, 'like the ripping of strong calico', echoed over the water. The *Ramada* was spared to fight another day, and continued to 'snore on' through the calm sea to Lunga.

There the nuns and priests were immediately put on a transport that was just leaving for Noumea, and the severely malnourished and malaria-ridden Rhoades and Schroder were repatriated to Australia, their duties as Coastwatchers more than fulfilled.

Mackenzie happily endured Vandegrift's wrath. He had gone against the general's direct orders, but was content in the knowledge he'd successfully rescued twenty people facing certain death at the hands of the Japanese. Moreover, he gave not a single indication that, should the situation arise again, he would be any more compliant.

Jack Read and Paul Mason continued their work, even as the Japanese – now twice defeated after two failed assaults on the Americans – became fixated on wiping them out. From his view atop Malabita Hill on Bougainville, Mason reported daily on the build-up of the Japanese naval anchorage in the Shortland Islands, which continually expanded with vessels of every size and description: '5 warships, either cruisers or large destroyers, suddenly started for the southeast at high speed at 1245,' he reported on 29 August. Then, to assuage the humiliation of Lunga, the Japanese began construction of an entirely new airstrip at Buin on Bougainville's southern tip. Hundreds of natives were pressed into service as labourers, including several of Mason's own scouts who reported back to him every detail, which he in turn relayed to the Marines:

… Kahili aerodrome state aerodrome is expected to be completed in a week's time … 27 lorries, 6 motorcars, 10 horses, 6 motorcycles, 4 tractors and aerodrome working equipment … stores and fuel under tarpaulins spread along foreshore from mouth of Ugumo River to mouth of Moliko River. Two anti-aircraft guns near mouth of Ugomo River in fuel and ammunition dump and one anti-aircraft gun on northwestern boundary of aerodrome. Wireless station on beach in front of aerodrome; also, eight new iron buildings. Priests and nuns interned in iron buildings on beach. Enemy troops in green uniforms with anchor badge on arm and on white hat. Scouts state about 440 enemy troops but Coolies too numerous to count. Weather too hazy to observe ships today …

Further north from his perch at Porapora, Jack Read continued to count the daily incursions of the Japanese aircraft as they desperately tried to neutralise Henderson Field:

August 29, 8.25 am: 18 twin engine bombers, 22 fighters now heading southeast.

August 30, 9.25 am: 15 planes, may be fighters, just passed going southeast via east coast.

September 1, 8.55 am: 18 bombers, 22 fighters going yours.

Reports on enemy shipping as it made its way south from Buka Passage were also supplied:

TRANSPORT AND DESTROYER LEFT 6 P.M., NOW MAKING SOUTH VIA WEST COAST. CRUISER, TWO DESTROYERS STILL HERE. LOT OF A.A. TESTING ON DROME. BELIEVE MORE GUNS MOUNTED.

On other occasions, Read was able to offer his own interpretation of Japanese activity, such as:

FIGHTERS VERY ACTIVE TO-DAY. SUCH USUALLY INDICATES GOING YOURS TOMORROW.

Around the clock, in the stifling atmosphere of the radio dugout at Lunga, the Marines listened out for the regular broadcasts of the Coastwatchers. Pencilled notes recorded each word, before the notes were rushed to the air controllers, now located in the specially built 'pagoda' so proudly admired by the former Japanese commander. The fighter aircraft would be alerted, warmed up, armed and readied, their pilots standing by. Then the message would be sent to the men at the anti-aircraft guns who would get to work setting the fuses of their ammunition to detonate at the estimated altitude of the attacking aircraft. Sometimes crowds would illegally gather outside the entrance to the radio room as the soldiers jostled to catch a snippet of the short, precise messages coming in over the airwaves, delivered always in a calm, unhurried voice, from somewhere deep amid the enemy.

At various intervals, an air-raid siren would crank up – powered by a furiously pedalling Marine on a fitted-up bicycle frame – giving the men as much as ninety minutes' warning. Just under an hour before the expected attack, the Wildcat and Kittyhawk fighters would take off, the pilots having time to reach altitude – the only possible advantage they could hope to have over the superior Zeros. Then, as the Japanese followed their predictable path to Lunga, the American pilots above would call out, peel over and zoom down through the formation, hurtling past the top cover, pressing their firing buttons to tear up the bombers. From their slit trenches, the Marines would gaze up, counting the smoke-streaming Bettys as they slumped towards the ground or, broken-winged, fluttered earthwards like falling autumn leaves.

The American pilots did not have it all their own way. Once the Zeros engaged, their speed and performance overcame the slower Wildcats, and rendered the heavier P-40 Kittyhawks all but useless. Once in a dogfight, the advantage shifted to the enemy, and the best chance of survival for the Marine airmen was to find refuge among the ubiquitous columns of cumulus which towered up from the jungle floor. Even so, casualties among the American pilots steadily mounted.

Then, in the middle of the September mayhem, Guadalcanal was greeted by the visit of a short, middle-aged man who, instead of a uniform, wore an immaculate Palm Beach suit and snappy Panama hat. Walter Brooksbank, assistant to the Director of Naval Intelligence, and one of the original architects of the Coastwatchers, had arrived at the behest of his boss, 'Cocky' Long. His task was to liaise with the Americans on how cooperation between them and the Coastwatchers might be enhanced. Between consultations with senior officers, however, he took time to visit some of the Marines, often venturing up to their foxholes to offer a joke or other words of encouragement. The bemused Marines remembered him as a friendly and charming man, who insisted on standing upright, refusing to duck, cower or give any other acknowledgement to the danger around him, despite the proximity of the Japanese, sometimes only a few hundred yards away in the jungle.

'With tourists like these hanging around,' remarked one soldier, 'things must be better than they seem.'

# Chapter 17

# CON PAGE'S FINAL STAND

By the middle of 1942, Eric Feldt was facing a mounting list of missing men, most of whom he had met, many that were close friends, and all of whom he had personally encouraged to join the Coastwatchers in the first place.

Perhaps no chapter in the Coastwatchers' saga is more poignant, more tragic, yet more maddeningly heroic, than that of Cornelius Lyons 'Con' Page.

In 1930, aged nineteen, Con's parents plucked their quiet son from his unremarkable life in suburban Sydney to set him to work on the new family venture, a trade store in the frontier of New Britain in the Australian-run settlement of Rabaul. Con's parents were concerned that their son being tied all day to a shop would lead him to pine for his old life in the city, but contrary to all expectations, he thrived.

Even from behind a shop counter, wrote Feldt, 'Con's eyes ranged far away beyond the hills that fringed the harbour. He met men who lived untrammelled lives (or so it seemed to him); recruiters, miners, planters. The glamour of far places in the islands called him insistently, whispering of white beaches and palms in moonlight and of hot, still jungle, but not of loneliness and melancholy.'

It was far more than tropical settings and promises of adventure that bewitched the young Con Page. Page began to embed himself in the culture of the island and its peoples in a way few whites of the time would dare. While some understanding of the natives was seen as essential to maintain the colonial status quo, to show too much interest – let alone *befriend* them – was looked on as distasteful, vulgar, even dangerous. Page went further still, heedless from the outset of the opinions belonging to the white colonial elite.

After leaving Rabaul, Page travelled to remote Mussau Island – one of the northernmost islands in New Guinea's far-flung archipelago beyond New Ireland – where he purchased land and grew coconuts for copra. Without European neighbours, he befriended the natives, learned several of their dialects, and slowly melded into their ways and laws. 'Personal freedom, complete freedom, was his,' says Feldt. 'Days, unmarked, drifted into months, and months to years … he came, imperceptibly, to regard Mussau, Kavieng, and the nearby islands as his country, indeed as his world, to feel that other places were nebulous and far away.'

Lost in the gap between two cultures, Page was unable to settle. He chased rumours of gold in the Tabar group off New Ireland's long northern coastline, then drifted between various jobs, never remaining long at any.

Stability came eventually in the form of a young native girl, Ansin Bulu, from a local village. At first he befriended her, and then she became his partner. Such interracial liaisons between white men and native women were accepted in colonial society if managed discreetly, but when Page took Bulu as his common law wife, he was dismissed as a peculiarity, an eccentric outlier who had succumbed to the heat of the tropics. Page, for his part, was content to live his life as he saw fit. All this would change with the coming of the war.

At first, the conflict seemed far removed from Page's world, but when the price of copra crashed, he took a job managing Pigibut, a plantation on another of the Tabar Group islands, Siberi, 20 miles off the New Ireland coast, after the owner had departed in search of more profitable pursuits. This previous owner had enrolled as a Coastwatcher and his Teleradio was still fully operational. Learning its function, including a rudimentary knowledge of Morse, Page eventually stepped into his former owner's shoes and accepted the offer to join the Coastwatchers himself. Observations now became a part of his daily routine. There was little of substance for him to report until the Japanese entered the war in late 1941.

Now, Page's 'inconsequential position in the outer nebula of New Guinea' was transformed into one of vital importance, as the Japanese pilots chose the easily identifiable Tabar group as their point of landfall along the long route from their bases in the Marianas to Rabaul. All of them, at one stage or another, passed directly over Con Page's head. On 9 December 1941 it was Page who first reported the reconnaissance flight which signalled Japan's earliest intentions in the Southwest Pacific and jolted the islanders from their tropical torpor.

On 10 January 1942, Page's warning that twenty-two bombers were en route to Rabaul gave the residents forty vital minutes' warning, undoubtedly saving lives. Later that day, he reported again, signalling the arrival of a group of Kawanishi flying boats.

After the Japanese landed and occupied Rabaul with minimal opposition, Page's position became highly precarious. A few days later, he reported an enemy destroyer lurking near his plantation on Simberi, though he had already had the presence of mind to relocate from the manager's quarters at

Pigibut to a camp in the jungle. His small island afforded little room to hide though. Nor was this Page's only problem. Just 2 miles away, the only other plantation on the island was under the management of Hans Oscar 'Sailor' Herterich, a German who had arrived in 1909 onboard the survey ship SMS *Planet*, and who for several years managed a number of plantations in the little Tabar group.

As with the Austrian Fred Urban, Feldt takes a dim view of Herterich, 'a lazy, unreliable man, who drifted along with the tide of life'. Herterich supposedly jumped ship then denounced his German allegiances before marrying a native woman to avoid deportation when German New Guinea was taken over by Australia after World War I. While Feldt's bias is perhaps understandable, there is little evidence to support it.

Herterich worked the islands extensively throughout World War I, and had saved several thousand marks to purchase a 100-hectare plantation of his own, but the sale was blocked by his own German district administrator. He did indeed marry a native woman, known as Naurpetau, and fathered a daughter, but this did not save him from being deported in 1921. After a few years running boats and businesses in Batavia, he was permitted to return to New Ireland.

According to Feldt, when the Japanese arrived, Herterich suddenly rediscovered his 'Germanic-ness', loudly declared his allegiance to his Japanese ally, and actively encouraged the natives to do the same. While this may have some validity, Herterich did not – as did some others of German extraction – support the Nazis, and his actions regarding his native workers could be interpreted as a way to shield them from Japanese reprisals, as well as to keep a low profile for himself.

Whatever the truth of the matter, Page did his utmost to assure the natives the Japanese would never arrive, and if they did, the Australians and Americans would soon force them out again. In any case, he told them, whatever transpired, he himself would never leave. The natives listened solemnly but gave little indication as to where their loyalties lay.

During this time, the Japanese were closing in on Page. Deploying radio-direction-finders, they began to narrow down his already shrinking world, and were confident that his infuriating broadcasts would soon cease.

In Townsville, the red pins Eric Feldt pushed into his map of New Guinea began to form an ever-tightening ring around Page's crumbling position on Simberi – 'a dot in a Japanese-held ocean', as he described – and so he advised Page cease transmission immediately.

'You have done magnificent work. Your position is now very dangerous if you continue reporting and under the present circumstances, reports are not of great value from your situation. Bury your Teleradio and join either party on New Ireland or take other measures for your safety. Good luck.'

Page ignored the warning, and actually increased his transmissions, determined that no detail of the Japanese invaders would pass unreported. On 15 February, he transmitted a long message giving details of Japanese ships in Kavieng Harbour, as well as the number and type of guns being used to bolster the harbour's defences. While invaluable, Feldt knew that every second Page spent on air was eating into his already borrowed time. 'Your reports appreciated,' he signalled again more urgently, 'but it is more important now to keep yourself free. Do not transmit except in extreme emergency. You will be ordered to report when information will be of greatest value.'

It is difficult to speculate on Page's actions, or indeed his state of mind. He can hardly have been unaware of the dangers, particularly in the event of his capture by the Japanese as, at that stage, he was without any rank of military protection. Whether his refusal to cease operating stemmed from a burning hatred of the Japanese; the love of his adopted home, which he had made a solemn promise not to abandon; or simply a stubborn resistance to being told what to do by anyone – even Feldt – we shall never know. Perhaps he came early to the conclusion that his chances of escaping the island had already passed, and so he decided to make the most of what little time remained for him to fight the enemy.

Despite Feldt imploring him to stay quiet, Page's reports came in, giving lists of Europeans taken prisoner, sightings of large ships, and the news that New Ireland's airstrip at Namatanai had been mined – information he gleaned from a fleeing native. Feldt continued to urge Page to flee. 'Proceed for Buka which is not in enemy hands,' he pleaded. Still Page resisted.

Then, in late March, Page sent a signal to Feldt hinting at 'trouble with the natives', and that he was 'going'. Perhaps, speculated Feldt, Page's native network had collapsed, and he had concluded his usefulness to the Coastwatchers was now at an end. In any event, a relieved Feldt advised caution and for Page to avoid the west coast of the island. A day or so later, Feldt received an indignant response: 'I never thought of ratting … I am flat out to get information, but intend to stay.' Despairing, Feldt advised Page that his escape routes were diminishing every day. By the beginning of April, Feldt had given up begging Page to leave and save himself, and simply informed him of the reality of his plight. 'Buka, Bougainville and Faisi now in enemy hands.' Yet, even in the face of his imminent annihilation, Page continued to deliver.

Other Coastwatchers in safer positions than Page listened in to his broadcasts and offered words of encouragement, even forwarding his fainter signals to Townsville and Port Moresby, lest his efforts be wasted. In the jungles of neighbouring New

Britain, Keith McCarthy later reflected that Page, knowing he was living on borrowed time, would end each wireless signal with a torrent of abuse directed at the Japanese, who he knew were listening. He was, said McCarthy, 'a man full of courage'.

Though frustrated by Page's pig-headedness, Feldt was philosophical in what drove his behaviour. 'Such disobedience,' he wrote, 'inconceivable in any other wartime operation, was not too surprising in an islander. We had to accept it, interwoven as it was with other traits so valuable.'

Still, Feldt continued to be amazed at Page's resilience, scarcely believing he had managed to evade capture up till now. In April, he managed to cleave through considerable red tape, and without having signed a single form nor sat for an interview, Page was awarded the rank of sub-lieutenant in the Royal Australian Navy Reserve. Feldt hoped this may shield him from the worst of the Japanese treatment if captured.

In May, Page signalled that he was losing the fight for the loyalty of the natives, who now refused to supply him and who, he suspected, would soon betray him to the Japanese. The irony of his years of devotion to the native islanders and their ways was not lost on him.

'Sailor' Herterich was now joined by another European former planter, Hans Pettersen, against whom evidence of treachery and violence is far more compelling. Feldt's ever-colourful description of him is as 'a half-caste, fat, sly swine of a man who had been in disrepute since boyhood'. Pettersen would further proselytise the native population into accepting the Japanese and later even produce crops for them, for which he was rewarded. He was later convicted of brutalising his native workers.

Even with such enemies within his orbit, Page refused to cease operating, dispatching instead a detailed shopping list of arms and supplies, which he requested be dropped by the

RAAF. 'Revolvers, money, quinine, flour, 15lb, fine cut tobacco and papers, sugar, tea, salt rum, kerosene, biscuits, jam … cap size 6⅞, boots size 9 …' He even nominated the spot the plane should head to for the drop. 'Am on beach Siberi Island at Napafur Village. Will have two canoes on beach and natives to attract plane waving from roof.'

A short time later, Page signalled his position was deteriorating further. Local natives, he said, were now wearing Japanese rising sun armbands, and sending out patrols of their own to round him up: 'position acute as friendly natives too scared. Include service rifles'. Finally, on 19 May, the drop was made from a low-flying Hudson bomber. Page managed to recover most of the stores but, to his dismay, the rifles were absent; the parcel had been hung up in the bomb bay of the aircraft – a grave misfortune that was realised only after the aircraft had returned to Darwin.

For a time, Page went silent, raising Feldt's hopes that an extended period of inactivity might convince the Japanese that he had left. Then, in late May, he resumed his signals. 'Big ship bearing north, course east. Possibly aircraft carrier,' he reported.

Finally, the Teleradio itself began to fail, and Page was unable to send spoken signals. Again, refusing to stop, he bypassed the fault and exposed two wires which he tapped together to send messages in a rough Morse code. Though difficult to decipher, the messages got through. A new part – the fault identified as a broken lead-in – was dropped to him in a later supply run, but by now Feldt knew that Page's only hope was via immediate evacuation. After a final appeal from Feldt, Page signalled back, finally sounding willing to accept the advice.

In a frantic series of requests and pleadings, Feldt managed to convince the US Navy to spare a submarine to rendezvous with Page and pluck him from a nominated beach on Simberi at the stroke of midnight. Feldt's emotions, which had ranged from grateful admiration to head-shaking despair, once again rode high on the expectation that, just perhaps, his maverick Coastwatcher might live to fight another day.

The rendezvous was set for midnight on 2 June. After dark, Page crept down to the beach and waited just offshore in a canoe as per the arrangement, signalling by torch out to sea, straining his eyes to catch the replying flash of a signal from his rescuers. He waited in vain. He returned the next night, and the one after that, but no welcoming light and no submarine appeared. Days later, Feldt learned that the American boat, old and worn out after the long Philippines campaign, developed engine trouble en route to Simberi, turned around and limped back to port.

Feldt seems to have been haunted by the tragic image of his Coastwatcher who, having at last agreed to save himself, was cruelly thwarted by luck, and abandoned. 'Every flash must have seemed an invitation to unseen enemies,' he wrote. 'Every ripple of the water must have made his heart leap with hope of friend or fear of foe. Those three nights must have been a fairly complete catalogue of hope, desperation, and triumph over panic.'

Page withdrew to the jungle once more, and reported the landing of a Japanese destroyer which, for four days, sent out parties of troops assisted by hostile natives to find him. '... Am hunted by dogs, natives, machine guns,' he signalled. 'Japanese left last night. They will return Thursday with more troops.' Page's sole chance for escape now was via air. The RAAF, their meagre resources already stretched, were reluctant to risk a precious Catalina and its crew for the sake of one man, however brave. But Feldt prevailed.

On the morning of 16 June, the CO of 11 Squadron, Squadron Leader Frank Chapman, took off from his base at Bowen in Queensland to Simberi, where he was to follow Page's instructions of setting his big Catalina down 'on the west side where there is small island and sandspit …' Chapman was told it was a dangerous mission, and to fly a non-direct route to confuse the Japanese. Arriving at dusk over the appointed spot, he flew low, and saw no sign of anyone save a few surly natives who refused to return the waves of the crew from the aircraft. At last, Chapman reluctantly gave up the search.

No transmission from Con Page was ever heard again.

Three years later, when the Japanese were finally being pushed back from New Guinea, an Australian sub-lieutenant, Stanley Bell, landed on newly liberated Tabar Island via a US patrol torpedo boat. While interviewing the native people about the Japanese occupation, he met a young student from Rabaul who, with a strong sense of history, had written down the story of Con Page's last days. It made for poignant reading.

On 16 June 1942, about the time Frank Chapman was taking off from Bowen, the Japanese – as Page had predicted – came ashore with a strong hunting party. Yet again, Page managed to flee, but four days later, a hostile native stumbled across his hideout and alerted the Japanese. After five months on the run, tormenting the Japanese at every available opportunity, Con Page was finally captured. His loyal wife, Ansin Bulu, was also taken, but separately, and interned in the native compound at Kavieng, while Page was incarcerated in the European prison. Here, he joined two other former district officers and Coastwatchers, Alan Kyle and Greg Benham, who had organised the escape of several Australian soldiers and civilians from Namatanai on New Ireland. Like Page, both Benham and Kyle had refused their chances of escape, preferring to stay together on the island.

It is unknown what Con Page was forced to endure in the weeks between his capture and murder by the Japanese.

Some sources state his death occurred in July, others cite early September. All agree that, along with Kyle, Benham, and several other Europeans, he was put onto a small boat and taken to Nago Island in Kavieng Harbour and executed. One of his fellow victims, never mentioned by historians, was 'Sailor' Herterich who, despite his supposed loyalty to the Japanese, was shown no favours. After the war, the bodies of Page, Kyle and Benham, along with other victims of Japanese brutality, were reinterred at the Bita Paka War Cemetery in Rabaul.

Eric Feldt seems to have been particularly affected by Page's story, and his death, which he saw early on as inevitable. 'A less skilful man would have been caught much earlier,' he wrote. 'A less courageous one would have retired in the first month.'

•

In the most poignant of epitaphs, on a subsequent visit to Kavieng in September 1945, Sub-lieutenant Bell was approached by a native woman, newly released by the Japanese. She looked thin, emaciated, and prematurely aged. Seeing his uniform, she stood in front of him and unfurled a tiny, crumpled scrap of paper upon which was pencilled a barely legible message:

> To CO. Allied Forces for Lieut-Co. E. A. Feldt R.A.N. from Sub-Lieut C. L. Page, R.A.N.V.R. 9th July.
> Re: The female Ansin Bulu, Nakapur Village, Simberi Island, Tabar.
> This female has been in my service 7 years. Has been of great value to me since Jan.
> Japs looted all she owned value £50 put her in prison and God knows what else.
> Her crime was she stuck.
> Sub-Lieut C. L. Page

# Chapter 18
# THE REMARKABLE SISTER FARLAND

Late one morning in mid-1942, Ruby Boye removed her sturdy but uncomfortable headphones and set them down on the large wooden table beside the grey metal case of her Teleradio. She felt justifiably satisfied with her morning's work. Moments earlier, she had delivered her second weather bulletin of the day to Port Vila in the New Hebrides, over 400 miles to the south. Today's report, she knew, would be of particular interest. Studying the view from the window, within the room in her large plantation home that she had dedicated solely to her broadcasting duties, she could see yet another storm was brewing over the wild and remote Santa Cruz islands. Boye knew this was information Allied intelligence urgently needed and that her broadcasts were the only means of letting them know.

Then, as she rose from the table, the Teleradio receiver suddenly hissed into life, and the needle on the frequency meter shunted abruptly to the right, indicating an incoming signal. This in itself was unusual, as Boye's communications with the outside world were almost always strictly on a one-way basis. What she heard next made her blood run cold.

'Calling Mrs Boye, calling Mrs Boye on Vanikoro,' said an accented voice speaking slowly and deliberately. 'Japanese commander say you get out … or else.' Then the signal went dead and the Teleradio was silent.

Her heart pounding, Boye stared at the set for some time. But, as unnerved by the enemy as she was, Ruby Boye, officially the only female in the Coastwatcher service, had no intention of going anywhere.

Born in Sydney in 1891, Ruby had followed her husband, Skov Boye, to Tulagi in 1928 when he took up a job as a Lever Brothers plantation manager. Eight years later, he scored a far more lucrative position with the Kauri Timber Company. The catch, however, was that he and Ruby would have to farewell Tulagi and relocate over 500 miles east to Vanikoro at the Solomons' wild outer edge in the remote Santa Cruz group. A region of storms, earthquakes and volcanoes, the locals dubbed it 'The Hurricane Belt'.

Vanikoro – a series of five volcanic islands ringed by a treacherous and poorly charted coral atoll – appeared to the Boyes on their arrival in 1936 as being at the very edge of civilisation. Nonetheless, they settled into the islands' close community of around twenty Europeans and several hundred Indigenous inhabitants. Standing at 5 foot 10, Ruby towered over most of them, but became well-liked for her warmth and genuine devotion to their wellbeing. Besides employing a good number of people, the Boyes crisscrossed the little archipelago, arbitrating local disputes, treating minor medical ailments and even pulling the occasional tooth.

For Vanikoro's location alone – way out into the Pacific and roughly equidistant between the Solomons and the New Hebrides – Eric Feldt had insisted a Coastwatcher station be established on the island early in the war. Hardly had his operator arrived when he announced his intention to transfer to the RAAF to become a pilot, leaving a gap in Feldt's Coastwatcher chain that would be difficult to fill. Therefore, at nearly fifty years of age, Ruby Boye stepped forward and offered herself as a replacement. Despite Feldt's reluctance to engage a woman, he had little choice but to accept.

After a perfunctory lesson on the function of the Teleradio, Boye began broadcasting weather information and other observations while maintaining her daily duties as the wife of a plantation manager. She also taught herself Morse code, becoming fully adept in just a few months. At the beginning of the Pacific War, her workload intensified: sometimes she reported to Allied headquarters in Tulagi up to four times a day. Then, in May 1942, a planter from the central Solomons arrived by boat with the alarming news that Tulagi had just fallen to the Japanese, who were expected to soon fan out to other islands. It was enough to prompt Vanikoro's Europeans to leave immediately, but Ruby and Skov Boye stayed put. 'My husband chose to remain for the company's interest,' explained Boye in an interview long after the war. 'I decided it was my duty to stay also to continue to operate the radio.'

As the Guadalcanal Campaign began, Boye's messages became of vital importance to the Americans, who came to rely on the meteorological data she sent from her remote and unpredictable corner of the Pacific. Apart from the reports, Boye continually relayed messages from other Coastwatchers further to the west, forwarding their fading signals to where they were needed at Allied Intelligence HQ.

The Japanese were aware of Ruby Boye and her work. When threats over the airwaves failed to dislodge her, reconnaissance flights began to appear over the islands, trying in vain to pinpoint her position. Then leaflets were dropped offering reward money to the locals for the capture or death of Vanikoro's 'European spy'. Yet all of them remained loyal.

At one stage, reports of a Japanese cruiser in the area were heard, and during the course of one memorable night, Ruby and Skov stood on their balcony and watched a series of lights attempting for several hours to probe through the atoll to the lagoon just below their property. Quietly in the dark, they discussed the details of their plan should the enemy find their way through. They had been friends with Percy Good and were under no illusion that their fate, if they were caught, would be just as brutal as his. Instead, they would head into the hills where a small cache of supplies had been prepared, but the couple calmly agreed that if faced with capture they would take their own lives rather than face torture, starvation and death at the hands of the Japanese.

As the tide of war turned, it was not Japanese ships but those of the US Navy which finally found their way through the atoll, eventually establishing a Catalina base at the lagoon. So impressed was the commander of the South Pacific Area, Admiral Halsey, with Ruby Boye's work, in 1943 he made a sudden visit to Vanikoro. As he emerged from his seaplane, he announced, 'I want to meet the wonderful lady who operates the radio here.'

Ruby Boye's enciphered meteorological reports were known to have been used by the American planners in the Battle of the Coral Sea and during the long Guadalcanal Campaign, as well as the engagement fought closest to her home, the Battle of Santa Cruz in late October 1942. While technically an American defeat with the loss of the carrier USS *Hornet*, Santa Cruz proved a pyrrhic victory for the Japanese, who suffered horrendous losses of irreplaceable aircrew, and effectively ended their naval dominance in the Southwest Pacific.

Despite his initial reluctance, Eric Feldt was so impressed with Boye that he appointed her an officer in the Women's Royal Australian Naval Service. Boye herself first came to know of it via a curious radio signal requesting – of all things – her dress size. A week or so later, an Australian Catalina dropped an amphibious canister into the lagoon. When opened, it was found to contain Ruby Boye's brand new naval uniform as a Third Officer, WRANS.

When Skov became seriously ill with leukaemia in 1947, Boye left the Solomons for Sydney, where Skov died two weeks later. Boye never returned. She remained phlegmatic about her wartime achievements – including being awarded the British Empire Medal in 1944. 'The mere fact that I was annoying the enemy sufficiently to have them warn me off was somewhat gratifying', she later said.

While officially the sole female in Feldt's organisation, Ruby Boye was not the only woman to risk her life providing invaluable service to the Coastwatchers during the war in the Pacific.

•

Henry Josselyn and John Keenan could not believe their thoroughly rotten luck.

In silence, they stared at the dials set in the dull grey metal casing, convincing themselves that their sheer willpower must, surely, force the Teleradio to work. But, after a full day of trying every trick they could muster from their limited repertoire of radio knowledge, they reluctantly admitted that their precious Teleradio, the sole purpose of their present existence, was broken. High on a hill in the steaming bush on the island of Vella Lavella, this was the dismal culmination of the most extraordinary fortnight of their lives.

Just a few weeks earlier, Hugh Mackenzie, who had recently taken over from Martin Clemens as the Coastwatcher boss on Guadalcanal, had revealed to Josselyn that there was a problem. As brilliant as the work being performed by men like Jack Read and Paul Mason was in warning of Japanese air attacks, an increasing number of raids were being missed.

A gap had opened up in the Coastwatcher network that needed to be plugged. At the top of The Slot, at least 40 miles of ocean separated the islands of Vella Lavella and Choiseul, through which the Japanese had begun sending ships and aircraft, unnoticed by the Coastwatchers on Bougainville further to the northwest. The build-up was on, it seemed, for another major assault on Henderson Field. A new team, or teams, needed to be inserted.

The Japanese were also reported to be well advanced in completing the airstrip at Buka on Bougainville, and had started another on New Georgia. Should either become operational, it would save the Japanese pilots at least 300 miles in their runs to Guadalcanal from Rabaul, and the peculiar balance, whereby the Japanese controlled the island but not its airfield, while the Americans held the airstrip but could not dislodge the Japanese from the remainder of Guadalcanal, could well be tipped in the enemy's favour. In this case, the Coastwatchers would be needed like never before.

Henry Josselyn, a former Guadalcanal officer, had waded ashore with the Marines in August and performed superbly as their guide, but now his knowledge was needed elsewhere. When Mackenzie enquired as to whether he would be prepared to establish a new Coastwatcher station on the northernmost island of the New Georgia group, Vella Lavella, he agreed immediately.

Eric Feldt had recently decided that the job of Coastwatching was too great a burden for any one man, and directed that teams would now consist of at least two operators. Fellow district officer John Keenan was chosen to accompany Josselyn, while the new Choiseul team covering the northern side of The

Slot would be headed up by District Officer Nick Waddell and Carden Seton, a planter from the Shortland Islands.

The four men were flown to Brisbane for training and to secure what few supplies they could take – only items that could fit through the 30-by-30-inch hatch of a US submarine. On an afternoon in October, wearing US Navy uniforms to blend in, and after a raucous send-off in town the night before, the four Coastwatchers quietly slipped away from Brisbane's New Farm wharf onboard the USS *Grampus* and headed north.

Being cooped up in the stifling conditions of the submarine was exhausting, and the men were in poor shape by the time they arrived at their first destination, Vella Lavella. In the dead of a still night, Josselyn and Keenan were loaded by the sub's crew into two inflatable boats, one of which immediately sprang a leak. Somehow, they managed to paddle the mile to shore, then hide their equipment just as the dawn came up. They spent a day eating and sleeping, but as Vella Lavella was firmly under the control of the Japanese, an ear was always cocked for signs of an enemy patrol.

With agonising slowness, Josselyn and Keenan hauled their equipment in batches to Mundi Mundi, a deserted copra plantation a few miles inland. The manager's house, while tempting, would not be an option, as the Japanese were sure to notice its sudden habitation.

Continuing a couple of miles up a stream, the men then scaled a 300-foot hill where they built a treetop hideout out of abandoned pieces of tin, and put up the aerial for their first broadcast. It had been over a week since their landing and they were ready to begin broadcasting. The Teleradio warmed up and functioned perfectly, just long enough to send a message to Feldt stating that they had arrived safely, before it failed completely.

It would not work the next day, nor the one after that, despite the two men toiling all day to try to fix it. There was no doubt about it, their brand-new Teleradio was dead. Their rancour bit hard as the largest formation of Japanese aircraft they had ever seen passed south over their heads down The Slot to attack Henderson Field, and there was nothing they could do to warn the Marines.

What they needed was a radio expert, and the nearest one of those was Coastwatcher Donald Kennedy, a man famed not merely for his courage and daring, but a complete and thorough knowledge of everything to do with radios. Kennedy was currently located at Segi, on the island of New Georgia, nearly 150 miles away. Josselyn and Keenan knew that one of them would have to remain at Vella Lavella, while the other took the errant radio set to Kennedy.

It was agreed Josselyn would make the journey. It would not be an easy one as they'd have to organise a series of canoe trips, provided by natives, all of whom had to be completely trustworthy. Up to this point, Josselyn and Keenan had seen absolutely no one – neither native, European nor Japanese – on the island at all.

Returning to the beach, the men decided to attract the attention of a passing native. After an hour, one passed by but failed to stop, making Josselyn feel deeply suspicious. Another hour passed, and around the headland came a large and stately canoe being paddled by six powerful men. Josselyn's luck was changing. The canoe's owner was Silas Lezstuni, an important and fiercely loyal chief from the nearby village of Paramata, and he was accompanied by six of his men.

Lezstuni not only seemed delighted to see Josselyn, but was full of information, such as the fact that the Japanese seemed to have set up a Coastwatching station of their own at Iringila, an elevated spot not terribly far away from where they now stood. He also told them that the New Zealand Methodist mission and hospital was still operating at Bilua on the island's southern tip, under Reverend Silvester. Silas could scarcely believe that Josselyn and Keenan had been on the island for ten days without his people knowing about it. Josselyn took this as a compliment and decided that, as Bilua was on the way to Kennedy at Segi, he would make his first stop the New Zealand mission. Silas Lezstuni immediately began picking men to be the first set of couriers, and promised to organise more.

On 26 October, travelling overnight by canoe along the coast, Josselyn nursed the faulty transmitter, careful not to drop it even when a Zero floatplane passed low overhead at dawn and he quickly slid to the bottom of the boat to conceal himself under some palm fronds.

A short while later, Josselyn stepped onto the little mission wharf, and for a moment thought he had been transported back to another world. In front of him was a calm oasis of clean, whitewashed buildings including a church, airily laid out on manicured lawns, and cheery native islanders speaking perfect English as they welcomed him ashore. Soon, a dapper, balding man in glasses appeared, equally pleased to see him. Somewhat surprised, Josselyn took the outstretched hand of the Reverend Archie Wharton 'Watty' Silvester, a New Zealander who had run the mission since 1935, building up a devoted following among the Vella Lavella natives. Watty said the Japanese had not visited the island in any strength so far, but he feared they were not far away, as a patrolling floatplane had recently shot up the mission's launch.

Silvester invited Josselyn to tea, imploring forgiveness for his enthusiasm, explaining that he was the first white visitor he had seen in months. As the two men chatted on the lawn over fine bone china cups and fresh cake delivered on polished silver servers, Josselyn explained his mission in conveying the precious Teleradio transmitter to Kennedy at Segi. Watty was delighted. Kennedy, he revealed, was a friend, and all the natives on the island could be trusted completely to take Josselyn there. Watty insisted on arranging the passage.

As Josselyn listened, he could not quite fight off the sensation that he was living a pleasant waking dream, a feeling amplified considerably when the reverend stood to introduce his assistant who, he said, also ran the hospital. Standing before Josselyn was a tall, elegant, and rather striking white woman.

•

Merle Stephanie Farland began her working life as a piano teacher in New Zealand, but when the Depression killed demand for her services, she retrained as a nurse at Auckland Hospital, becoming a State Registered Nurse in 1934. Four years later, she accepted a role at the Helena Goldie Hospital at the New Zealand Methodist Mission in the Solomons, arriving, she would later say, 'when the Pacific was untroubled'. At Bilua, Farland found the mission was well set up by Watty Silvester, with the hospital in its own compound comprising an operating theatre, wards and even an outpatients clinic to cater for the large number of Solomon Islanders from Vella Lavella and many other islands who had come to depend on it. Although part of a team comprising a doctor, his wife, and another nurse, Farland soon found the demands on her skills extended far beyond simple nursing. Injections and inoculations, bone-setting, lancing abscesses, delivering babies, training native nurses and pulling teeth would all form part of her daily routine.

Robust and unflappable, Farland thrived in the tropics. She learned the local dialect, and would often attend to patients on outlying islands by paddling her own canoe. She was particularly taken with the local children who she later recalled as 'more beautiful than ours'.

After three years in the job, she had earned a six-month furlough back home in New Zealand, returning to Bilua just as Pearl Harbor was bombed in December 1941. While most Europeans in the Solomons – including the hospital doctor and his wife, as well as the other nurse – joined the panicking exodus, Farland and Silvester decided to stay put. Considering herself neither brave nor fearless, Farland outlined her reasons in a letter to a friend: 'It is surely not consistent with Christian service that our medical work should be completely dropped because things are a little difficult. I am the only medical person left. Therefore I stay. There is no other course.'

As the Solomons fell, piece by piece, to the Japanese, a government motor launch was sent to collect Farland as she tended orphans on Choiseul Island. She instead asked the astonished launch driver to thank the resident commissioner for the thought, but she had no intention of abandoning her patients and was not going anywhere. 'I simply said I couldn't leave them until they could be cared for by some other arrangement,' Farland recounted later. A journalist would add that 'Nobody depended on her in New Zealand, but a home full of brown babies, most of whom she had delivered herself, needed her in Choiseul.' The launch driver shrugged his shoulders and turned the boat around.

For a while, the life of the mission continued unchanged. As the Japanese drew closer to Vella Lavella, however, the regular shipments of provisions ceased, and Farland and Silvester began eating the natives' staples of banana and sweet potato. Japanese reconnaisance aircraft began to appear overhead, and Farland thought it prudent to swap her highly visible starched white nurse's uniform for the closest thing she could find to camouflage, a green floral dress. Both she and Silvester knew their survival would depend on concealing their presence from the Japanese for as long as possible. So far, due in large part to the intense loyalty of the Vella Lavella natives, the ruse had worked. But neither believed that it could last forever.

•

Henry Josselyn had had no idea of Farland's presence on Vella Lavella, and was pretty sure nobody else had either.

Taking in this remarkable woman over tea at the mission, he was struck by her confidence, her straightforward sense of authority, and even humour, as well as her complete acceptance of the terrible danger she faced as the sole white woman for hundreds of miles in the Japanese-occupied Solomon Islands.

Nor, he discovered, was the running of a tropical hospital Farland and Silvester's sole responsibility at Bilua. Both were active – albeit informal – operators in the local Coastwatcher system. Sometime earlier, they had agreed to assist Donald Kennedy on New Georgia by contributing observations of Japanese ships and aircraft of their own. In this they were ably assisted by just about every native on the island who had rallied to the powerful personality of Reverend Silvester in his hour of need. He had even established native spies on other occupied islands. 'They were 100 per cent loyal,' recalled Farland later. 'They were our saving.'

They likewise proved the saving of Henry Josselyn who, for the next three nights, was shuttled in stages across the enemy-occupied waters surrounding New Georgia to Don Kennedy's camp at Segi by a network of native oarsmen fiercely loyal to Reverend Silvester. Josselyn would forever wonder at how it was all arranged, but at each rendezvous point he was amazed to be greeted by a new canoe which emerged from the gloom precisely as planned, ready to carry him and his precious radio on to the next village and the next set of paddlers. On the first night, he was taken across Vella Gulf, then down Blackett

Strait. At one stage, a Japanese barge chugged by, fully laden with men and materiel, barely 20 yards away. Holed up for the day at Mandou village, he watched the smoke of Japanese camp fires on an adjacent beach, just a few hundred yards away. However, the notion of passing the new Japanese stronghold at Viru Harbour was considered by the local villagers to be too dangerous. Instead, Josselyn was dropped on shore and guided across New Georgia on foot to pick up yet another canoe which finally deposited him on Don Kennedy's little dock at Segi on 2 November. Both men welcomed each other's company, and Kennedy quickly diagnosed Josselyn's radio fault as a broken transformer. As a solution, he gave Josselyn his own, and built another for himself from parts salvaged from a downed Japanese bomber. Henry Josselyn would return to Vella Lavella where he would continue his invaluable Coastwatcher duties.

Farland and Silvester could have used a Teleradio of their own, for while their ageing shortwave set — which Farland operated — could receive, it was unable to transmit. Every report to Kennedy therefore had to be carried down the chain of islands by many of those same native runners in canoes who had spirited Josselyn through the night.

Of the many tests Farland faced during her time on Vella Lavella and beyond, one of the most urgent occurred a month later when, in the middle of a November night, Watty Silvester burst into her quarters announcing a B-17 bomber had been shot down over the sea, with a number of her surviving crew currently sheltering at the village of Paramata, on the other side of the island. Furthermore, some of the airmen were reportedly in need of medical attention. Silvester requested Farland prepare sheets and bedding while he grabbed a first-aid kit and organised a canoe to take him there. Farland sat up in bed, planted her feet firmly on the ground and rose in her nightgown.

No, she informed him, that simply would not do. There was one person on the island qualified to administer medical assistance: herself. Reverend Silvester's efforts would be far better spent on looking to the bedding while she made her way to the downed airmen. In the face of such fearsome logic, Silvester could only agree.

By 6 a.m., Farland had arranged a series of native bearers, packed a first-aid kit, and, after a gulp of tea, was off.

•

For the airmen of the US 26th Bombardment Squadron, it had been a torrid twenty-four hours. They had taken off from Henderson Field as part of a mixed formation of eighteen Fortress and Marauder bombers, tasked with flying 300 miles northwest to Tonolei Harbour at the southern tip of Bougainville to try to hit some of those wretched Japanese ships which, in their brazen nightly supply runs down The Slot, were causing headaches for the exhausted Marines of Guadalcanal. Piloting the lead Fortress, 41-24531, Major Allan J. Sewart was fully cognisant of the dangers of facing the concentrated firepower of massed shipping but was under the added pressure of carrying the overall Bombardment Group commander, Colonel Laverne Saunders, to orchestrate the raid over the radio.

They encountered no opposition when approaching the target and the ship's gunners below seemed to have been caught by surprise. Sewart started to believe they may have scored an easy 'milk run'. Then one of the formation's B-17s' bombs got hung up in the bomb bay and Colonel Saunders – unbelievably – ordered the formation to swing around, line up, and make the run again. Whatever element of surprise they might have enjoyed was now well and truly gone. Just as the lead bombardier lined up the ships in his bomb sight, a formation of fifteen Zeros pounced.

Concentrating on the bomber's poorly protected nose, the Zeros made two slashing passes, killing Sewart where he sat and wounding his co-pilot, Jack Lee, as well as setting fire to the two left engines. Colonel Saunders, himself wounded in the thigh, pulled the dead Sewart out of his seat and managed to fly for another 30 miles before making a water landing off Baga Island near Vella Lavella. Scrambling into their life raft, the men came ashore, where Lee soon died and was buried on the beach. A group of passing natives in a canoe came ashore briefly, but a cursing Saunders despaired at not being able to communicate with them, and they departed.

In fact, the natives headed straight to Coastwatcher Jack Keenan's station a few miles away, alerted him to the emergency, and brought him back to the Americans three hours later. Saunders watched the canoe approach, and was speechless when a smiling, well-dressed Keenan stepped out onto the beach and – in a moment of perfect sangfroid – handed the American officer his card.

That night, the six survivors of Sewart's crew were transferred to the village of Paramata where, to their continued surprise, the local chief Silas Lezstuni – who had previously warmly greeted Henry Josselyn – had ordered the preparation of a cooked meal to be served with proper cutlery, as well as provided beds with blankets, courtesy of a local mission station.

•

Well on her way by dawn, Merle Farland faced a trek of over 20 miles to the opposite side of the island from the mission at Bilua. The rough path crossed a range of steep hills and several rivers and gorges. Riding atop the shoulders of guides for the river crossings, she emerged at the coast by midday, then paddled a canoe for several miles. The last section of the journey required her to pick her way over an extended section of slippery coastal rocks, eventually arriving into Paramata mid-afternoon.

The Americans were stunned to see a European woman approaching – apparently from the sea – and open a first-aid kit to begin treating their injuries. Bandages were produced, and a gash in a wounded airman's leg cleaned and bound. Barely an hour after her arrival, the sound of large aircraft could be heard, and a PBY Catalina touched down just off the shore. Alerted by Coastwatcher radio, Hugh Mackenzie at Henderson had wasted no time in dispatching the rescue aircraft, and the entire operation was completed with remarkable efficiency.

As the men were loaded into the aircraft, Farland noted the navigator's pain from a bullet wound, and shoved a syringe of morphine into his backside. As Farland said later in life, 'it was a long way to go just to deliver a shot in the buttocks', but the system of Coastwatchers operating beside a loyal network of natives, saving the lives of several valuable airmen, was shown to work with brilliant efficiency.

A few weeks later, hearing of her exploits and recalling that Farland had once declared being prepared to do 'anything, anywhere', Coastwatcher Donald Kennedy enquired of Silvester whether Sister Farland might be spared from Bilua to watch over his radio while he reconnoitred increasing Japanese activity on New Georgia. Farland jumped at the chance, and on 3 December set off by canoe with a native oarsman on a perilous, three-day journey which would take them through the heart of the Japanese-occupied Solomons. They could hear the deep throbbing of motorised barges shuttling back and forth within the darkness nearby. When dawn came up, Farland was shocked by the volume of Japanese sea traffic she could see all around her, but somehow managed to avoid being discovered. At one point, she hid under a native umbrella to avoid a patrolling aircraft, as her oarsman offered the pilot an innocent wave. In the middle of the final night, her oarsman cut through the glassy black water of a lagoon, passing to within a stone's throw of a small hut which – too late – they realised was a Japanese lookout post. Holding their breath, they watched as a bored sentry emerged from the hut, stared blankly at them for a few moments, then went back inside. On 6 December, she finally reached Segi.

Donald Kennedy was delighted to see Farland and insisted on immediately training her up in the use of a gun, at which she proved herself an excellent shot with both the Webley .38 service revolver and the American Colt .44. But as he prepared to leave the station in her hands, one of the first messages Farland decoded was one ordering her own removal. Both she and Kennedy were stunned.

Resident Commissioner Marchant, still nominally running what was left of the British Solomons Protectorate after his hurried and unedifying exit from Tulagi, had somehow caught wind of Farland's presence and was aghast to learn her earlier evacuation had slipped through his administration's fingers. 'Arrangements being made to evacuate Sister Farland. Have you any news of other members of the mission?' he declared. Farland was crestfallen, and Kennedy furious. In vain he tried to argue her case to remain, but Marchant was adamant, citing 'present restrictions on white women remaining in the Protectorate'.

Kennedy contrived to be called away, supposedly to attend the rescue of a downed airman, and in an act of defiance, left Farland to run the Segi operation on her own for three days, in which she proved herself to be a skilled and resourceful operator. Just in case, a loaded Thompson submachine gun –

the use in which she had also been instructed – never left her side.

On 21 December, on the same flight that took away Kennedy's Japanese prisoners, Merle Farland was removed from the Solomons via Catalina flying boat. En route to the safety of Noumea, she stayed a night on Henderson Field, where she created a sensation. Riding in a Jeep through the garrison on her way to her quarters, the troops stood silent and stared at the only white female among 30 000 troops. Like wildfire, the rumour tore through the camp that Amelia Earhart, the famous American aviator who had vanished in this part of the Pacific five years earlier, had amazingly been found. In later life, the story continued to bemuse her and she admitted to a journalist, 'I suppose I did look a little like her.'

After a year of exemplary service performed in the shadow of the Japanese, Merle Farland's reward was to be shunted away by her own people solely because of her sex.

She continued to be of service to the war effort. In the large US base at Noumea, the Americans – who evidently valued her skills more highly than her own countrymen – feted her as a celebrity, inviting her to the most exclusive parties where she rubbed shoulders with generals and their wives. It was a far cry from her previous existence on Vella Lavella. She later became attached to US Army HQ Noumea, where her deep knowledge of Solomons geography was put to good use deciphering aerial photographic reconnaissance images. One photograph, she recalled in later life, baffled the Americans completely, capturing as it did a mysterious white strip in the middle of a field at Munda in New Georgia. After endless poring over the image, the Americans were convinced they were looking at part of a previously unknown Japanese military installation. Someone then handed it to Farland. Through the stereo viewer, she studied the photograph carefully, then quietly explained that what they were looking at was what was generally referred to as a cricket pitch.

Farland returned to the Solomons, as well as to nursing, finishing the war at a New Zealand Army-run casualty station in Honiara. Although awarded the OBE, as well as the Pacific Star campaign medal, it is perhaps indicative of the times that Eric Feldt's monumental work on the Coastwatchers mentions her just three times, in passing, omits her feats almost completely, and even misspells her name.

Settling back to a quiet civilian life after the war, Farland spoke little about her exploits as one of the only female Coastwatcher in the Solomons and, as nobody seemed to ask her about it, she remained quiet about her war almost until the end of her life in the 1990s. Her heroism and dedication to duty are still mostly unknown to this day.

# Chapter 19
# NEW GEORGIA'S 'CAPTAIN BLIGH'

If Merle Farland was surprised when Donald Kennedy insisted she first familiarise herself with the use of a gun after her arrival on Segi, the reason soon became apparent.

When she first stepped ashore on 6 December, she was surprised to be greeted by native men who were standing at attention and armed with rifles captured, she later learned, from the Japanese. As they marched beside her, she noticed their decidedly military gait. Kennedy then appeared, immediately insisting on a tour of his large and elegant headquarters. He also pointed out a mess room, and even an arsenal containing a variety of weapons, almost all – again – courtesy of the enemy. A short distance off was a secure-looking shed, outside which stood an armed and serious-looking native sentry. 'The lock-up,' said Kennedy in answer to Farland's enquiring glance. He could see she thought it might be reserved for local miscreants, so he corrected her. 'For the Japanese.' Farland was stunned. Kennedy then revealed that more than a dozen captured Japanese aircrew were currently incarcerated within his compound which, to Farland, resembled a military barracks. Kennedy explained how it was almost impossible for his prisoners to escape as he had them under the guard of two sentries, one inside and one outside. As soon as transport could be arranged, they would be on their way to interrogation centres and POW camps. The chances of them escaping were remote, he said, but even so, he would prefer her to know how to use a gun.

Clearly, this was no ordinary Coastwatcher station.

•

To this day, Donald Gilbert Kennedy remains one of the most brilliant yet most controversial figures among Feldt's hidden army of Coastwatchers. Certainly a man of powerful intellect and unquestionable bravery, a superb soldier, organiser and leader of men, Kennedy was the first – but by no means the last – to throw aside Feldt's pacifist Ferdinand doctrine and take the fight directly to the enemy.

What began as a small force of native volunteers, established to protect his precious position at Segi from discovery, eventually grew into a private army, conducting deadly ambush and guerrilla raids, and inflicting considerable casualties on the enemy. Kennedy's brutality was not confined to the Japanese, and his treatment of those under his command forever tarnished his wartime career. Such was the resentment he engendered in some of his own people that the closest he came to being killed in action was from a bullet fired by one of his own men.

As one of his ex-wives described him:

He was an extraordinary character – utterly charming, with a great presence and a tremendous sense of humour, extremely erudite and interesting with it. A very clear thinking and brilliant brain, but almost paranoiac. If he thought his authority or pride were touched in any way he became violent. And, of course, being an alcoholic didn't help. His years of isolation on the islands made it difficult for him to adjust to civilised living where his authority could be questioned.

Kennedy's behaviour was protected – even excused – by his unquestionable success as a Coastwatcher. Feldt treads warily in his own account of the man, who he personally recruited, talking up his achievements, but little more than hinting at his flaws. The regard he was held in by the Americans at Guadalcanal, for whom Kennedy's information became vital, remained unequivocal.

Within the first weeks of his timely arrival at Segi, Kennedy's reports, according to the US air commander at Guadalcanal, General Roy Geiger, 'resulted in the destruction of more than forty enemy aircraft'. Physically closer to Guadalcanal than either Mason or Read on Bougainville, Kennedy's alerts became instrumental in creating the early warning system which, over six months, helped the Americans repel the repeated and increasingly desperate efforts of the Japanese to dislodge them.

One of Kennedy's signals, for example, sent on 10 October, informed the Americans that a group of thirty-five enemy planes had just passed over his position on New Georgia, allowing them time to ready their aircraft for an engagement in which Toshio Ota – the famous playboy Zero fighter pilot and, with thirty-four kills to his credit, the Imperial Japanese Navy's fourth highest-scoring ace of the war – was shot down and killed.

Kennedy also regularly reported on Japanese sea traffic and troop movements, and rescued dozens of downed US airmen.

The exactness of his information was always highly valued, for example:

One barge passed Vakabo island heading SE through Marovo Lagoon about midnight …

Scout reports about thirty Japs at Sombiro Gatukai have wireless in village church which is larger of two isolated houses in clearing on hill. Japs live in other village houses. Fifteen at Penjuku all moved to camp about one mile to south in garden clearing on low hill near shore …

Capt. J. E. Swett USMC, shot down off Lingutu Entrance a.m. eleventh now here. Unhurt. Am sending over in about half hour …

•

Born in Invercargill, New Zealand, in 1898, Donald Kennedy enrolled in the army as a lieutenant, but World War I ended before he saw action. Retraining as a teacher in the colonial service, he taught in, then later ran, schools throughout the 1920s and 1930s in Fiji and the Gilbert and Ellice Islands. His pupils remembered him as a harsh taskmaster quick to use a cricket bat to enforce discipline. From a young age, Kennedy developed a deep and lifelong interest in radios as well as a thorough knowledge of their workings. In his classrooms, he would supervise the building of wet cell batteries – completely from scratch – using old beer bottles and lead from melted cans.

When war came, he transferred to the British Solomon Islands as a district officer on Santa Isabel, responsible for much of the northwest, and was awarded the rank of captain in the local defence force. In 1941, he was recruited by Feldt into the Coastwatcher service and began forming his own wide-ranging sub-network of planters, government officials, and even missionaries such as Reverend Silvester on Vella Lavella, to complement his reports with observations of their own. Still nominally running the civil administration of a large swathe of the western islands, Kennedy also recruited many locals into his network which, by the time the Japanese entered the war, extended across much of the northern Solomons.

In May, Kennedy's alerts about Japanese vessels off Santa Isabel provided warning to the government in Tulagi to begin evacuating. After the fall of the capital, he elected to stay and fight the invaders any way he could. For several months, he was effectively on the run, living in his own motor launch, both evading the Japanese and searching for the best position to establish a Coastwatcher post to observe them. He returned to Santa Isabel but soon realised he was too far removed, and would need to risk moving closer to the enemy.

Studying the local admiralty charts, which he had had the foresight to grab from his office, Kennedy's eyes caught the ominous notation 'foul ground' describing the Segi Passage, on the southern tip of New Georgia separating it from the island of Vangunu. He also saw it to be 'partially examined'. The Japanese, he reasoned, relying on these same maps, would be unlikely to show interest in this corner of the country.

Kennedy also knew Segi to be the site of the property of Harold Markham, known locally as 'Old Marko', and regarded as the doyen of planters in the western Solomons. Markham had arrived from England in 1908, married the daughter of a local chief and built a successful 800-acre copra plantation including a large home, famous for a tropical garden which was the envy of many in the region. Wealthy, and now in his later years, Old Marko had been evacuated to Sydney at the beginning of the war, leaving the big house vacant.

Though much of the Segi channel was reef bound, Kennedy discovered a navigable passage through the coral, leading to a deeper channel which could accommodate a flying boat. There was also a series of interconnected lagoons with passages to some of the natives' primary canoe routes which, from the ocean side, were undetectable.

In July 1941, Kennedy moved into the Markham plantation, bringing some of his recruits with him, and began transforming it into a quasi-military base extending far beyond the boundaries of the property. But first he needed to stamp his authority on the local population. 'These islands are British and they are to remain British,' he declared in a message delivered to every native village in the area. 'The government is not leaving. Even if the Japanese come, we shall stay with you and in the end they will be driven out.' Much of the local population was reassured, while others clamoured to join him.

Kennedy's vital Teleradio was concealed in a shack hidden half a mile or so into the bush, its location a secret to everyone but himself. He also established reserve radio huts and caches of food up to 10 miles inland; a series of hidden canoes were stashed in mangroves to facilitate escape, and 'getaway roads' spread away through the jungle in several directions.

Combining his background in teaching as well as the military, Kennedy trained his raw men along strict military lines, melding them into a virtual private militia. His second-in-command, William 'Billy Bennett', a talented mixed-race man of twenty-two, proved himself a proficient sailor, mechanic and medical dresser, as well as an inspirational motivator to his fellow islanders, exhorting them to resist the Japanese invaders.

For several weeks after setting up Segi, there was little for Kennedy's army to do. While he was now close enough to the centre of Japanese activity to report on air and sea traffic, New Georgia itself remained relatively undisturbed.

Then, on the afternoon of 24 November, Kennedy's spies reported a group of enemy warships anchoring off Munda Point on the island's southwest coast. That night, the Japanese began landings and all sorts of equipment were brought to shore by a flotilla of small boats. The enemy were planning to build another airstrip at the site of the Lambeti copra plantation, and were determined not to repeat their mistakes of the past.

Here, at Munda, no native labour was to be used, with any local caught in the area to be severely punished. To make sure this airstrip would not be discovered by the prying Allied reconnaissance flights, Japanese engineers cut off the tree crowns and suspended them on wires in situ while construction workers toiled underneath. For several vital weeks, the ruse succeeded.

Kennedy's scouts reported more Japanese landings on New Georgia, at Wickham Anchorage to the east, Ramada Island to the north, and at Kolombangara to the west, all of which he was able to report to Hugh Mackenzie who was 250 miles away at Henderson Field.

As a result of Kennedy's reporting, an airstrike was launched against the Japanese at Wickham Anchorage, resulting in the sinking of a number of ships. Kennedy's scouts recovered several tons of food from the flotsam, which was fortunate as his army had steadily grown to several dozen and supplying them with food was becoming an issue. This went some way towards negating Kennedy's dependence on the Americans at Lunga for supplies.

As enemy aircraft began to be shot down in numbers – once again thanks largely to the Coastwatchers' reporting – Kennedy's men started to also collect Japanese pilots, albeit as extremely reluctant prisoners. For every downed airman – whether friend or foe – his native scouts brought in from the neighbouring areas, Kennedy supplied the standard reward of a case of tinned meat and a bag of rice. In all, it is estimated that twenty-two American and twenty Japanese aviators were collected by his scouts. While the American pilots and crews were soon back with their units, the Japanese were kept under guard in Kennedy's homemade stockade, where they complained bitterly about everything from the food to the toilet paper, before being loaded, wrists tied, onto a flying boat to be taken away for interrogation and the humiliation of incarceration as a prisoner of war.

Kennedy suspected the Japanese knew of his existence but not his strength or precise location, and he intended to keep it that way. Any Japanese soldiers found within a few miles of the plantation – what Kennedy dubbed the 'forbidden zone' – whether actively looking for him or not, were to be wiped out, completely, with no exceptions, lest any of them escape to reveal his location. If, in such cases, supplies of food or arms could also be secured, so much the better.

Ably assisted by Billy Bennett, Kennedy trained and disciplined his men. Like a sporting coach, Bennett would rouse them to fever pitch with florid oratory, reminding them their fathers and grandfathers had been headhunters, noted among the fiercest warriors in the world, and they were their successors. Now, it was their turn to invoke their warrior blood to throw out the Japanese invader. The men responded with calls and cries of enthusiasm. How they would behave in actual combat was yet to be tested.

Then, one morning in November, a runner came with the startling news that a Japanese Daihatsu motor barge filled with soldiers had anchored among mangroves 5 miles to the north and that the Japanese were sleeping onboard. Gathering twenty-three of his best men – as well as a couple of downed American flyers who were itching to join the patrol – they set off at dusk and trekked north. Stealthily, without a word being spoken among them, the party stalked the unsuspecting Japanese, and quietly set up a captured enemy heavy machine gun. At 7 p.m., on Kennedy's signal, they attacked, taking the Japanese completely by surprise with a savage onslaught of fire.

Like a pirate, Billy Bennett was the first to board the barge, but was jumped by a crouching Japanese soldier as he attempted to lower the ramp. Struck on the head, Bennett managed to ram a bayonet into the soldier's chest, and resistance thereafter ceased. Without incurring a single casualty, Kennedy's men, in their first combat, had wiped out an enemy formation with an enthusiasm that surprised even him. Valuable food and arms were recovered from the barge, which was then towed out into the water and sunk, along with its complement of Japanese corpses, with 'the sharks acting as undertakers'.

A day or so later, another barge was reported and the action was repeated in a similar night ambush. This time captured hand grenades were hurled into the mass of soldiers and, once again, the fearsome Billy Bennett leaped onboard. In the darkness, he noticed the outline of a Japanese soldier aiming a rifle but, firing first, removed most of the man's head with a single shot from his own. When sounds were heard from the engine room below, he lifted the hatch, hurled more grenades inside and, somewhat rashly, sat on the hatch. After the explosion – which Bennett somehow survived – no further resistance was recorded, and another cache of weapons was recovered.

If Donald Kennedy had harboured any doubts about his men's ability to fight, they had been quickly dispelled in the mangroves north of Segi. Soon, news of the massacre spread through the island. Native men, young and old, tired of the brutality of the Japanese and their occupation, and newly emboldened by Kennedy's successes, clamoured to join his militia, arriving to register at Segi faster than he could process them.

Some began undertaking their own patrols, armed with whatever antique or captured firearm they could muster. Seni, a chief from a small group of islands called the Mindi Mindi, was inspired to single-handedly ambush a party of six Japanese, killing one and taking his rifle, which he handed to another man before both travelled to Kennedy to enlist.

Seni then attracted followers of his own and, reviving the war canoe traditions of old, prowled the lagoons, seeking out the enemy. On one occasion, his canoe rounded an outcrop of mangroves and came face to face with another filled with Japanese. Seni immediately opened fire, and a running battle erupted across the still water. The Japanese were better shots, but less adept at handling their stolen canoe. One by one, Seni's men picked them off until all five were dead, and five more rifles were presented to an impressed Donald Kennedy.

Some of the new recruits did not even need weapons. Another local chief, Ngato, sought Kennedy's permission to attack a five-man Japanese reconnaissance team stationed on a nearby island, but was told there were no guns to spare. Ngato smiled and told Kennedy to leave the matter with him. The next morning, with six other villagers, he paddled up to the island and befriended the Japanese, even prepared their evening meal. That night as they slept, Ngato and his men crept into the Japanese tents and stole their rifles. When the Japanese realised they had been duped the next day, a fight broke out, with two of the Japanese proving themselves skilled in jujitsu. The local villagers seized the moment and overpowered the unarmed Japanese. Instead of shooting them, Ngato ordered the prisoners to be trussed like livestock and delivered back to an astonished Kennedy, who threw them into his prison, prior to them being removed via flying boat for questioning.

Soon, Kennedy had a core of over 100 warriors whom he drilled and trained relentlessly, always beginning the day with reveille and parade until, in the words of one historian, 'they could go through the manual of arms like a Guards Regiment'.

He also developed stricter discipline, until his relationship with even his most loyal acolytes began to sour.

Not content to let military success bolster morale and discipline, Kennedy employed violence and intimidation. Men suspected of disloyalty or displaying any insubordination were placed 'across the drum', a 44-gallon barrel, feet and hands touching the ground, and flogged with a belt. So as to avoid accusations of racial injustice, Kennedy was careful never to administer the punishments himself, always passing the role off to a native. But the humiliation, for a proud people already risking their lives in the defence of their country, cut deep.

Relations were further exacerbated by Kennedy's slow descent into drinking which, with the stress of leadership, became heavier, bringing on bouts of paranoia in which he would rail at his men, accusing them of spying and betrayal. On one occasion, he even put the uncle of his assistant, Billy Bennett, across the drum. For the shocked men, this proved a turning point.

Still, the war with the Japanese continued. In more and more frequent encounters, Kennedy and his men would patrol the 'forbidden zone' for signs of enemy patrols. Those outside the zone were usually left unmolested, but those who ventured closer to the compound were taken mercilessly.

Kennedy never shirked physical danger himself. As his captured arsenal grew to include a 20-millimetre cannon, eight heavy machine guns, two submachine guns, twelve pistols and sixty rifles, he also gathered a flotilla of no less than three working Japanese Daihatsu motorised barges. Two had been tied up on the island when strafed by an American fighter as the crew were ashore patrolling. Returning, they found one partially sunk, the other with a wrecked engine. As the Japanese trudged back on foot, Kennedy's scouts emerged, plugged the leaks, refloated the sunken barge and towed both of them back to Segi. When, a day later, a third barge turned up with a replacement engine, they managed to steal that too.

From a nearby Seventh Day Adventist mission, Kennedy also acquired a 10-ton schooner, the *Dundavata*, which featured in Kennedy's most dramatic engagement, an extraordinary skirmish unofficially known as the Battle of Marova Lagoon.

On the evening of 19 May 1943, a breathless scout reported that a whaleboat filled with at least twenty Japanese troops was heading straight for Segi Point via a lagoon called Marova. Gathering twenty men, Kennedy pushed off in the *Dundavata* to intercept, having armed the little boat with a half-inch calibre machine gun from a downed B-24 Liberator bomber in the bow, and two smaller guns stripped from a crashed Zero in the stern.

In the still water of the lagoon, the moonlight revealed the Japanese boat probing the shoreline for an anchorage. Kennedy, who had as usual been drinking, directed Billy Bennett at the helm to sail straight towards it. At 500 yards, Kennedy opened up with his machine gun, expending two full belts before it jammed. The Japanese fired back and Kennedy's right thigh was struck with two bullets. Bloodied but undeterred, he limped aft with little more than a grumble, and opened up with the stern guns.

As the vessels drew closer, he shouted at Bennett to ram the whaleboat, but the Japanese hurled a grenade at the *Dundavata* which exploded on the deck. Seconds later, the schooner smashed into the side of the whaler, overturning it and throwing the Japanese into the water. Kennedy made sure that not one of them was spared. Some of his men were hit by grenade fragments, but none seriously, and they eventually accounted for all twenty enemy dead.

Back at Segi, Kennedy chose to treat his own wounds, and carried on his very private war.

Kennedy insisted his headquarters at Old Marko's plantation house be spared none of the luxuries of peacetime. In early 1943, a visiting party of Marines, having heard of his exploits, arrived expecting something like a primitive jungle hideout. Instead, they were treated to a well-prepared dinner served precisely at 8 p.m., presented on the finest white linen, bone china and silver by jacketed waiting staff, preceded by drinks on the balcony. As they sat, they were suddenly joined by an exquisite-looking Polynesian girl who smiled but said little. Afterwards, a decanter of the finest single malt Scotch was produced. Later it was revealed that Kennedy had fathered a child with the girl, who was from the southernmost Solomons province of Rennell and Bellona.

Kennedy, according to the visiting Marines, was impeccably polite but somewhat aloof, as if conscious of the show he was putting on for his guests, with whom he never quite seemed at ease. The next day, the display continued with a parade, followed by a firing drill and stripping down of a .50 calibre machine gun which, in the words of one of the Americans, would 'put any Marine gun crew to shame'.

Finally, in mid-June 1943, Kennedy heard reports of a new Japanese commander, Major Hara, who had set out with a platoon of soldiers with orders to locate his garrison once and for all. Tipped off by his scouts, Kennedy planned another night-time ambush. Although some of the Japanese escaped in the darkness this time, they left behind diaries, sketches and handwritten orders. From these, Kennedy was able to confirm that the Japanese had indeed discovered his exact location and were intent on wiping it out.

On 20 June, he radioed Hugh Mackenzie to tell him the game was up, and that he would need to either evacuate or hide in the hills. The reply he received was immediate and astonishing.

*No!* Segi was *not* to be evacuated under *any circumstances*, came the clear direct order from Admiral Turner, in charge of the US Navy's amphibious operations. Unbeknown to Kennedy, the plantation at Markham had already been earmarked as the site for a new American fighter strip, and Marines were due to land there in just ten days' time. Under the circumstances, this schedule would need to be brought forward. This was all very well, responded a concerned Kennedy – who was now expecting an imminent Japanese attack – but would it be possible to clarify when, exactly, the Americans might be arriving? Again, an immediate reply came back: *Now!*

By dawn the next morning, 400 Marines had been packed onto destroyer transports and landing craft and were ashore at Segi, having several times scraped their hulls on the reefs of the poorly charted waters off Segi Point. As the US commander, Colonel Currin, waded ashore in the early light, he was greeted by an exhausted-looking man in singlet and khaki shorts with a rifle slung casually over his shoulder. The colonel accepted the man's outstretched hand, curious as to who this stranger might be. 'Captain Donald Kennedy,' the haggard figure said quietly.

For a while, Kennedy remained on Segi, but as the American construction battalions arrived with their bulldozers, followed by several thousand infantry, his position of authority evaporated and his men – some deeply embittered – dispersed home. His private war at Segi was over.

After the war, as a decorated hero holding the Distinguished Service Order as well as the US Navy Cross, Kennedy returned to the colonial administrative service, but his drinking, as well as his erratic behaviour – undoubtedly exacerbated by shell shock, or what would later be referred to as Post Traumatic Stress Disorder (PTSD) – upset his superiors.

Ever a source of contradiction, Kennedy, though a fierce disciplinarian among the natives under his command, would later take their side in their postwar struggles to break free of colonial rule, infuriating his bosses further. Eventually, he came to be regarded as something of an embarrassment within the service and he retired back to New Zealand.

In later years, Sir Colin Allan, the last Governor of the Solomon Islands before its independence in 1978, was so appalled by Kennedy's legacy, he thought it preferable to leave his story unwritten 'rather than have some of the details of his personal behaviour offered to a general readership'.

Little wonder American historian Richard B. Frank described Kennedy as the 'Captain Bligh' of New Georgia.

Only in the late 1980s, well after Kennedy's death, did his erstwhile lieutenant, Billy Bennett, finally confess that it was not Japanese bullets which struck Kennedy's thigh but Bennett's, fired in the dark at the height of battle in May 1943 onboard the schooner *Dundavata*. It was an act of revenge, he said, for the humiliation Kennedy had meted out to his uncle over the notorious 'drum'.

It was, perhaps, the final, melancholy instalment in the saga of the Coastwatchers' most flawed hero.

# Chapter 20
# THE SISTERS OF THE *NAUTILUS*

Lieutenant Commander William H. Brockman Junior, commander of the sturdy but somewhat ageing submarine USS *Nautilus*, read the piece of paper upon which was scratched the hurriedly decoded words, rubbed his eyes, and read them again. Without question, it was the strangest order he had ever received. A glance at his watch told him it was one minute past four on 29 December 1942, but whether it was morning or afternoon, he had no idea. Day and night tended to blur over the long hours when the sub ran submerged, and sleep was snatched in greedy handfuls of minutes when the demands of the boat permitted.

Brockman, who would eventually climb to the rank of rear admiral and command an entire submarine division, had already packed a great deal of action into just a few months of war. As a sub man, he was completely fearless, exasperatingly stubborn, and prepared to try absolutely anything to get at the enemy. The officers and men of his crew adored him.

In the last week of May, Brockman had steered the *Nautilus* out of Pearl Harbor then set course northwest towards an inconsequential speck of sand in the middle of the Pacific

Ocean called Midway Island, to begin his first war patrol. A week later, one of the greatest naval battles in history erupted around him.

On the morning of 4 June, surfacing to peer through the periscope, he sighted the outline of a Japanese warship, lined up his boat and let go two torpedoes. One of them misfired, the other simply missed. At the same moment, he was spotted by several Japanese aircraft that promptly attacked the *Nautilus* with a brace of depth charges. Undeterred, Brockman hid deep for a while, then returned to periscope depth where, this time, it was an enemy aircraft carrier that filled his sights. Almost feeling the Navy Cross being pinned to his chest, he fired another spread of four torpedoes, but once again the infamous failings of the US Mark XIV torpedo conspired to foil him. With a speed of just 28 knots, this notorious 1920s-era weapon ran slower than almost any Japanese vessel it could be aimed at, and often simply failed to explode. One of Brockman's 'fish' refused to emerge from its tube, while two more set off in opposite directions. The fourth torpedo made it all the way to the enemy carrier, but harmlessly broke in two as it hit the hull. Brockman, however, could consider himself lucky, as another trait of the infamous Mark XIV was its tendency to veer off in a large circle and double back towards the unfortunate vessel which had launched it. In any case, unbeknown to Brockman, the Japanese carrier – probably the *Kaga* – was already doomed and sinking, its crew in the process of abandoning ship. Brockman's only achievement was to provoke another sustained Japanese attack that lasted many hours and in which no less than forty-two depth charge explosions were recorded, all of which the *Nautilus* survived. Suspecting the old boat had probably expended its supply of luck for the moment, the navy withdrew Brockman to the west.

In August, he was involved in a further folly known as the Makin Raid, in which he and another sub deposited a couple of companies of Marines on a tiny atoll in the Gilbert and Ellice Islands to draw the Japanese away from their attack on the Solomons. It not only failed to achieve this but cost the lives of nine brave young Marines for no purpose whatsoever.

By the end of the year, now with four patrols under his belt, Brockman had sunk three small Japanese merchant ships and a number of sampans, and survived even more bouts of depth-charging. On Christmas Day, he found himself patrolling up and down the coast of Bougainville looking for targets of opportunity, so far unsuccessfully. A couple of days later, a message came with a high level of priority, right from the top, from COMSOPAC, Commander, South Pacific Area – Admiral William F. Halsey himself.

Brockman read it one more time, then his brain cleared. It was, in fact, 4 a.m.

*Nautilus* was ordered to proceed directly to a tiny bay in an obscure harbour on the lonely northeast tip of Bougainville – it sounded very much like a mercy dash. Brockman summoned his stores officer, Ensign George Davis. Having recently been caught smoking a pipe in the forward torpedo room, Davis made his way midships expecting a further dressing-down by the boss.

'Davis,' said the captain.

'Sir,' he answered.

'How many women can you take care of?'

There was a pause.

'Sir?' replied Davis, unsure he'd heard correctly.

'Women, Davis. How many can you take care of?'

'Any number, sir!' answered a suddenly animated Davis.

The women who would soon be coming aboard were somewhat different from those envisaged by Davis, but on New Year's Eve 1942 the US submarine *Nautilus* would play the central role in one of the most unusual yet spectacular of all the Coastwatcher missions of the Pacific War.

•

The Sisters of St Joseph of Orange, the California chapter of the venerable Roman Catholic Sisters of St Joseph, had only been founded thirty years earlier, but their French roots stretched back to the middle of the seventeenth century. Their mission was to assist in the betterment of women all over the world. In December 1940, at the request of Thomas Wade, the Marist Bishop of faraway Bougainville, the sisters decided to send four missionary pioneers – two teachers and two nurses – to continue their good work. None of them had ever been there, nor anywhere in the South Pacific previously, and all of them were of middle age.

From their mission in the village of Hanahan on the lonely northeast coast of Buka Island, the sisters plunged into the work, establishing a school, giving medical care, and generally delivering good cheer with a sense of purpose and optimism. Sister Mary Isabelle Aubin of Newport, who spoke and taught French, was a natural organiser, and could play both trumpet and violin to reasonable proficiency, was the obvious choice as Superior of the group of four nuns, including Sister Mary Celestine Belanger of Massachusetts, Sister Mary Irene Alton of California, and Sister Mary Hedda Jaeger of Saskatchewan, Canada.

The sisters took the challenges of the tropics in their strides, never complaining, and even attempting to learn several local dialects. They travelled to various villages on Buka by bicycle, becoming a well-loved sight as they tore along jungle tracks, their habits and robes flowing out behind.

It all changed drastically when Japan entered the war in late 1941. Initially, the sisters remained oblivious, believing life would continue as before. As Japan marched inexorably towards the Solomons in the new year, Sister Hedda began to keep a daily and detailed diary which has endured as a record of the events that would soon engulf their lives. Initially, Hedda seemed to anticipate occupation by the Japanese as one might welcome a new employer. 'We wonder if the new officials will be staying at Buka Passage, and just what we are meant to do to fulfil our role as neutrals,' she wrote, even looking forward to the prospect of ordering new rubber tyres for her bicycle 'from Sydney or Tokyo'.

Sharing no such naivety, Coastwatcher Jack Read did his best to urge the sisters – as he did all civilians – to evacuate, regarding their presence on the island as both a hindrance and a danger. But, like many Europeans, the Sisters of St Joseph, as well as their missionary in charge, Father Joseph Lamarre, had managed to convince themselves of the sanctity of their neutrality, and carried on as normal.

Gradually however, their unease began to grow. As the Japanese approached, Sister Hedda wrote, 'The natives are all very much concerned about our welfare, and some have even expressed the wish that they could give us their black skin so we could pass unseen. We do not know what the future holds for us.'

The scales would finally fall in March when the Japanese began landing on Buka, and executed local planter and Coastwatcher Percy Good, and another American priest, Father James T. Hennessy, vanished from his mission just 17 miles away.

This was too much for Father Lamarre, who immediately ordered the four women south, under the escort of the American-born Bishop of the Diocese of Bougainville, Thomas Wade, who was nearly fifty years of age and had been in the job since 1930. Once in Bougainville, Wade thought it prudent to split the women up, depositing Sisters Hedda and Celestine in the village of Asitavi, while Sisters Isabelle and Irene were sent to a small inland mission at Monetai.

For a while, the women settled in and resumed their roles of teaching and medicine, believing they may be able to avoid the war, and the Japanese, after all. Then, in July, Bougainville's administrative capital, Kieta, was occupied, and Bishop Wade arrested. The timing of his incarceration was fortunate, as he was released after a month, just before the American landings at Guadalcanal in August when Japanese tolerance of Europeans in the areas under their control abruptly ceased. The five remaining priests on Buka – including Father Lamarre – were rounded up, their missions ransacked and closed down.

In late August, the Japanese suffered their first major defeat of the Guadalcanal Campaign at the mouth of the Tenaru River. In the massacre that followed, the Japanese command was stunned and bewildered. Shortly after, the mission of the Society of Mary at the village of Ruavatu, just 20 miles east of the Tenaru, was visited. Having previously shown tolerance towards the missionaries, the Japanese now demanded they make their way to the American lines and warn them of the overwhelming Japanese might which would soon be turned against them. American Father Arthur C. Duhamel, Dutch Father Henry Oude-Engberink, French nun Sister Sylvia, and Sister Odilia from Italy, all politely refused, stating their role could never be anything but neutral. Infuriated, the Japanese imprisoned and starved them for a week. When the four still refused to do their bidding, they were bayoneted through the throat, further tortured and finally murdered.

When news of the atrocity reached Bishop Wade, he realised the time for self-delusion was over, and the sisters had to be evacuated. There was only one person he could think of who knew the country well enough to take the women to safety: the priest in charge of another mission at Tinputz on Bougainville's northeast coast, Father Albert Lebel. Originally from Maine, Lebel had spent thirteen years in the Solomons and knew every track, so much so that he had successfully evaded the Japanese attempts to round him up, and was still administering medicine to the many villages he frequented. Aged forty but still fit, he had also displayed remarkable nerve in the face of the enemy. In March 1942, Lebel had watched a Japanese destroyer anchor just off his mission at Tinputz Harbour but instead of fleeing, he donned his full ecclesiastical robes and swaggered down the beach to meet the landing party. Such was his show of confidence, the young Japanese lieutenant in charge was embarrassed at his poor English, and even invited Lebel back to the wardroom of the destroyer for tea, despite Lebel openly admitting to being an American. According to Jack Read, Lebel 'put on a first class show for the enemy'. As Japanese officers bowed with respect, Lebel answered questions 'of no special importance' and was escorted back to the beach, where he was assured he could carry on his work if he promised not to leave the mission.

The Japanese would not remain so chivalrous. The massacre at Ruavatu had convinced all remaining nuns and clergy that staying on the island now meant almost certain death. In a short time there were more women to take care of and Lebel was determined to evacuate all of them. Word was sent out in strict secrecy through his local network for people to make their way to the village of Tsipatavai, where they would assemble, then proceed to Teop Harbour, which was deep enough for a small boat or Catalina flying boat to swoop in and land.

Soon, four more sisters from the Marist mission at Soveli, deep in the interior, arrived, having been escorted the entire 90 miles by another priest who had escaped from Buin. Here, they were joined by the four St Joseph sisters, who were once again united.

The list of escapees would grow longer still. At a mission at Tarlena, deep inside the Japanese-controlled Buka Passage area, Lebel learned of two priests and three nuns currently under house arrest, well guarded, and forbidden to leave the property. Two of the sisters were so sick they could barely walk, but Lebel vowed to bring them all to safety if he could. In late November, he set out with a party of seven of his most trusted native guides for the 30-mile trek to Tarlena, avoiding a direct approach and travelling instead via the lesser-used coastal track. This route happened to take him through a former coffee plantation called Rugen, where he intended to rest. To his surprise, the first person who greeted him here was the principal Coastwatcher of northern Bougainville, Jack Read, who was using Rugen as his base. The two men sat, and Lebel outlined the plot now unfolding. Read listened quietly but seemed less than enamoured of the plan.

'It's a big risk, Father,' he said after a silence.

Surprised, Lebel assured him that he appreciated the danger but intended to carry through with the escape. Read was silent again. At length, he wryly asked the priest how he felt about finally dragging the Church into the war. 'Now, you're on this side of the fence,' he added. Lebel smiled.

Reflecting on the irony of his earlier pleadings for the island's clergy to leave when it was still relatively safe, Read then asked what he could do to help.

When he reached Tarlena a short distance down the track, Lebel could not believe his luck: the Japanese guards were nowhere to be seen, apparently having taken the night off. Alerting Father McConville, the head priest at Tarlena, Lebel implored him to quickly round up the women. And so, just as the sisters were preparing for bed, McConville burst in with the astonishing news that the Saviour had answered their prayers, and the vehicle of their deliverance had arrived in the form of two hurriedly put together cane chairs lashed with vines. Sister Mary Alton later recalled that, 'Father Lebel gave orders that each of us could only take one small package or bag. We were not told how the evacuation was to be effected. We assumed that it would be by plane – but we never dreamed we would be liberated from the island by submarine.'

Sisters Claire and Remy, both old and partially infirmed with exhaustion and bad knees – not to mention bewildered by the sudden appearance of their rescuers – dutifully mounted the bamboo chairs which were borne on the shoulders of the native carriers. From the darkness more figures emerged to join the exodus. Bobby Pitt, a mixed-race man who had been living in fear of the Japanese discovering his previous work for the Allies, appeared from nowhere with his wife and five children in tow. They were joined by a blind native girl and her companion, as well as one or two other stragglers who wished to leave. Lebel threw a look of enquiry to McConville, who simply shrugged his shoulders.

The enlarged party set out, making its way from the west coast back to the east, arriving at Tsipatavai on 26 November. To the party's relief, Lebel's natives had prepared food and even comfortable accommodation, further cementing his faith in their loyalty.

Now the original four St Joseph sisters as well as those from Soveli needed to be brought up the 25 miles from their village of Asitavi, a feat achieved by a motor launch lent – at enormous personal risk – by a local Chinese trader. On the trip, the nuns refused to remove their conspicuous habits, but were prepared to compromise by donning blue veils to make themselves less visible from the air.

More people began to trickle into Lebel's holding camp at Tsipatavai. The last of the European planters, so recently contemptuous of those fleeing, now realised their mistake and sought a place in Lebel's evacuation plan. Of particular surprise to Jack Read was the sight of the planter Claude Campbell, accompanied by his wife, who had earlier refused to evacuate on account of her husband being unwell. While Mr Campbell had apparently recovered, it was now his wife who looked broken and exhausted. For months, the couple had managed to lie low and live life largely as before on their magnificent 7000-acre plantation at Rauna on the north coast. Then, just a few days earlier the Japanese, having ignored them for months, suddenly sent a raiding party to Rauna, which the Campbells barely managed to escape by fleeing into the jungle, diving into a river and hiding in a native hut. The Japanese burned their house to the ground and left a note saying they would be back in a few days to kill them, along with 'all the English'. In desperation, the Campbells sent a note to Father Lebel, pleading for help.

As Lebel's party of refugees grew, the question of what to do with them became paramount, and in Townsville, the powers were of little help. Whenever Jack Read radioed requests for the ever-expanding group to be taken off by ship or plane, the answer was always the same: sit tight and wait – nothing can be spared at the moment.

Even Eric Feldt remained obdurate, seemingly happy to let these stubborn civilians stew for a while after they'd refused earlier help when it had been freely offered. With the Japanese strengthening their grip on Bougainville, he was less willing to risk men and resources to accommodate their change of heart.

Lebel was in a quandary. If the party became much larger, it would be too unwieldy to be evacuated; it was already becoming harder to feed and protect. He knew the largesse of his native village friends would only stretch so far. By Christmas Eve, the Japanese had sent raiding parties even closer – to the mission at Tinputz Harbour itself – in their efforts to root out the Coastwatchers.

In desperation, Lebel decided to fall back on his nationality. As an American looking after primarily American Catholic nuns, he decided to appeal directly to another American, Admiral William F. Halsey Junior, commander of all Allied forces, South Pacific Area. Jack Read, who hated bureaucracy, nevertheless demurred at the idea of going so far over Eric Feldt's head but suggested seeking permission to contact Halsey.

No reply came immediately, but both Read and Lebel sensed this was simply the bewilderment experienced by large organisations in responding to unorthodox requests.

As Lebel conducted midnight mass in the village, a runner arrived with news that the Japanese were back at Tinputz Harbour and heading inland towards them. Lebel halted the service, turned to his small congregation and told them to pack and leave *now*. 'Be prepared to be cold, wet and hungry,' he warned. 'I want you to cooperate with everything I ask you to do. Move quickly and be ready for anything.' By 1.30 Christmas morning, they were on the move, heading up along a trail that led into the mountains.

Holding flickering hurricane lamps, the women stumbled over rocks and roots, holding each other's arms when needed, encouraging, cajoling, offering army biscuits and occasional cups of tea from a thermos as they climbed into the darkness. All they had in the world was now on their own backs or those of the loyal natives who refused to leave their sides. The two older sisters were borne away in their chairs again, and even when the party had to climb into a ravine then tackle the near vertical ascent on the other side, the footing of the native bearers never faltered.

By dawn, they could afford to rest and survey the view below them. They were high enough to spot the ocean far below through the trees. But even here, Lebel would not let them rest for long.

Adding one more ravine between them and the Japanese, Lebel chose a flat plateau, ordered rest, and collapsed, having not slept for over two days. Later that Christmas Day 1942, they sang the 'Magnificat' under the stars.

The next day, Lebel received a belated Christmas gift as a runner handed him a note from Read, who had made his way back to his camp at Porapora, informing him that permission had been granted to contact Admiral Halsey, with the caveat that the message must not exceed 200 letters. Read, said the messenger, awaited his instructions. Lebel penned the message carefully: 'Urgently request immediate evacuation of American women from Bougainville stop fear repetition of crimes on Guadalcanal stop Teop and Tinputz Harbor safe and convenient stop eternally grateful.'

About to put his own name to it, he thought the power of his superior might just carry more weight, so signed off in the name Bishop Wade. Wishing the runner God's speed, he sent him off, and prayed. After a day's rest, and word that the Japanese had left Tinputz empty-handed, he prepared his exhausted party for the trek down to Tsipatavai.

The response came quickly in words Lebel could scarcely believe he was reading. No ship was available, but a *submarine* would be sent to Teop this very night, 28 December. Having waited an eternity, events were now moving too fast, and Lebel begged for more time to gather a few more stragglers, not to mention Read himself, who was now a day's journey away. Somehow, the word fanned out that departure was imminent, and more people accepted Read's order to join the exodus including the recalcitrant Campbells and Mrs Falkner, the wealthy widow whose plantation happened to be set just back from the evacuation beach at Teop. Fred Urban, the Austrian manager of Hakau plantation, was officially the only male evacuee, and was going against his will. Read had long suspected him of collaborating with the Japanese and decided he had no future in Bougainville. Several native policemen were therefore sent to escort him to the departure, by force if necessary. Urban pleaded with Read to stay, fearing internment in Australia, but to no avail.

By noon on 31 December, the party had assembled a few miles behind the beach at Teop. Jack Read had gone ahead to assemble the Teleradio and send out the message that all were in position and awaiting further instructions, which he thought could not come soon enough. Looking at the nuns, he was amazed at their cheer and optimism which, even at the worst of times, had remained unbreakable. Many fit young men, he knew, had been broken by lesser trials than those endured by these remarkable ladies. Some were in terrible physical shape – malnourished, sunburned, blistered and exhausted, their shoes either falling apart or non-existent. One sister flopped about in a pair of tennis shoes given to her by Bishop Wade that were close to disintegration. And yet, according to Read, 'with never a murmur of complaint'.

At 5 p.m., the party moved off in single file towards the beach, Lebel staying behind to gather up any latecomers. Moving through a village, they passed Read, headphones on, hunched intensely over his Teleradio dials. 'Probably tonight,' he muttered, glancing up at Father McConville as he passed. It was not until 8 p.m. that Read received the confirmation that the pick-up was indeed imminent. He also instructed that two fires would be lit on the beach at precisely 10 p.m., positioned to mark the gap in the offshore reef. All a small boat needed to do was line up the fires and head into shore unimpeded. Then it would be up to the escapees themselves, and luck. Now, in darkness dotted only by the occasional lamp, the party stumbled on, blind, tripping in mud holes and bumping into roots, clinging for dear life to the garments of the invisible person in front. Read began to urge them on, warning that their rescuers could not afford to wait.

Finally, the path ended, and everyone emerged onto a fine, sandy moonlit beach. Others, having heard of the operation, had turned up of their own accord. Looking at the number of men who had arrived, Read felt compelled to remind them that this was essentially an evacuation of women and children, and any males wishing to board the submarine – except Urban who was being forcibly removed – would be admitted at the discretion of the captain.

A servant of Mrs Falkner appeared, offering the four Sisters of St Joseph use of her house in which to freshen up before the trip. Bedraggled, and in their filthy clothes, the nuns walked, hushed, into the wealthy family living room, a world of velvet cushions, waxed teak floorboards, oil lamps and Persian rugs, with bowls of sweet-smelling frangipanis on the sideboard. Then, in a black lace evening dress, Mrs Falkner herself appeared, the perfect hostess. After what the nuns had been through, it was surreal.

Down on the beach, fires were lit at precisely 10 p.m., and two pillars of flame roared up from the sand into the night sky. Some of Lieutenant Mackie's Independent Company men – now essentially guerrilla fighters – emerged to assist with the embarkation. Conversations rose, and a new sense of optimism lent the occasion something of a party atmosphere as people shared news and tales of ordeals, taking it in turns to thank those who had run the terrible risk to organise it all. Some of the ladies apologised to Read for all the trouble they had caused, and expressed their undying gratitude that he had driven them hard. The tough Read was genuinely moved but could not take his eyes off the sea. It was now after 11 p.m. Where was the submarine?

•

All that day, the *Nautilus* had remained submerged 10 miles out on the bottom of Teop Harbour. Lieutenant-Commander Brockman had regularly scanned the beach and horizon for signs of the Japanese, as well as the white sheets that were supposed to be raised by the Coastwatchers to indicate the coast was clear. Somehow, this part of the message had failed to get through to Jack Read.

Brockman was anxious. If discovered in the shallows by the enemy, a few well-placed depth charges would mean a quick end to both himself and the *Nautilus*. After searching in vain for the white sheets through the periscope, Brockman waited till nightfall then, just before 8 p.m., brought the sub to within 3 miles of the beach, cursing the paucity of the charts he was forced to use.

A three-man landing party was assembled, with the sub's gangly, 6-foot-tall gunnery and torpedo officer Lieutenant Richard B. Lynch in charge of two old hands and excellent small boat handlers, Petty Officers Killgor and Porterfield. The sub's heavy deck hatches were removed, and the whaleboat brought up from the holds by a boom which had to be assembled on the deck – a difficult job even in daylight. When the cursing sailors finally placed it in the water, its flooded engine refused to start. The smaller launch was then readied, but Brockman was now over an hour late. At last the little boat set out, only to immediately return with a defective rudder. Another hour was lost in repairs. When finally underway again, Lieutenant Lynch forgot his instructions to line up the launch with the two signal fires marking the reef opening, slammed into a shelf of coral and capsized. Thankfully, the water at this point was only up to the men's knees. The drenched sailors righted the boat and, cursing their sheepish lieutenant in the colourful language of old sailors, bailed out water with their helmets.

On the beach, Read was told that all evacuees were accounted for, minus just two. Scanning the list, he cursed quietly to himself when he saw it was none other than the Campbells. They had returned to collect some 'essentials' from what was left of their home but assured Read they would be there at the appointed time. Father Lebel then emerged onto the beach, informing Read the couple were on their way, but exhausted and lagging behind. Read sent a party of natives and one of Mackie's men to urge them along. It was now nearly midnight, and still no sign of the submarine. He was then told that Mrs Falkner had changed her mind and was refusing to go. This was too much for Read. Marching straight for the house, he confronted his wavering passenger and did not mince his words. 'I had worked too hard on this project to remove all the non-native women from the island,' he later wrote. 'I had no intention of being handicapped in the future by having Mrs Falkner on my hands ... I informed her that if she did not go voluntarily, she would be forcibly carried aboard the submarine.' After a pause, Mrs Falkner politely agreed to swap her lace evening gown for something more suited to travel and made her way down to the beach.

Standing at the shore, Sergeant Dolby shushed for silence. With one ear cocked, he beckoned Read. Now, he could hear it too: voices, somewhere out there on the water. Quickly calling up a canoe, the two men were paddled out and, after a short time, came up to Lieutenant Lynch and the launch, still being bailed out.

'Happy New Year,' one of the sailors dryly remarked as the canoe pulled up.

Soon they had the boat off the reef and were heading to shore, the last shallow hundred yards having to be walked. Once on the beach, the trio of sailors glanced up, aghast at the smiling crowd of people in front of them. Lynch looked to Read.

'Yes,' he responded coyly. 'There are … one or two more than I had planned.' Lynch was speechless. Instead of the four American nuns plus – perhaps – a handful of others, he would now have to tell Brockman that the list had grown to twenty-nine women, children and, contrary to the arrangement, even some men, all of whom needed to be accommodated on a very crowded submarine. Shaking his head, Lynch warned Read to be prepared to have to leave a few of them behind.

The Campbells now showed up, along with a couple of servants, all towing sufficient luggage for an ocean cruise, the apparent cause of their tardiness. Read instructed it be left on the shore but Mrs Campbell dug in her heels, insisting none of it be left behind or she would refuse to board. An argument ensued but, for once, the steely Jack Read relented. In any case, the prospect of Mrs Campbell remaining on the island was simply too much to bear.

Lynch suggested taking just a few people back to the submarine before asking permission from the captain to return for the rest, but Read demurred, believing his best chance was in presenting Brockman with a fait accompli. He directed the boat be filled with as many women and children as it could hold.

After Father Lebel conducted a quick service of thanks on the beach, the civilians piled into canoes to be transported to the launch. 'What if I fall in?' asked a nervous Sister Irene as she placed herself in the bottom of the boat. The native oarsman smiled, assuring her that he'd simply haul her out. As it pulled away, Jack Read noticed that among the women, a single man had quietly inserted himself: Claude Campbell. For a moment in the half light he caught Read's eye, then quickly glanced away. Read sighed and ordered the boat to go.

On the deck of the *Nautilus*, William Brockman was anxiously waiting. It was now 3 a.m., long past their scheduled departure time and only a couple of hours till dawn. The boat was submerged as low in the water as it could be, and all deck guns were manned and ready, with repeated reminders for the crew to keep their eyes peeled. Finally, a sailor on lookout at the bow called, 'Sir!' And the faint noise of an engine could be heard approaching in the dark. All guns trained towards it, then relief as the launch pulled up alongside, filled with – Brockman could barely count them – twenty-one people. Lynch explained the situation, then asked how many more people Brockman was willing to take.

Brockman looked at him steadily for a moment, then consulted his watch. 'Go get 'em all,' he said. 'And hurry.' If Lynch was not back by 4.30, Brockman said, he would leave without him.

As he prepared to pull away, a sailor passed down a crate, telling Lynch it was for Jack Read.

Willing the slow boat on, Lynch raced back to Teop, this time remembering to find the gap in the reef. The hopeful men waiting on the beach were delighted to learn that the captain was welcoming them also. The last eight evacuees – five male planters, two Catholic priests and Fred Urban – piled into the boat as Lynch turned around and headed out to sea. Now the wind had come up and the launch had to plough into a mild chop, slowing her pace further. Trying to consult a compass in the dark, Lynch noticed the first blush of dawn as his watch told him it was 4.35.

At last, at 4.41 a.m., Lynch pulled up alongside the *Nautilus*. Brockman was still there, shaking his head as the extra refugees were helped up from the launch, which then had to be extracted from the water and stowed. Only at 5.37 a.m., in the clear light of dawn, could the *Nautilus* sound her diving klaxon, submerge to 100 feet, and edge her way out of the harbour.

Below, Brockman was presented with a sight he had never thought to see: his boat crowded with sailors and civilians, laughing, smiling and chatting in whatever space they could squeeze into. The crew gave up their bunks to those who needed rest. One priest found a cot in the forward torpedo room and settled himself there. Brockman's wardroom was filled with exhausted but smiling nuns in habits. 'Make the submarine your home,' he announced to all.

Shortly afterwards, he signalled the success of the evacuation, then received a reply from COMSOPAC which vindicated his caution: 'Congratulations *Nautilus*, you were just ahead of the sheriff. Jap destroyer entered Teop Harbor shortly after you left.'

For the next three days, the relief and novelty of the successful operation permeated the ship with good humour. Despite the stifling 96 degrees Fahrenheit of the sub's interior, games of cards and cribbage were played, and even a birthday party organised, complete with wrapped presents for the children. From the planters, Brockman was able to extract valuable knowledge about local conditions, tides and reefs, as well as Japanese shipping traffic and the fact that a Japanese floatplane conducted a daily circumnavigation of the island, regular as clockwork, at 7 a.m.

Brockman was ordered to proceed to a point off Tulagi where his 'guests' would be transferred to a patrol craft, a small ship whose usual job was hunting enemy submarines.

Just before 3 a.m. on 4 January, the *Nautilus* flashed its challenge, and received the correct reply as the outline of the patrol craft slid up alongside. As the passengers made their sincere farewells, the crew of the sub watched in amusement the faces of the crew of the patrol craft as they took onboard their unlikely cargo. With nothing visible in the dark except the sisters' white habits and veils, the sailors initially believed sacks of flour were being carried aboard. In a few days, they would step ashore at the large US base in Noumea, having taken part in one of the most unusual evacuations of the war.

•

A strange and sudden silence descended on the beach as the last of the evacuees departed on New Year's Eve. In the darkness, Jack Read stood with a handful of natives and some of Lieutenant Mackie's men, watching the shadow of the boat disappear, silently wishing them safe passage. Next to him was the crate which Lynch had given him as he pulled away. 'Compliments of the *Nautilus*,' he had said with a wave.

A few hours earlier, Brockman had organised a few supplies for Read, asking the stores officer what could be spared – a couple of cans of boneless chicken and some corned beef. Then, as word went around the boat that the cache was intended for Jack Read – one of those legendary Coastwatchers who, day after day from their stinking jungle hideouts had given the Guadalcanal Marines the jump on Japanese air attacks – the sailors began rifling through their meagre lockers. They threw in everything they could spare and much they could not: soap, small bottles of brandy, toothpaste, a scout knife. One young ensign even surrendered his precious pipe tobacco and pouch.

In the light of dawn, Jack Read opened the crate and reverently inspected the gifts, each one of them a luxury he had not seen in over a year.

There would be little time to enjoy them, as in early 1943, the Coastwatchers of New Guinea and the Solomons would face their greatest challenge of the war as the Japanese determined to wipe them out once and for all.

# Chapter 21

# TIGHTENING THE SCREW

After the war, Jack Read would write:

> I have always maintained, and still do, that the Japanese
> were never any menace to our coast-watching activities.
> We could hide in the jungle, within a few yards of them.
> They were not trackers. However, it became a different
> proposition when the enemy gained the allegiance of
> natives who really knew the island and who could read the
> telltale tracks of our every movement like an open book.

By the end of 1942, Guadalcanal had become an obsession
for the Japanese – no cost would be considered too high to
expel the Americans from their precious foothold around the
airfield at Lunga. So far, they had tried everything: full-frontal
assaults, multi-pronged night offensives, bombardment from
the sea and the air, even invading other parts of the Solomons
as a diversion. Each effort was repulsed, usually with
catastrophic losses to the Japanese, and still the American
Marines clung on to their little ribbon of beach and jungle
like barnacles.

Following the massacre on the banks of the Tenaru River in August, the Japanese regrouped and sent 3000 men storming across a grassy half-mile-wide plateau called Edson's Ridge. The American lines wavered, even appearing to break in places, but held. In one desperate, headlong frontal attack after another, the Americans mowed the Japanese down, killing 850 for a loss of fifty-nine to themselves.

There would be other attacks, similarly brutally repulsed. In mid-November, another 15 000 fresh Japanese troops were earmarked to storm Henderson Field yet again. This time, the Japanese changed their tactics, allowing large ships to enter the battle area to cover the landings and keep the Americans under pressure by bombarding the airstrip from the sea. To the north in Bougainville, Coastwatcher Paul Mason kept the Americans updated on the enemy naval build-up around Buin. To identify Japanese vessels, pages of *Jane's Fighting Ships* were torn out and delivered to him in supply drops. Later, these would be supplemented by hand-drawn silhouettes. So armed, Mason was able to deliver highly accurate information, correctly identifying the cruisers *Aoba* and *Mogami* among a fleet of: '61 ship in the area … 2 sloops, 33 destroyers, 17 cargoes, 2 tankers, 1 passenger liner of 8,000 tons'.

Eventually, after nearly 20 000 dead and the loss of scores of ships and hundreds of aircraft along with their irreplaceable crews, the Japanese Emperor, on the last day of 1942, endorsed his generals' bitter decision to face the inevitable and evacuate their remaining 10 000 exhausted troops from Guadalcanal.

One of the causes of their defeat, they now increasingly suspected, was the network of Allied spies secreted in the jungle, reporting on their every move, robbing them of any advantage of surprise. The spies had not been properly dealt with on Guadalcanal, and the Japanese soldiers and airmen had suffered the consequences. It was now time to rid them from

Japan's other Pacific conquests, beginning with Bougainville. Determined patrols would now be pushed deep inland from the coast to root out these wretched spies, one by one, and neither they nor those natives helping them would be shown any mercy. All remaining Europeans would be treated likewise.

On Bougainville, the Japanese would bring to bear their deadliest tactic in fighting the Coastwatchers: the pitting of native against native.

As early as November, the Japanese, possibly sensing the direction in which the Guadalcanal campaign was headed, began to reinforce their presence in Bougainville. From his station at Buin on the island's southern tip, Paul Mason began to hear reports of Japanese landing parties bringing ashore their beds, indicating a long stay. As Mason later recalled: '... from our lookout post we spotted more than just beds. Tractors, lorries, heavy guns, and war materiel of all kinds were being unloaded. I quickly decided that this was a good time to get moving.'

This new activity pointed to the familiar conclusion that yet another airstrip was being planned, and the Japanese began a campaign to win over the local villagers by coercion and, if need be, force.

Like the persuasive Terushige Ishimoto, whose success in wooing the native population on Guadalcanal was cut short while bathing on a beach in October by a bullet from an American soldier, Tsunesuke Tashiro had likewise spent many years in the South Pacific and was fluent in several languages, including English and Pidgin.

In March 1942, following the occupation of Bougainville, Tashiro was given an office in the Burns, Philp building in Kieta, working with the 1st Naval Force's sinisterly titled Native Pacification Section. From here, he travelled across the island translating, organising native labour, recruiting and advising on sites for the construction of bases and airstrips. He also began to work with a shadowy figure, about whom little is known besides one of his names, Harada. Some records indicate Harada to have been a naval petty officer, others that he was an army lieutenant. Others claim him as a member of the Tokkei-Tai, the naval version of Imperial Japan's dreaded secret police, the Kempei-Tai. Harada kept a far lower profile than Tashiro, but was charged with hunting down and eliminating all anti-Japanese elements and resistance on Bougainville, primarily by recruiting and organising disaffected and renegade natives into violent bands to attack Japan's enemies. To instil an added note of terror, he named them the Black Dogs.

Essentially little more than hired gangs, primarily from the coastal village areas around Kieta, the Black Dogs were charged with enforcing general obedience to Japan, with emphasis on eliminating the Coastwatchers and their native support networks, as well as the few remaining Europeans and Chinese. They were encouraged to use any method they chose, including rape, killing, looting and the burning of other villages. As Jack Read described them: 'They ravaged and pillaged the villages of all friendly and neutral tribes. These other natives said over and over again, "It is not the Jap who is bad: it is the Kieta native."'

In December 1942, the Black Dogs' first task would be the elimination of perhaps the most dangerous Coastwatcher of them all, Paul Mason.

Mason had already moved his camp 20 miles to the north to a river valley halfway between Buin and Kieta, but he received word from his native network that three separate enemy patrols were moving against him inland from the coast. Clearly, it was again time to leave, and Mason banked on the most difficult route as being the safest.

'The enemy appeared to be closing in on us fast. We knew that the Japs were not fond of travelling in the high country, so we elected to cross some of the roughest terrain in Bougainville – the southeast end of the Crown Prince Range.'

It was, in Feldt's words, 'an arduous, breathtaking climb', but Mason's instincts were correct. The Japanese sent two patrols to block both the north and south ends of the valley, and, with the third party being guided by Black Dog natives, discovered his camp. They were, however, three days too late.

Instead, they set upon one of the last remaining Europeans in the area, an elderly planter named Tom Ebery, a Bougainville resident since 1915. Ebery had been keen to work with Jack Read as a Coastwatcher, but his Teleradio had been confiscated by the administration during its flight from Tulagi. Mason remembered Ebery as: '... the sort of man who helped everybody. He became a father figure to all the natives – attending to the sick and judging their arguments.'

Despite his lack of radio, Ebery was always ready to supply Mason and Read with any information he could glean regarding the Japanese, and he had shown considerable skill in evading them until now.

Despite only recently having recovered from a long illness, Ebery was arrested by the Black Dogs, beaten, then handed over to the Japanese, who were convinced he knew of Mason's whereabouts. In fact, he had not seen Mason for months. Uphill, across gorge and river, the wretched man was driven, beaten and tormented until, possibly of his own volition, he fell into a stream as it was being crossed and drowned. Later, his body was recovered and buried on the bank by sympathetic natives.

Mason found himself pursued into rough country where food was already running low with no prospect of aerial resupply. His native helpers' home villages were now being threatened by the Black Dogs' reign of terror, which included the confiscation of food from village gardens. Many of Mason's men had no choice but to return and defend them. In tearful farewells, they gripped Mason's hands, wished him the best of luck, and headed back down the mountains.

At Guadalcanal, Hugh Mackenzie, who had recently been placed in charge of all the Bougainville Coastwatchers, remembered the tragic last stand of Con Page, and urged Mason to set aside all notion of heroics, destroy his Teleradio and head north to join up with Jack Read at his relatively secure camp at Porapora at the top end of the island. Also, a detachment of fresh commandos would soon be on their way to assist. Mackenzie also reminded Mason that he had already done more than his share.

Watching the situation deteriorate around him, Mason needed no encouragement to leave. With the Japanese in pursuit, he set out on the 100-mile trek to the opposite end of the island with a small party including a couple of native police boys acting as guides and lookouts. To assist him, Read sent some of Mackie's AIF men south to link up with Mason and offer protection. Mason's opinion of soldier Coastwatchers was poor so he requested Mackie keep his soldiers and just send him down some weapons, particularly a couple of Thompson submachine guns. Mackie would have none of it. The weapons came with the soldiers, he said, or not at all.

Mason and his men pushed their way along little-used tracks, avoiding villages where possible and sleeping in the jungle to avoid the Japanese patrols and the Black Dog gangs now spreading through the southern part of the island. At one stage, a patrol of eighty Japanese on bicycles came within a few hundred yards of Mason's campsite. While it was no longer possible to assume the loyalty of the native villagers, Mason was forever grateful that those from around Buin, where he had worked these many months, never betrayed him, even when threatened directly.

'When asked my location, they would point to the south and say, "Sydney, Sydney",' he would later recall with pride. Further north, he was finding it to be a very different story: '... with the help of the Kieta natives, the enemy had turned the local natives into treacherous servants of the Empire.'

Having made it as far as Mainuki in the very centre of Bougainville, Mason told his party to rest for a couple of days while he visited a Chinese friend, Wong Yu, at a village five hours away to gain some local information. Spending only a few hours with Wong Yu, Mason borrowed a blanket to sleep in the jungle but, not wishing to compromise his friend, left during the night, walking barefooted so as not to leave the telltale footprints of a European boot. In the darkness, he ripped the instep of his left foot on the needle-like barbs of the notorious wait-a-while vine. In searing pain, he struggled back into his boots, then managed to find shelter at the hut of another friend, gold miner Frank Roche, who had worked with Mason at his Inus plantation in what now seemed like another world: before the war.

When Mason pulled off his boots, the skin on his rapidly infecting foot came agonisingly away. Roche unhesitatingly put him up for several days so he had a chance to heal. Mason continually urged Roche to evacuate, but the old miner was loath to abandon his valuable equipment and believed he could continue to evade the Japanese. Limping away from Roche's hut, Mason turned to wave, sensing he would never see his friend again.

Just weeks later, Roche's hut was revealed to the Black Dog gangs who brought him to the Japanese. Frank Roche was tied up, dragged through the jungle and beheaded beside a river.

A month after fleeing his camp in the south, Mason having travelled the last part of the journey by native canoe, arrived at Lieutenant Mackie's AIF camp at Namatoa in the north of the island, where he was united with the remainder of his entourage whom he had left at Mainuki. Although congratulated heartily, Mason was appalled by the level of luxury the soldiers were enjoying, much of it apparently derived from the pilfering of the abandoned homes of planters. He even recognised some of his own furniture and other items scattered through the camp. More infuriating was the soldiers' sloppy habits, such as burning bright kerosene lamps at night, which could undoubtedly be seen for miles. It did nothing to repair Mason's view of the AIF soldiers.

A few days later, on 28 January 1943, Mason reached Jack Read's camp at Porapora, and the two Coastwatchers – who between them had achieved so much in confounding the enemy – met face to face for the first time in twelve months. As they related stories and compared notes and methods, a firm friendship was established.

Mason stayed with Read for a fortnight while his foot healed.

The AIF men had reached the end of their rope, and Lieutenant Mackie signalled Mackenzie at Guadalcanal to request they be evacuated. After months in the jungle, they were demoralised, physically spent, and of little further use to the Coastwatchers. In his somewhat jittery signal, Mackie concluded by saying he could '... accept no responsibility as to fate of section if nothing done. Acknowledge immediately.'

Mackenzie quietly sought Mason's and Read's opinions as to the state of the men. Mason was forthright, saying they should indeed be removed along with all the AIF soldiers as the lot of them, in his view, were useless as Coastwatchers in any case. Jack Read was more sympathetic, pointing out that, without the benefit of proper training, Lieutenant Mackie and his men had been operating in the harshness of the jungle without rest for eighteen months: 'It must be remembered that the capacity to endure the sort of existence under which we were forced to live can only be acquired by many years of experience in the tropics. People unaccustomed to this kind of life become somewhat awed with the jungle ...'

Eric Feldt even chipped in, stating that 'the soldiers, not salted to the climate as Read and Mason, were now weary and splenetic; in fact, a little "troppo"'. Feldt offered to send in a replacement detachment of new men, over which Read would be placed in overall command. Read readily accepted.

Another evacuation was organised, again from Teop Harbour, for the night of 28 March 1943, this time courtesy of the US submarine *Gato*, whose captain dispensed with the necessity of long ferry trips by closing to within 100 metres of the shore. Read once again oversaw the evacuation, in which fifty-one weary civilians, priests and nuns, as well as the remaining twelve original AIF commandos, were lifted off the beach to safety. Taking their places were fourteen fresh men of the newly formed M Special Unit who had at least been better trained for jungle conditions than their predecessors. Read also finally took the opportunity to send off the financial and banking records of the Buka and Kieta districts, which he had now been carrying with him for nearly a year.

These new soldiers, it was assumed by Feldt, would relieve Mason and Read after their year of continual operation in the jungle. But Mason and Read saw things differently and had no intention of leaving the island. Read instead saw the new men as the perfect opportunity to re-establish the Coastwatcher network in the southern part of Bougainville and on 1 May, he instructed Mason to return to Buin with a new party of police boys, scouts and native constables. He was also to take some of the new soldiers, who would travel down the coast independently and join him later. Mason complained loudly but his protests fell on deaf ears. Read's and Mason's views on the efficacy of the soldiers on Bougainville would continue to differ. As far as Read was concerned: 'I was most impressed by the physical standard and the keen enthusiasm of Lieut Bedkober and his men. They were fresh and eager for the job and they were actually a great tonic for us all.'

Mason was somewhat less complimentary: 'Besides a sapper, a private, and three careless signalmen, the Army lads included three sergeants – one in charge of the detachment, one in charge of supplies, and one who thought he should be in charge of everything.'

On their journey down from the north, he continued: '... these guys had been having a great time as they leisurely meandered along the coast. Under the sharp eyes of Japanese pilots, these raw troops had been joyriding in native canoes, tossing hand grenades in the water to catch fish and shooting their rifles for sport.'

Mason formed a far better opinion of some of the men's officers, particularly those who, like himself, had experienced the islands as government administrators. He was especially impressed with Lieutenant Doug Bedkober, as well as a former patrol officer, Lieutenant George Stevenson, from Brisbane, who had married just prior to his departure from Australia. Stevenson was a gifted leader who quickly galvanised his men with a fearless contempt of the Japanese. At one abandoned plantation he came across at Puruata, which had been ransacked by the enemy – Japanese characters had been scrawled on the walls, with *Keep Out* written in English. Stevenson, in large letters, inscribed a reply of his own: *Like Hell!*

Jack Read remained in the north of the island and, a few weeks later, oversaw another of the now regular submarine extractions which took away virtually the last of the Bougainville Chinese civilians and missionaries, including Bishop Wade, who Read now barely recognised since he was 'a broken man, mentally and physically: and he could not do otherwise than accede to my desire that he be evacuated.'

Read was glad to be rid of the civilians, but as the loyal army of native bearers filed away from the beach, he sensed their unease. For over a year they had been told the Americans were close and the Japanese would soon be expelled. But the only people fleeing were the planters, soldiers and missionaries. Perhaps Mr Tsunesuke Tashiro, that very clever Japanese officer, was correct when he explained to them the war was over and that Bougainville was now part of Nippon's great empire?

'The situation was deteriorating,' wrote Feldt, 'and everybody knew it.' Many of the natives were in an invidious position, threatened by both sides for cooperating with the other. As more and more of the island fell under the sway of Tashiro, his gangs, and the Japanese Army, the Coastwatchers began to live on borrowed time. To deter the native population from helping the enemy, strafing and bombing raids were carried out against villages known to have assisted the enemy, a foolish and poorly thought-out exercise which did more harm than good.

In the north, one Buka village known to have betrayed several loyal natives became too much for Read, who requested it be bombed as a deterrent. Feldt agreed and requested an RAAF Catalina to make the run. To ensure the correct village was targeted, some of the commandos, guided by several of Read's scouts, risked lighting fires to guide the Catalina in as the sound of its motors loomed out of the night. The raid caused a good deal of noise and flames, but – to Read and Mason's relief – just a single casualty, one slightly wounded native man. The village may have been deterred from supporting the Japanese, but the larger battle was one Read could not win.

The Japanese had their own methods of coercion, which were far more direct in their brutality. At one stage, the local Japanese commander ordered the chiefs of the area to his headquarters at Mosigetta and forced them to witness the execution of a number of natives who had helped Stevenson and his commandos. Demoralised and terrorised, the local people felt damned either way, but many now swayed to the Japanese side in fear of their lives.

Even as the island became lost to them, Mason and Read continued patrolling. By April, the Japanese had occupied large swathes of the east coast and established several more strongholds, using their troops recently evacuated from Guadalcanal for the purpose. Mason's scouts now reported the Japanese were patrolling everywhere, assisted by more and more natives.

In late June, Lieutenant Stevenson's camp at Dubonami at the foot of the Crown Prince Range of hills was attacked. With both paths leading to the small and isolated village well-guarded, the Japanese were guided by a sympathetic native to a third, unwatched path used only to spirit the village women and children to safety in times of strife.

In the middle of the afternoon, gunfire was heard, and Japanese in green fatigues burst into the camp from the unwatched 'women's path'. Stevenson and his party of AIF and natives were all taken by surprise. A firefight ensued, in which five Japanese were killed and the remainder eventually driven off, but Stevenson, whose shelter lay closest to the path, was felled with a bullet to the heart. At his side, the redoubtable Fijian Usaia Sotutu attempted to drag his body away, firing back at the enemy as he did, but the young officer was already dead.

After the Japanese had left, a group of Stevenson's native men caught the villager who had betrayed them. As Mason himself later recounted: 'As they escaped, they came across a native who had been organising for the Japs. The traitor begged for his life, saying that … the five Japs killed on the ridge were enough people for one day. My lads thought not and executed him on the spot.'

# Chapter 22
# THE LIEUTENANT

In almost pitch darkness, eleven men clung as best they could to what used to be their ship of war. It was no easy task. Slowly but surely, the angle of the deck was tilting. Soon, they presumed, it would topple over completely. What they were supposed to do then was anyone's guess. Their captain, a skinny 26-year-old sub-lieutenant, did his best to keep his crew's spirits up with small talk and bravado. Luck, he reassured them, was already on their side. Amazingly, eleven of the crew of thirteen had survived the impact of the collision with a Japanese destroyer, and almost all of them were in good shape. Not so for Pat McMahon, however. Although still dark, the lieutenant could tell the burns to McMahon's arms and legs were terrible. The fact that he wasn't uttering a sound somehow made it worse.

Hours earlier, McMahon hadn't even heard the lieutenant suddenly shout, 'Sound general quarters!' He'd been down in the noisy engine room, putting his hand on the manifolds to make sure they weren't overheating as the boat idled, then he'd opened one of the scoop controls to let a bit more seawater through the system to cool things down a little. He'd just pulled himself up over one of the engines to peer at a gauge, when a tremendous jolt threw him across the room against a bulkhead and onto the oily floor next to the auxiliary generator. Then, in disbelief, he watched a river of flame and water pouring towards him from the day room. In a lucid moment of foresight, he regretted having rolled up his dungarees, then felt the searing pain of heat as the flames stuck to the skin of his arms and legs.

Farewelling everything he had come to know in his short life, McMahon was suddenly plunged into darkness. A few seconds later, as the weight of the engines carried the aft section of the boat to the bottom with a grinding, tearing sound, he bobbed up to the surface like a released cork, gasping for air, trying to process the searing pain now coursing through his body, and wondering why his head felt like it was being crushed.

Charlie Harris was immediately beside him, talking to him, but still McMahon couldn't see a thing. His head was twisted and Harris's face was next to his, illuminated by a nearby sea of flame. Harris was grinning, holding up McMahon's helmet that had been jammed tight onto his head in the crash. Harris tossed it into the water.

Now the lieutenant was beside him too, talking, pulling him away, assuring him that he was alive, and commending him for not having removed his kapok life jacket, which had propelled him up through the water to life, as the rear of the boat fell away. Now the breeze, thank God, was dispersing the burning fuel from the wreckage. The lieutenant was right. Luck was on their side.

Another PT boat would soon be along to pick them up, the lieutenant said. But as the hours slipped by, even the lieutenant began to have doubts. Where was the rest of the flotilla? Surely they had seen the explosion and the fire? And why had that imbecile of a commanding officer, who had never once been out on a patrol himself, insisted on radio silence on a completely dark night when it was simply impossible to see anything at all?

The broken bow section, severed somewhere down there below the waterline, gave another lurch. Soon the men would have nothing to hold onto, and the lieutenant would have to make a decision.

Oh, the irony, he thought to himself; while the newspapers and the women adored the PT boats and their crews, the reality was starkly different. Though, come to think of it, he'd been fooled himself: the press stories of racing across the sea at 40 knots, dashing in among the enemy and letting loose a brace of torpedoes before disappearing again into the night, had been the very reason he'd pulled every string he knew – and those strings were considerable – to join the navy's PTs in the first place.

Perhaps if, like the Germans, the navy had built their PT boats with sturdy steel hulls, or as with the famous E-boats, equipped them with reliable diesel engines, they might have performed better. Instead, with the 80-foot, 40-ton Electric Launch Company ELCO Motor Torpedo Boats, the navy had shackled themselves to a dud.

Instead of diesels, PT boats were driven by three temperamental Packard 1350 horsepower engines which, when not broken down, guzzled highly inflammable 100-octane aviation fuel by the ton. More alarmingly, the boats' hulls were made not from welded steel, but plywood, which punctured easily from bullets and shrapnel easily igniting the 3000-gallon fuel tank inside, and for which no armour plate had been supplied. Armament consisted of little more than rifles and these were derided by their crews as *fifty calibres at fifty paces*. Even Japan's cheap and ubiquitous Daihatsu motorised barges performed better.

Despite warnings from US Navy trainers that PTs were unsuitable for night operations, in early 1943 they were thrown into the South Pacific in great numbers, charged with interdicting the nocturnal Japanese troop and supply runs of the Tokyo Express, a task for which they soon proved completely incapable.

'The glamour of the PTs just isn't, except to the outsider,' wrote the young lieutenant to his sister after a few months operating in the Russell Islands to the northwest of Guadalcanal. Night after night, they were sent out to find the Japanese destroyers in poorly coordinated operations in which the enemy was hardly ever found and almost never successfully attacked. In a twelve-day period in July, the lieutenant journeyed out on five separate patrols and failed to encounter a single Japanese vessel.

The boats themselves, however, often provided lurid targets for the enemy. On more than one occasion, a PT's deck-mounted torpedo tubes would catch fire, providing a beacon for the Japanese ship gunners, though bizarrely, the PTs' main nocturnal enemy was enemy floatplanes on their low-level night patrols. The Pacific waters around the Solomons produce a phosphorescence when disturbed by a churning motion – such as that of a ship – presenting any aerial observer with the glowing lines of a ship's wake. The Kawanishi pilots would sometimes just have to follow this to the apex and drop their bombs blind with a fair chance of hitting something. To avoid this, the captains would reduce power to a crawl, thereby negating the PT's primary feature, speed.

Nor were the PT crews respected by the remainder of the US naval establishment, who labelled them the *hooligan navy*, and limited the promotion path of their officers. One PT squadron commander later reflected that much of the navy regarded the PTs as a joke, and not a single wartime PT boat officer ever advanced to flag rank. A common joke among veterans was that the author of the famous book *They Were Expendable* ought to have penned a sequel, *They Were Useless*.

But the night of the lieutenant's near-demise – 1 August 1943 – was the PTs' greatest joke of all. Determined to replicate the tactics which had failed so demonstrably over the previous nineteen months of the war, but on a bigger scale, the commander of the PTs' most forward base on the island of Rendova in the New Georgia Group, Lieutenant-Commander Thomas Warfield, decided to send out every serviceable boat he could find in the largest – and the most forgettable – PT boat operation of the entire Solomons Campaign.

That day, a Japanese signal had been decoded, suggesting four destroyers of the Tokyo Express – *Hagikaze*, *Arashi*, *Shigure*, with *Amagiri* as escort – would be sailing at high speed down the southwest side of Kolombangara from Rabaul to resupply their forces at Vila. The fifteen PT boats Warfield had managed to muster would be divided into four groups, each with a group leader who would be the only boat equipped with radar. The groups were instructed to act as one, intercepting the Japanese destroyers at high speed and unleashing their four torpedoes in mass attacks that would overwhelm the Japanese ship defences. Although each PT boat used radio, Warfield, for reasons which have bewildered historians since, demanded that strict radio silence be observed throughout the entire operation except in an emergency.

At 6.30 p.m., just after sunset, the flotilla set out from Rendova into one of the blackest nights anyone could remember. Thick cloud blocked out the stars of an already moonless sky, and even an outstretched hand placed in front of one's face could barely be seen. Patrolling the waters of Blackett Strait, the boats spread out across the 5-mile channel between Kolombangara and the island of Gizo, lying in ambush for the Japanese ships expected later in the evening. Barely had the boats settled into their positions, however, when blips began to appear on the radar screens of the lead boats.

As the main Japanese destroyer force was not expected for several hours, it was assumed small motor barges were making their way down the channel and ripe for attack. So quickly did many of the lead boats open their throttles and roar off into the darkness, however, that the skippers of the remaining boats were caught unawares, with no idea where their leaders had just disappeared to.

Then, as the lead boats zeroed in on the 'blips', anticipating an easy kill, they were suddenly illuminated by a bank of powerful searchlights, and large shells began to explode around them in the water. Clearly these were no barges but the four destroyers, travelling at high speed, far earlier than anticipated, and catching the Americans completely off guard.

Hours of confusion ensued. The PT boats lost contact with each other and blindly let loose their torpedoes at a radar bearing alone. Most, though, had little idea of what was happening, and simply idled their engines or sailed in circles, oblivious to the location of friend and enemy alike. As the procession of destroyers passed by, the Japanese gunners opened fire, illuminating the night with bright orange flashes, but nobody could be certain of who was shooting at who. The chaos was compounded by another of Wakefield's peculiar orders: his instruction for the lead boats to return to base as soon as their torpedoes had been expended, leaving the remaining vessels – literally – in the dark. Of at least thirty torpedoes fired by the American PT boats that night not a single hit was registered.

•

In the early hours of the next day, 2 August, the lieutenant was running slowly towards the west with two other boats of his group a mile to either side. For him, too, the night had been confusing. He had long been left behind when his group leader, Lieutenant Brantingham, sped off suddenly into the night, and though he had observed gun flashes in the distance had no idea whether they emanated from ship or shore. Due to the radio silence, no word had reached him about the earlier action, nor could he know that some boats were already on their way home, or that there were Japanese ships in the vicinity.

Whenever he dared to send a signal to Rendova for advice, a brusque message came back, 'Keep patrolling'.

At 2.30 a.m., the lieutenant had reduced the PT boat to just one engine to avoid creating the telltale wake and to enable the crew to listen out for enemy vessels or, for that matter, friendly ones. One or two of his crew of thirteen were off duty and lying down wherever they could find a flat surface. In Charlie Harris's case, this was the nook between the day-room canopy and one of the starboard torpedo tubes. He had taken off his life jacket and was using it as a pillow. William Johnston was likewise snoozing near the engine room hatch and Andrew Kirksey was resting on the starboard deck aft. In the forward gun turret, Harry Marney – known for his excellent night vision – was more alert, peering into the darkness. The lieutenant had the helm in the small wheelhouse as he chatted softly with the radio man. Up front was Barney Ross, who had joined the crew at the last minute as a spare. He peered over the bow, right next to the 37-millimetre anti-tank gun which the lieutenant had snaffled from some army friends and lashed to the deck to give the boat some extra firepower.

Little could be made out in the gloom, but, if anything was expected, it was more likely another friendly PT boat. So quietly was the boat moving that Barney Ross heard nothing but the breeze and the gentle slap of the sea against the hull, and imagined he was sailing.

Then, 'Ship at two o'clock!' shouted Harry Marney. All looked to starboard. Blacker than the black night, the outline of a ship's bow could be seen, bearing down at great speed, a pale glow of phosphorescence betraying its passage straight towards them through the water. In the dark, the scale of the scene was deceptive, and for a few vital, irretrievable seconds, the lieutenant believed it to be a fellow PT boat. A mile or so away, two other boats had seen the silhouette of the Japanese ship as well. One later claimed to have sent out a radio alert, but no such warning was received.

'Sound general quarters!' called the lieutenant when he realised what it was. Spinning the wheel around, he tried to manoeuvre, but the lag in the idling engines condemned the boat to remain virtually stationary. Seconds ticked by. One of the men attempted to ready the torpedoes, but even had he managed to do so, they were incorrectly fused for such a short distance, and would have failed to detonate had they been fired.

Then the great steel bow of the Japanese destroyer *Amagiri*, the last of four ships returning to Rabaul from their supply run to Vila, and aiming to ram the Americans, loomed over the little wooden vessel. No one onboard would ever forget the sound of wrenching metal and splintering timber as it slammed into the boat's starboard side, slicing diagonally a few feet behind the wheelhouse. Harry Marney took the full impact in the turret, along with the prone Andrew Kirksey behind him. Both men were crushed to death instantly, their bodies never recovered.

The boat spun violently with the impact and, in the wheelhouse, the lieutenant was flung against a rear bulkhead. Helpless, he looked directly up as a moving wall of steel passed him barely inches away, followed by the low raked outline of a funnel. *This is how it feels to be killed*, he thought. Then it was gone. Like a knife, the 1700-ton *Amagiri*'s bow had sheared off the entire rear section of the boat, somehow spewing out Pat McMahon as it did so.

Towards the stern, Ray Starkey was flung clean out of the boat and into the water. At the bow, Barney Ross grabbed onto the 37-millimetre gun as the boat rolled over to the right. 'It was like what I imagine it would be like to be hit by a train,' he would later recall.

A mile or so off in the darkness, the skipper of another PT boat witnessed the explosion and heard the awful tearing sound of the collision. All he could do was bury his face in his hands and sob, 'My God, my God!'

The ship's fuel tanks were torn open; flames erupted everywhere as the crew leaped over the side or were washed into the sea. Some remembered the sound of excited Japanese voices on the deck of the destroyer as it passed above their heads. Just as quickly, it had disappeared back into the invisible night. Instinctively, all swam away from the blazing wreck until the lieutenant pulled them up with a shout. The wind, he could see, was blowing the fire away from them, and something was still afloat. He urged all his men to swim towards it.

Men called for each other by name, some diving into the black water to tow a shocked crewmate back to the wreck. Ensign Lenny Thom, a friendly blond-headed giant of a man who had been a champion college athlete, made several trips to retrieve his disorientated crewmates. Clambering onto the crazily tilting bow section, they braced their feet against anything they could find to stay upright. The lieutenant did a headcount. McMahon was terribly burned, but otherwise eleven men out of a crew of thirteen had miraculously survived, essentially unharmed, although William Johnston had to be pulled in, having ingested some of the petrol floating on the water and sick with the fumes. All that could be done now was to sit in the darkness, and wait.

Hours passed, and still the longed-for sound of an approaching PT boat eluded them. The lieutenant was disbelieving. Was it possible the rest of the squadron had not seen the explosion? Had they really turned around and headed back to the base, without even attempting a rescue? He recalled that no plan, no contingency, had been discussed regarding the rescue of survivors. Slowly, the lieutenant accepted the reality that they were alone – probably already written off as dead. As the darkness faded, he knew the day would bring an entirely new set of problems.

The men of PT-109 were not alone, however. Although they had no way of yet knowing it, on a hill barely 3 miles away they were being watched, and the seeds of the rescue had already been planted.

•

Arthur Reginald 'Reg' Evans, in his own words, grew up 'sea-minded and ship crazy', and so felt destined to join the navy. The moment he was old enough, Evans applied to join the cadet course at the Royal Australian Naval College at Jervis Bay, and was promptly rejected. The reasons were never explained, but Evans suspected his lowly state school education and humble upbringing in the outer suburbs of Sydney might have played a part. As these were things he could never change, Evans saw no point in reapplying so joined the army cadets, then his local militia, and became a lieutenant. Army life never really suited him though and, still pining for the ocean, in 1929, aged twenty-four, he left Australia for the exotic New Hebrides, to work as assistant manager of a coconut plantation. It would prove the beginning of a love affair with the Pacific Islands that would endure his entire life.

When the property changed hands a year or so later, Evans was made redundant and returned to Sydney. He walked into the Burns, Philp head office in Bridge Street and immediately pestered for another job. A quiet but engaging man with a memorable smile, his persistence paid off, and he was dispatched to the Solomons, working for the next ten years in a variety of managerial roles. It was on the inter-island trader *Manutu* that Evans 'got to know the islands like an old friend'.

When World War II began, Evans was certain his knowledge and experience would see his beloved navy come begging for his services. Once again he applied to join the RAN, and once again he was knocked back. Dejected, Evans again signed up for the army and sailed to the Middle East to take part in the Syrian Campaign just as it came to an abrupt halt in July 1941. When Japan entered the war in December, his regiment was hastily brought back to Australia. By this time, inter-service transfers had become possible and, unable to bear the army a day longer, Evans yet again applied for the navy. 'They weren't so fussy this time,' he later reflected and – third time lucky – he was accepted.

A few weeks later, scanning the list of the navy's newest additions, the finger of Walter Brooksbank, the Coastwatcher pioneer and assistant to Australia's intelligence chief 'Cocky' Long, stopped at the name of Reg Evans. 'They knew more about my background than I did,' said Evans when brought in to be interviewed for an organisation so secret he could not even be properly informed as to its purpose. After a year in the dust of the Middle East, the promise of a return to his beloved islands was enough to make him sign the bottom of the form and join the mysterious Coastwatchers.

By February 1943, the only island Evans had seen very much of was Guadalcanal, where he worked in the headquarters of Hugh Mackenzie, learning the basics of the Coastwatcher craft. He might have spent the remainder of the war there had intelligence not revealed the Japanese were constructing a landing strip at the old Vila coconut plantation on the southern tip of the island of Kolombangara in the northern part of the Solomons. This was alarming, as it was most likely intended as a satellite strip for the larger Japanese base across the Blackett Strait at Munda on the southwest tip of New Georgia.

At Munda, the enemy's trick of screening their workers from the air with the severed and suspended crowns of coconut trees had worked completely, and the Allies were determined not to be so fooled again. A new Coastwatching station on Kolombangara was considered essential, and Reg Evans was given the job. He was more than ready for the challenge. In March 1943, Evans was flown to Don Kennedy's Segi headquarters, where he was further briefed, and he recruited a native oarsman and interpreter, Malanga, who took him the remaining 80-odd miles by canoe to Kolombangara, one of the most breathtaking islands in the entire Solomons. 'Think of an olive green pyramid thrusting high out of the sea,' recounted Evans years later, 'twenty-five miles round, and covered with jungle.'

But Evans had not been sent to enjoy the scenery. Travelling northwest in stages from Segi, and hoisting a sail to take advantage of the night breezes, he and Malanga passed so close to the Japanese base at Munda that the sound of trucks and vehicles working in virtual darkness to avoid Allied air attack could clearly be heard.

Arriving on the south coast of Kolombangara on 21 March, Evans was surprised by the large reception laid on by the island's venerable hereditary Chief Rovu, who not only welcomed Evans warmly but, to his surprise, promptly nominated himself as his second-in-command. As encouraging as this was, what Evans needed was knowledge of the island's interior and he was perplexed to discover that almost all

Kolombangara's 500 inhabitants were beach-dwellers crammed into the southwest coast. Almost all knew as little about the interior as Evans did. And while they had seen the occasional ship, they would be unable to tell a local trading steamer from a battleship.

While Evans was familiar with none of the Kolombangara natives, they all seemed to know him from before the war, and their cooperation would prove vital in the months ahead. 'They were in my corner from the start,' he would say. 'I had their goodwill.'

Under the direction of the one man who did know every rock of the island, the sixty-year-old Chief Rovu, a hut was established near Kolombangara's 1500-foot volcanic peak of Mount Veve, from where Evans could observe all the sea approaches and keep an eye on the 10000-man Japanese garrison on the island's only flat land at the Vila plantation.

From his lonely hilltop, every move of the surrounding enemy was observed and, in a few weeks, so thoroughly had Evans instructed his team of enthusiastic scouts in the minutiae of Japanese military materiel that they could soon discern enemy ships and barges, guns and aircraft type with reliable accuracy. Every piece of information gleaned was then sent by Teleradio straight to Henderson Field, an hour away by air, giving the Americans just enough time to prepare their defence.

'We had [the Japanese] dry-gulched,' Evans later said. 'They might as well have been heading into an ambush.' More than once, as he peered down at the enemy garrison, it occurred to him that he was the only Allied military personnel on an island with thousands of armed Japanese soldiers living what seemed a very short way down the hill.

One night six weeks into his mission, Evans was awakened at 3 a.m. by the sound of explosions from the direction of the sea. Unable to see anything, he slept on till dawn when the astonishing sight was revealed of one sinking Japanese destroyer, two others ablaze, and an undamaged fourth busily picking up survivors – all just a few miles from his post. During the night, the ships, on their nightly supply run down The Slot, had slammed straight into a recently laid marine minefield. So close was Evans that he barely needed the use of his binoculars to observe the scene.

An urgent message was sent to Guadalcanal, a little over 200 miles away. A short time later, the drone of aircraft engines was heard from the south, and Evans watched nineteen Dauntless dive-bombers make short work of the helpless destroyers, sending all four to the bottom in what seemed like minutes, before they wheeled around and headed home.

'It was grim,' he later said, 'but it was the job.'

On this same day, as it happened, Evans, to his surprise, was joined by an assistant. Having built up an efficient system with the locals on Kolombangara, Evans would have been quite happy to remain operating on his own, but larger forces were in play. The retaking of New Georgia, an operation codenamed 'Toenails', was in the advanced stages of planning, and was to begin with a large amphibious landing to take the Japanese airstrip at Munda. Evans's position nearby at Kolombangara would be close to the epicentre of battle, and more than one operator would be needed to observe the expected Japanese build-up and counterattack.

The choice of Evans's assistant was an unusual one in Corporal Benjamin Franklin Nash – one of the small number of Americans to join the Coastwatchers' ranks. Feldt lists two dozen or so US personnel as having worked for his organisation, but most of these never left the headquarters at Henderson Field. In early 1943, Nash – a tall Colorado cattle man – belonged to an Airfield Signals Unit but longed to be closer to the action, so he lobbied Mackenzie personally to join the Coastwatchers, who by now were acquiring almost superhuman status among the Americans. Mackenzie agreed, and without even waiting for his transfer to go through, Nash – as he would say after the war – 'sort of deserted'.

Corporal Nash's arrival at Kolombangara just as the Japanese began to strengthen their base at Vila for the coming showdown on New Georgia was timely. Enemy sea traffic was increasing, and Evans knew that much of it to the west and south was being missed. He therefore proposed relocating to the tiny island of Gomu between Kolombangara and Wana Wana 10 miles further west, while Nash remained on Kolombangara.

On the night of 1 August, while still awaiting the confirmation of the relocation to Gomu, Evans and Nash sat mesmerised at their high observation post on Mount Veve, grappling to understand what they were looking at. To the southwest, another series of intermittent gun flashes lit up the pitch-black night. It had been going on like this now for a couple of hours, more like a drawn-out skirmish than the short, sharp action of an actual battle. Then, at around 2.30, both gasped as a sudden flash erupted, followed by a pillar of fire which rose to over 100 feet before subsiding to the water. Evans tried to focus his binoculars then made his way to a telescope mounted on a tree. 'I thought I saw the wreckage of a boat and figures moving on it,' he would later recount, 'but in the darkness it was too far away to see properly, and I thought I was only imagining the figures.'

At first light after a few hours' sleep, Evans was back at the observation post and could just make out a distant object floating in Blackett Strait. Firing up the Teleradio, he reported the sighting to Guadalcanal, suggesting it might be the remains of a Japanese barge.

Whether through bad communication or simple dim-wittedness, the receivers at Henderson failed to correlate Evans's sighting to their now missing navy PT boat. Only at 9.30 did they think to inform Evans that one of their boats had failed to return from last night's operation conducted on his very doorstep.

PT BOAT ONE OWE NINE LOST IN ACTION IN BLACKETT STRAIT TWO MILES SW MERESU COVE. CREW OF TWELVE. REQUEST ANY INFORMATION.

In fact, the navy's number of missing crew members was one short, as they were yet unaware that Barney Ross had only joined the lieutenant at the last minute when his boat was pulling away from the dock.

Evans read the message and cursed before swinging into action. Some nagging voice had told him that the mysterious black object – which he could still just make out through his glasses – was important. He immediately dispatched all his native scouts to begin scouring the area in a search for survivors. Some went straight out to the larger island of Gizo, while others searched the beaches closer to Kolombangara. No sailors – American or otherwise – encountered, but several spent and lethally primed torpedoes were found washed up around the beaches.

By early in the afternoon, the wreckage had slipped from Evans's sight.

•

The legend of Sub-lieutenant John Fitzgerald Kennedy and his crew of PT-109 and their week-long saga of survival in the remote Solomon Islands has been recounted in books and even a Hollywood film, and forms an enduring part of the myth of the brilliant, flawed and complex 35th President of the United States. The exact details of the saga, however, are infinitely variable, and no two of the myriad accounts ever appear to be precisely the same. While briefly grabbing headlines at the time, the story then became lost for nearly twenty years, only to be exhumed to bolster JFK's political capital against rival Hubert Humphrey in the 1960 Democratic Party presidential primaries. Lagging considerably in the polls for the important West Virginia race, the revelation of Kennedy's forgotten wartime heroism erupted in dazzling brilliance beside Humphrey's unexciting – though wholly legitimate – medical exemption from war service due to colour blindness and a double hernia.

Political machinations aside, little can detract from Kennedy's unquestionable bravery, superb leadership, dedication to his men, and the almost superhuman energy he conjured the moment his vessel was struck and severed in two by the Japanese destroyer *Amagiri* on the night of 1 August 1943.

Still clinging to the upturned bow in the early afternoon of 2 August, Kennedy had all but given up hope of an immediate rescue, and now faced the real possibility of being seen by the Japanese, or else being pulled by the tide towards their base on New Georgia, or directly out to sea. In any case, the watertight compartments keeping the piece of the boat upright were beginning to fail, and it would soon turn turtle in the water. Spotting an island several miles off which appeared too small for a Japanese outpost but large enough on which to hide, Kennedy pointed and announced, 'We've got to swim to that.' Grabbing various pieces of flotsam, some men kicked their feet behind an 8-foot wooden plank, while Kennedy held a strap of the life jacket of the badly burned McMahon in his teeth and towed him, swimming breaststroke, non-stop for four hours.

A reconnaissance aircraft was in fact dispatched from Henderson to search for PT-109, but, inexplicably, did not take off until nearly dark. Its New Zealand aircrew managed to spot the bow section, but Kennedy and his crew were long gone.

With barely enough energy to stagger up the sand from the shoreline, Kennedy's eleven men collapsed onto the beach on what turned out to be Plum Pudding Island, a speck of sand devoid of anything save a few coconut trees. There was not a drop of fresh water to be found. As the men hid in the jungle and found what they could to settle in for the night, Kennedy donned his life jacket once more and swam back out to a channel known as Ferguson Passage, holding a battle lantern, hoping to flag down a patrolling PT boat as if hailing a taxi on a busy street corner. His efforts, along with his numerous subsequent attempts, would be wasted, as just that day the PTs' patrolling routes had changed to the north, and none came his way.

With his men surviving as best they could on green coconuts and rainwater caught in leaves, Kennedy on 4 August led them back into the water to another island named Olasana, a half-mile distant, where coconuts appeared more abundant. From there, Kennedy set off with Barney Ross to reconnoitre yet another island, Naru, a further mile distant. As they walked the beach here, they came upon a large tin marked with Japanese writing and containing – to their enormous relief – boiled sweets and hard crackers. Further along, a concealed canoe and 50-gallon drum of fresh water were found, one of the several emergency stashes secreted by Reg Evans and his scouts in the area.

As Kennedy and Ross prepared to depart with their booty back to the men still over at Olasana, they noticed a wrecked Japanese vessel just offshore high on a reef. As they approached it, two natives emerged from its interior. On sighting each other, all four men were startled and, as if in a comedy, fled in opposite directions into the scrub.

Biuku Gasa and Eroni Kumana, two of Reg Evans's most trusted scouts – both trained by the British in search and detection – had been patrolling the islands for two days as per his instructions, searching for any sign of survivors from the wreck of the American boat. So far, they had found nothing. Passing Naru one afternoon, they noticed the wreck of a previously unexplored Japanese barge wedged on the coral. Tying up their large dugout canoe close by, they salvaged a little fuel before satisfying themselves the wreck's interior would yield little more of interest. As they clambered out, they were startled by two rather wild-looking white men staring at them from the beach. Convinced they must be Japanese, Gasa and Kumana leaped into the jungle, then doubled back to their canoe and paddled off at speed.

Kennedy and Ross, somehow managing to convince themselves the natives were Japanese spies, likewise retreated, hastily scrambling into the bushes. Ross remained on the island that night while Kennedy returned to his men over at Olasana in the canoe with the water and Japanese rations, only to discover the same two native 'spies' had arrived ahead of him, and were now happily conversing in sign language with his men. Paddling up to Olasana, Gasa and Kumana had initially believed this larger group must also be Japanese and began to paddle away when Ensign Thom had the inspiration to point skywards shouting, 'White star, white star!' Hearing the description of the marking common to all American aircraft, the two men were convinced and came ashore. The first news they imparted was of the two dangerous Japanese spies they had just seen over on Naru, and that the Americans should be beware.

After Kennedy arrived all remaining confusion was cleared up. The next morning, 6 August, the two scouts paddled him back to Naru to retrieve Ross who, amazingly, was collected en route in the sea, making his own way back to Olasana.

Back on Olasana, Kennedy had an idea. Pointing to the distant mountainous peak of Rendova 38 miles to the southeast, he communicated his desire for Gasa and Kumana to sail to the Americans there and raise the alarm. Speaking almost no English, the two men eventually comprehended what was being asked of them and nodded in agreement.

Thom then wrote out a detailed note on a blank Burns, Philp invoice he had found on the beach with a pencil stub one of the sailors happened to have in his pocket. Kennedy looked it over and approved, but Gasa seemed concerned the flimsy paper would not survive the journey. Kumana agreed and immediately climbed an adjacent coconut tree and picked one. Cleaving the hard outer husk, he handed it to Kennedy and indicated he should scratch a note on it. Nodding in appreciation at the genius of the idea, Kennedy pulled out his penknife and went to work:

NAURO ISL
COMMANDER ... NATIVE KNOWS POS'IT
HE CAN PILOT ... 11 ALIVE
NEED SMALL BOAT ... KENNEDY

With both notes preciously secured in the canoe, Gasa and Kumana solemnly shook each man's hand, then pushed their boat into the water and departed into the dusk, carrying the hopes of eleven desperate men with them. In silence, the crew watched them paddle away until the light faded completely. For what it was worth, Kennedy and Ross then decided to once more try their luck in flagging down a PT boat out in Ferguson Passage. Again, they were unsuccessful, and a wave eventually overturned their canoe onto a reef. They were lucky to make it back to Naru, utterly exhausted.

Gasa and Kumana meanwhile paddled steadily through the night, but detoured to Wana Wana Island, where they made contact with Reg Evans's principal scout, Benjamin Kevu, a man whose English was not only perfect but delivered in a finely clipped British accent. Amazed by the news of the survivors, he encouraged the two scouts to continue their fifteen-hour journey to Rendova posthaste, while Kevu sent another man to inform Evans, who had just arrived at his new post on the little island of Gomu. Evans finally learned, around 11 p.m. on 6 August, that eleven Americans were alive on an island between Gizo and Ferguson Passage. Consulting his charts, he concluded – incorrectly – the island to be Naru, sometimes known as Gross Island.

Events now moved quickly. At first light, Evans requested Kevu organise a strong team of six paddlers in a large war canoe to bring provisions and a note to the men on Naru. Then, tuning his Teleradio, he tapped out the incredible news to Guadalcanal, who quickly relayed it to the stunned Americans at Rendova:

ELEVEN SURVIVORS PT BOAT ON GROSS IS. HAVE SENT FOOD AND LETTER ADVISING SENIOR COME HERE WITHOUT DELAY. WARN AVIATION OF CANOE CROSSING FERGUSON.

Kevu and his team made fast work of Ferguson Passage, but quickly realised Evans's error. No one was on tiny Naru Island so they instead paddled the half-mile over to Olasana. Here too, however, they found no one. Heading inland, it took two hours to eventually locate Kennedy and his men hiding in a jungle clearing. All stood in surprise as Kevu strode confidently up to Kennedy.

'I have a letter for you, sir,' said Kevu calmly in his perfect English.

Kennedy, half-naked, bearded and haggard, his hair matted, sunburned skin cut all over with festering coral wounds, who had not smiled in a week, now broke into a wide grin as Kevu handed him a crisp white envelope marked 'On His Majesty's Service'. Evans's note began:

To Senior Officer, Gross Is.
Friday, 11 pm. Have just learned of your presence on Gross Is. and also that two natives have taken news to Rendova. I strongly advise you return immediately to here in this canoe and by the time you arrive here I will be in radio communication with authorities at Rendova and we can finalise plans to collect balance of your party.
A R Evans Sub-Lt.
RANVR
Will warn aviation of your crossing Ferguson Passage.

Back on the beach, Kevu's men prepared the first meal the crew of PT-109 had eaten in a week, consisting of yams, roast beef and potatoes. In no time, they had also constructed – from branches and leaves – a shaded lean-to for the badly burned McMahon.

By mid-afternoon, Kennedy was once more in a canoe, being paddled to Gomu to meet Reg Evans, assuring the remaining men that he would soon be back to rescue them. Kevu insisted Kennedy conceal himself at the bottom of the boat under a bed of palm fronds – a wise move, as halfway across the strait, several Japanese aircraft appeared and began circling low overhead. From under his screen of fronds, Kennedy asked if he could poke his head out and take a look. Kevu firmly told him to stay where he was, then stood up in the canoe and gave the Japanese pilots a friendly wave. Convinced they were looking at nothing more than some local fishermen, they flew away. Kevu and his men began to sing hymns in thanks.

At 6 p.m., the little boat pulled up at the beach on Gomu. Emerging from under the foliage, Kennedy was greeted by a smiling and besuited man, and could think of nothing to say other than, 'Man, am I glad to see you.' Evans smiled again. 'And I'm bloody glad to see you too,' he said. 'Come to my tent and have a cup of tea.'

Meanwhile, Gasa and Kumana had braved Japanese-infested waters to paddle through the night to Rendova, where they handed both Kennedy's coconut and Thom's note to the American authorities, confirming the information received from Reg Evans.

At 11.20 that night, more than an hour past the agreed pick-up time, Kennedy heard the approach of engines, and the bow of PT-157 loomed into view.

'Hey, Jack!' called a familiar voice from the deck.

'Where the hell you been?' Kennedy gruffly replied.

Onboard were Gasa and Kumana, who had faultlessly guided the boat from Rendova.

A short time later, exactly a week since the night of the collision, PT-157 poked its way cautiously through the reef surrounding Olasana Island. Kennedy waded ashore and called out but no reply was heard. A moment of horror passed over him as the prospects of the Japanese having arrived before him crossed his mind. Then he heard the stirring of the first of his astonished men, all of whom had been sound asleep.

●

Jack's illustrious father, Joseph Kennedy, made sure his son's heroics were in the headlines, and for his efforts the navy awarded the young lieutenant both the Navy and Marine Corps

Medal and the Purple Heart. He is still the only US president to be so awarded. Perhaps the most significant moment of his life came a year later, however, when his older brother, Joseph Junior – in whom the Kennedys' hopes and ambitions truly lay – was killed in Europe flying a B-24 Liberator bomber. Now, it would be the younger brother who would take up the mantle to forge both his own history and one of the great chapters of the twentieth century.

After becoming president in 1960, JFK reclaimed the heroics of his youth and would adore retelling the story of the crew of PT-109 and their amazing week of survival to anyone who wished to hear it. He particularly loved to screen the Hollywood movie of the story to his White House guests, loudly pointing out the many exaggerations and inaccuracies.

Due to the restrictions on revealing Coastwatchers' identities, Reg Evans's name was not recorded in the initial flurry of press around the PT-109 story. Only seventeen years later, upon Kennedy's ascension to the presidency, when Evans himself – now a quiet accountant working in an office in Sydney – sent a congratulatory card to the new president, was his identity revealed. JFK, delighted by the discovery, immediately invited Evans to visit the White House, and on 1 May 1961, they met once again in a much-publicised reunion.

Biuku Gasa and Eroni Kumana, the two devoted Melanesian scouts who had arguably done more than any to secure the rescue, were also invited to visit the United States. The Solomons governor, however, blocked the application, citing their English as being too poor. Another opportunity was extended later, but this was cut short by larger historical events. Upon hearing the news of Kennedy's assassination, Biuku and Eroni were overwhelmed with sadness, having carried the story of their meeting with the young lieutenant on a lonely island of the Solomons their entire lives.

## Chapter 23
# THE END ON BOUGAINVILLE

With the keenly felt loss of Lieutenant George Stevenson, combined with attacks on other camps, the situation for Coastwatchers in Bougainville was fast approaching untenable. Read reflected: 'Weighing up the position of the whole of our parties, it was apparent that effective coast-watching in Bougainville had at last reached the end of its tether. We had enjoyed a pretty good innings over a far longer period than one would have ever thought possible.'

On 25 June, Read signalled Mackenzie at Guadalcanal:

My duty to now report that position here vitally serious. After fifteen months occupation almost whole island pro-Japanese. Initial enemy patrols plus hordes pro-Japanese natives have completely disorganised us. Position will not ease. Believe no hope reorganised. Our intelligence value nil in last fortnight. All parties have been either attacked or forced to quit. Reluctantly urge immediate evacuation.

The signal was passed to headquarters in Brisbane, and the decision was made to withdraw all the Bougainville

Coastwatchers. Read, in the north, was already close to the evacuation beaches, but Mason, still in the central south at his new camp near a hill called Mom, was over 80 miles away. Once again, he was ordered to pack up, turn around and head north.

His destination was Kereaka in the island's northwest. Here, he would meet up with a detachment of commandos led by a Sergeant McPhee, where further arrangements would be made for a final evacuation. He was also warned that the Japanese were becoming more numerous, and more desperate, and to be careful.

Then, as if the gods themselves were conspiring against the Coastwatchers, the organisation's two most pivotal figures were suddenly removed from the picture. On Guadalcanal, the indefatigable Hugh Mackenzie, running the network from his bunker on a now secure Henderson Field, was struck down with the dreaded malarial complication blackwater fever. After hovering close to death for a week, he was forced into an extended recuperation.

At almost the same time, Eric Feldt, upon completing a successful tour of Guadalcanal, was preparing to fly out to Malaita when seized by terrible chest pain, and treated by the US Army. Lying in his hospital bed in Tulagi, he read the words *coronary thrombosis* the doctor had written on his chart and knew his service with the Coastwatchers was over.

Having exhausted his energy in building up the network from virtual scratch at the beginning of the war, then enduring the gnawing stress of long periods of silence as he sent Coastwatchers into the jungle, followed in many cases by the grief of their deaths at the hands of the enemy, Feldt's constitution proved itself human after all.

Paul Mason's final trek north would unfold into a nightmare odyssey with the enemy constantly in pursuit, and death and danger faced at every turn of the endlessly winding jungle tracks. Having initially resented the order to again pack up and withdraw north, he soon understood why it had been given. Reports and evidence of Japanese patrols were everywhere. Experienced as Mason was, even he was shocked at the speed with which the enemy now moved into areas they had previously left untouched. Sometimes they were in front of him, sometimes just hours to the rear. At every step, he prepared to encounter them around the very next bend.

As his loyal scouts and police boys probed ahead, the news came back that all his previous routes to the north were now blocked with Japanese, or natives in their service. He had no choice but to head into the higher – unimaginably rough – country to the island's west, 'a place', writes author Walter Lord, 'of gorges that seemed made for ambush, paths almost lost in lawyervine, chilling ridges and steaming swamps'.

To make matters more difficult, his party, enlarged by the remnants of Stevenson's scattered company, as well as a number of natives known to have helped the Allies and who now feared for their lives, had swelled to an unwieldy fifty. Nevertheless, a path was found and followed for a day without incident. In the centre of the group, the precious Teleradio was carried in its various components, ready to be hidden in the jungle if attacked. With the Japanese and their radio-direction-finding equipment so close, the idea of using it was now out of the question. Mason was totally cut off.

On the second day, 29 June, just as Mason had begun to dare hope that the track might take them all the way to McPhee's men, they crossed a gorge below a village at Meridau, disturbing a number of patrolling Japanese soldiers camped there. The Japanese quickly opened fire with rifle and machine gun. Shepherding the men off the track, Mason directed fire upwards into a native hut and the machine gun abruptly stopped. Suddenly, four Japanese came charging down the hill. One of them was killed by a single shot from a native policeman, but some of Mason's carriers bolted, abandoning their gear. Making a firing withdrawal, Mason cut down to a stream, then led the way along the creek bed to avoid leaving footprints, following it into a deep gorge, in which they were forced to spend a wet and miserable night. To his disgust, much of the gear, including the rations box which had to last the entire party three weeks, had been abandoned along the track. This thankfully was recovered, but most of the components of the Teleradio were lost forever, rendering Mason silent for the first time in over a year.

Even some of the soldiers had fled into the nearby jungle, including a fearsome, one-eyed sergeant who, despite having a skull and crossbones tattooed across his chest, had abandoned his pack and hidden as soon as the firing had started. 'Of such stuff were these soldiers made,' Mason later lamented. The sergeant later quietly found his way back to the group, apparently having left much of his bravado in the jungle.

After a miserable night spent in the open in pouring rain, Mason's party – which now comprised eight soldiers, Usaia Sotutu, six police boys and a dozen native carriers – pushed ahead at first light and were untroubled the rest of that day, even managing to scrounge a meal of taro from a native garden. The following morning they were stopped at the far end of the gorge adjacent to a village by three native sentries apparently looking out for them. Mason crept forward and managed to grab two of the boys, who turned out to be brothers, telling one to go and inform his village that his brother would be 'treated as a Japanese spy' unless Mason and his men were allowed to pass unmolested. The ploy worked and, to the sound of women wailing, Mason led his hostage past the village, releasing him unharmed once they were out of sight. Far from shaken by the ordeal, the young lad volunteered to remain with Mason as a guide for the next two days.

At the beginning of a valley, Mason again came under fire from a Japanese ambush, but his men fired back and held them off while yet again slipping through the net, unharmed. When Mason conducted a headcount, however, a further ten had fled. Another dismal night was spent in the rainy jungle. Mason ordered the column to continue and led the way with a luminous compass, instructing each man to attach a piece of phosphorescent moss to his body so the man behind could keep contact in the dark. Pushing ever onwards, they discovered a native garden, and having not eaten for thirty-six hours, fell upon a crop of taro, even risking a small fire to cook it, choosing possible discovery by the enemy over certain collapse from starvation.

By the second day of July, Mason and his men had reached the island's main east–west track, which he knew would be heavily patrolled by the Japanese. At one point, a single soldier emerged from a smaller path directly in front of them not more than 30 yards ahead.

'Until that moment,' he recalled, 'I had not realised how near we were to the main trail. Some of the troops foolishly ducked, but I remained immobile until the Jap passed.'

Mason could not be sure if they had been seen, but erred on the side of caution and ordered the march to continue through the night.

Every ounce of Mason's energy was now directed to simple survival. Scouts constantly ran ahead to locate the Japanese and report back. Sometimes the enemy was just an hour behind him, or camped over a ridge or on the other side of an escarpment. Not once did they manage to pinpoint Mason and his party.

Native gardens were raided for a few vegetables, but everyone was constantly hungry and what little that could be

314 • AUSTRALIA'S SECRET ARMY

found was insufficient to sustain the men for the journey. Every man particularly craved salt.

Climbing higher, the grade became almost vertical and their bodies were torn by the savage barbs of the ubiquitous wait-a-while vine. When night fell, they rested high on a ledge in the cliff, scooping out a step to prevent themselves from rolling off. The cold was bitter. Far below, Mason could see the fires from a Japanese camp.

On 6 July, they were lucky enough to find a couple of pigs to slaughter and cook, enjoying their most substantial food in weeks. While replenishing their exhausted bodies on roast pig, one of Mason's missing carriers caught up with him, brandishing a note given to him by another native, purportedly written by the local Japanese commander:

MY DEAR ANSACS
WE JAPANESE TROOPS ADMIRE FOR YOUR BRAVE ACTS. YOU HAVE ALL DONE YOUR BEST FOR THE GLORY OF GREAT BRITON.

BUT YOU ARE NOW SURROUNDED BY OUR ARMY TROOPS ANYWHERE YOU GO, YOU WILL SEE THE EYE OF WATCHING. YOU HAVE DROPPED IN TRAPS LAID BY US. ALL THE SMALL ROAD AND JUNGLE ARE NOW WATCHING BY OUR SOLDIERS AND THE MORE SHARPER EYE OF THE NATIVES. ALL YOUR ATTEMPTS TO RUN AWAY OR TO GO IN TOGETHER WITH OTHER YOUR TROOPS IN BUKA ARE IN VAIN.

NOW YOU CAN ONLY WAITING DEATH OF HUNERY IN THE JUNGLE. NOW SOME OF YOUR CAMERADS HAS BEEN SACRIFICED AND CAUGHT BY US. YOU MAY FEAR FOR CRUELLY OF JAPANESE TROOPS BUT WE ARE NOT CRUEL.

THIS IS PROVAGANDA OF U.S.A. OFTEN SPEAK
ILL OF US. WE DARE ADVICE YOU – SURRENDER
TO US!! COME TO US AND YOUR ALIVES SHALL
BE KEPT ALIVE ASSURDLY.
CAPTAIN ITO
JAPANESE TROOPS

Similar notes had on occasions been left by the Japanese,
but this time Captain Ito had done Mason a favour by
confirming that the 'troops in Buka' were still free. The
scout who brought the note also reported that the Japanese
had captured the famous Fijian, Usaia Sotutu. At this, Mason
laughed and looked over to Usaia, who was standing next
to him, smiling like an outlaw admiring his own WANTED
poster.

'Come and get us!' shouted Sergeant Ken Thorpe into the
surrounding wall of jungle, defiantly brandishing his Tommy
gun. Emboldened by full stomachs, Mason's party set off
again. The tide, however, was turning. Many native people
now ignored Mason and his party or fled at the sight of them
as they entered their village.

By 12 July, they were facing the toughest climb to date,
scaling the ridges of the Emperor Range running along the
spine of the island. Mason recalled that:

The journey was difficult, dangerous and monotonous.
Despite increasing fatigue, we were forced to climb again
and again to heights of 5000 feet – then plunge downward
to the dry river coursed between the peaks. Hiking through
continual tropical rainstorms and having no blankets for
the cold, we slept at night alongside our fires, letting the
smoke dry out our clothes.

To Mason and everyone else in the party, this was unknown territory. Villagers here had never encountered either a white person or a Japanese person, and the children fled from these strange-looking creatures in terror. At one stop Mason was asked if he was Japanese or English. Upon his answer of the latter, he and his men were invited to help themselves to the garden and treated as honoured, if unexpected, guests.

Conquering one jagged limestone ridge, the party descended into a gorge, then hours later climbed their way out, exhaustedly looking back at the previous peak, which now seemed but a small distance behind them. The pattern was repeated as they made their way across the ancient mountain range. After a week, the relief of reaching the foothills was palpable, although as they progressed north, there was once again evidence of recent Japanese patrols.

On 16 July, Mason looked at the state of his men. The natives were exhausted, with all but one of the eight commandos in a far worse state, debilitated by the endless hunger, cold, tropical ulcers and infections. Mason himself, despite being the oldest among them, was in better shape even than these supposedly fit young men. Arriving at a flat, grassy plain, he awarded everyone with a day's rest. The news was greeted as a gift from heaven.

Just as they settled, a native from an adjacent village arrived to announce that another party of white men was camped a day's walk up the track. With little faith in the native's ability to distinguish Europeans from Japanese, Mason was wary. Two police boys, stripped of anything written on their person, were cautiously sent ahead. The next day they returned accompanied by two native guides bearing rations, a note from Coastwatcher Jack Keenan and, unbelievably, flasks of hot tea. Mason was far closer to his goal of Kereaka than he had realised and Keenan had been searching for him. On 19 July, Mason and his party arrived at Kereaka, having pulled off the miracle of a three-week, 80-mile trek over some of the most impossible territory on earth, evading, for a second time, the net the Japanese had so carefully set for him.

•

Keenan signalled Guadalcanal that Mason and his party had at last shown up. The now familiar request then passed from the Coastwatchers in Guadalcanal, to Townsville, then Brisbane, then up through the various chains of command to the US Navy who once again laid on a submarine. The rendezvous point this time would be Atsilima Bay on Bougainville's rugged west coast, in four nights' time. That day, a long white sheet was to be unfurled and suspended between two poles for the sub to spot, and a sentry posted at both approaches to the beach to report any Japanese activity. At nightfall, two signal fires were to be lit to guide the submarine to shore.

Mason was given command of the evacuation, and in a few days began moving down to the coast at Atsilima Bay. In his charge was an eclectic collection of humanity: twenty-two Australian commandos, a couple of RAAF airmen survivors from a Catalina crash, twenty-four native scouts and police boys, seven fleeing Chinese, a single Fijian and various other native men along with their wives and children. Conspicuous by his absence was Jack Read and his own party who, like Mason, had spent the last few weeks being hunted by the Japanese and hostile native villagers across the north of the island. Read was currently just a few miles to the east but informed headquarters that his path west was blocked by Japanese. If the submarine was able to return for a second trip, he said he should be able to meet it in a few days' time. On hearing of Read's plight, Usaia Sotutu and five native scouts immediately left Mason's company to assist him through the Japanese positions.

Read's ordeal of the past weeks, as the Japanese began to infiltrate north as well as south, had been no less dramatic than Mason's. On one occasion, camped high on a ridge on the northeast of the island at the village of Sikoriapaia, he continued his Coastwatching even as Japanese patrols could be seen hunting him below. Scouts kept a constant eye on the Japanese through binoculars, ready to raise the alarm should they be seen to discover the small and secret track which led up to their camp on the escarpment. Closer to home, dried and shredded bamboo husks had been laid on the approaching tracks, designed to crackle underfoot and alert the listening sentries in the dark.

One night in late June, a shout went up as a sharp-eared sentry challenged whoever had set off the bamboo warning. Receiving no answer, he fired a single shot, and the reply came in a sudden burst of automatic weapon fire. Eighty Japanese and forty Black Dog natives stormed into the camp, firing guns and lobbing grenades in every direction. Caught unawares, Read and another Coastwatcher, Captain Eric Robinson, slid down the rocky escarpment, feeling their way in the dark until they reached a small ledge, beyond which Read thought it prudent not to venture. Above them, the shouts and cries of a battle continued, then the gunfire gave way to the sounds of Japanese and hostile natives calling for Read by name, urging him and his men to reappear and surrender.

Throughout the bleak night, the two men huddled on the bitterly cold ledge, reflecting on the old man who had wandered into camp that afternoon seeking to barter. He did not fit the normal description of a spy but was possibly met by some Japanese who demanded to know where he had obtained the cigarette papers he was using.

Finally, the pre-dawn light revealed Read's wisdom in having proceeded no further, as the two men found themselves staring over a precipice of many hundreds of feet to the valley floor below.

In the village above, the sounds of the searching Japanese could still be heard. Another day, then yet another night was spent on the ledge. Finally, after two days, the two men slowly clambered back up to the camp to find it ransacked and burned to the ground with all the stores taken or destroyed. Read called out, and slowly some of his men emerged from hiding. Then more appeared. After a quick count, Read was amazed to realise that not a single man had been lost. Someone shouted that the Teleradio had not been discovered and was still operable. Read came down the mountain, headed over to the commando base at Aita, and was back on the air the same day.

•

On 24 July, after sailing submerged up and down the coast the entire day, the navigation officer of the US submarine *Guardfish* had all but exhausted himself peering through the periscope for any sign of the white cloth signal at Atsilima Bay. Cursing the vague and ancient German maps he was forced to use – not to mention his own navy for failing to provide him with anything better – he was close to telling his captain that it was a 'no show'. Commander Norvell Ward urged him to be patient and keep looking. After all, he had been through this before as executive officer on the *Gato* back in March when several dozen refugees had come aboard. Ward knew full well that operations involving the Coastwatchers didn't usually run to schedule.

Then, just before 4 p.m., the navigator caught sight of a pale smudge standing out against the endless line of jungle green where it met the sand. Satisfied, Ward ordered the sub to settle on the sandy bottom until nightfall.

A few hours later, the operation went off without a hitch, with Ward managing to reverse his boat close to shore for a speedy embarkation. On the beach, Mason had directed the operation well, readying his excited people to quickly take to the eight inflatable boats that emerged through the breakers and nosed up onto the sand. Two trips, and half an hour later, all were safely inside the *Guardfish* with an incredulous Ward now having to find room for sixty-two people on his crowded submarine. 'We gathered a bit more of a crowd than we'd anticipated,' offered up the very last soul to come aboard, Paul Mason.

Inside the sub, the smell of brewing coffee and fresh white bread was akin to a dream. One of Mason's men mentioned that it was a pity Jack Read had been cut off by the enemy and unable to make it. Mason simply smiled a conspiratorial smile, and assured the man that Jack would be just fine.

•

Ten miles away, Jack Read waited for the signal confirming the *Guardfish* had successfully departed, then began making preparations to head to the coast. There were no Japanese blocking his passage and Read could have made the rendezvous with time to spare. He was not, however, prepared to abandon the twenty-two natives who had risked their lives to stay by his side these past seventeen months, protecting him, and without whom he could not have survived for a week. He knew that once the captain declared the submarine full, the natives would be the first to be left on the beach.

Almost as soon as the *Guardfish* had pulled away from the beach, headquarters was informed that, by some miracle, Read had managed to find his way through the Japanese line and was now on his way to the coast. As soon as the sub had departed the danger area and offloaded her guests to another ship, which would take them on to Guadalcanal and beyond, it would turn around and come back for Jack Read.

In the early hours of 28 July 1943, the *Guardfish* sealed its hatches once again, and with a hissing of its ballast tanks, slid beneath the surface off Kunua, 30 miles up the coast from Mason's departure point four nights earlier. Theirs would be a far roomier trip, as Read and his party numbered a relatively modest twenty-three, including Sergeant Yauwika and Usaia Sotutu, neither of whom had faltered for a moment in their bravery and devotion.

As the boat pulled away from the shores of Bougainville, Read felt a mixture of emotions. It was true he and the Coastwatchers were being forced off the island, but at this moment he sensed more strongly their many victories which, though small individually, had combined to wield the power of a mighty army.

•

With little more than guts, a cumbersome radio and the help of some devoted locals, the Coastwatchers of the Pacific covered a network stretching across half a million miles of ocean, recorded hundreds of aircraft sightings, identified the ships of secret enemy convoys, announced Japanese troop movements, provided vital and otherwise unobtainable weather information, spirited away hundreds of civilians, soldiers and missionaries to safety, and provided a continual flow of intelligence which denied the Japanese the ability to either defend or attack without the Allies knowing their every move.

When the enemy belatedly came to realise the damage this handful of irregulars were inflicting on their mighty military aspirations, their humiliation, as well as their fury, were immeasurable.

Coastwatching would continue following the departures of Mason and Read, as well as the exit of Eric Feldt due to ill health, but with the waning of Japanese power in the Southwest Pacific, it evolved into a native-augmented guerrilla force, under the direction of the Australian commandos of the special forces. Facing the Japanese directly in battle, they would eventually be credited with the killing of nearly 5500 enemy soldiers, with seventy-four captured.

After the war, it was estimated the Coastwatchers rescued 601 military personnel including over 300 downed airmen and 280 naval men from sunken ships. The total number of civilians they arranged to be extracted – soldiers, planters, missionaries, Chinese, as well as native men, women and children – exceeded 450.

However, fifty-six Coastwatchers – thirty-six European and twenty native – died in action, in often barbaric circumstances at the hands of the Japanese.

In a report after the war, Mason was modest in his assessment:

It had actually been a pretty hard existence on Bougainville – such as few realise ... Reviewing the course of our operations, coast-watching on that most northerly peg of the Solomons had fulfilled its mission long before we were driven out – and to a far greater effect than even we realised.

•

When Lieutenant-Commander Ward introduced himself to Jack onboard the *Guardfish*, he reminded him that they had met previously, back in March, in the shadows of the bridge of the *Gato* during one of the evacuations from Teop Harbour. On that occasion, Read had remained behind on the beach, his duty still incomplete. For the first time in over a year, Jack did not have to look over his shoulder, nor be constantly primed for the shout of a native scout raising an alarm, nor an aircraft engine prowling overhead. Now, the only sound he needed to hear was the deep and comforting throb of the submarine's engines as they took him away to safety beneath the warm waves of the Pacific.

# Chapter 24
# A LEGACY FORGOTTEN

The Japanese victory over the Coastwatchers in mid-1943 was short-lived. On the first day of November, the US Third Marine Division came ashore to little resistance at Cape Torokina at the northern end of Empress Augusta Bay – not far from the spot where Paul Mason and his party had departed – to begin the slow, slogging Bougainville Campaign, which would drag on till the end of the war in August 1945. Long before this, Japan's Pacific empire – forged in death and violence – had begun to fall apart.

Amazingly, Paul Mason's war was far from over. After a brief recuperation in Australia, he returned to Bougainville in late November to galvanise native resistance to the Japanese and even commanded a guerrilla army which accounted for over 2000 enemy casualties. It was a one-sided affair, with the once mighty Japanese soldier already broken, and resigned to defeat and death.

Mason's reappearance electrified the natives of Bougainville, who saw in him an almost divine aura of authority and indestructibility, enhanced further when he forbade any harsh measures against those natives who had helped the Japanese.

One of his guerrilla fighters remarked that Mason was always the last to eat after sharing his food with his native comrades. He treated their wounds and illnesses, and he took particular care of the native women and children. 'Paul had a saying, "Courtesy is understood in any language".'

One of the few Coastwatchers to be decorated for his services by Australia, Mason was awarded the navy's Distinguished Service Cross in 1945. The lure of the islands persisted even after his wartime ordeals. Demobilised from the navy in 1946, and now something of a celebrity, he married a year later and returned to his old plantation at Inus, founding several businesses and eventually representing his area in the Territory's Legislative Council. Although he penned the occasional article, and would spend more than half his life in the islands, Mason never wrote about his war in any detail.

Jack Read likewise returned to New Guinea, becoming a district officer at Kavieng on New Ireland. In 1951, he was lured back to a navy job in Melbourne but within a year had thrown it in and was back on the islands, now as a civilian, taking up the position of native land commissioner where he spent years recording local Indigenous histories and advocating for native peoples' land rights. While awarded the United States Distinguished Service Cross, his service remained unrecognised by Australia his entire life – he died aged eighty-seven.

Eric Feldt, the Coastwatchers' founder and mentor, suffered the effects of his damaged heart the rest of his life. His sole award, an OBE, was received in 1944, but for years he fought to have his service pension increased from its miserly 30 per cent. In 1946, he published *The Coast Watchers*, which remains the definitive account of the spy ring he founded, one of the most successful in history.

If the Australian government was slow to recognise the importance of the Coastwatchers, the Americans were not. For the rest of his life, the formidable, bull-necked commander of US forces in the South Pacific, Admiral William F. Halsey Junior, never lost an opportunity to praise Feldt and his organisation. At an anniversary in 1954, he stated to an Australian newspaper: 'Read and Mason saved Guadalcanal and Guadalcanal saved the Pacific. I could get down on my knees every night and thank God for Commander Eric Feldt.'

More than ten years earlier, in August 1943, when Halsey caught wind that the recently extricated Mason and Read were on an aircraft returning to Australia, he ordered it diverted to Noumea in order to thank them personally.

Finding himself unexpectedly on the ground during the unscheduled stopover, an unsure Paul Mason was ushered into the anteroom outside Halsey's office. When the door opened and the great man entered, Mason stood. Immediately, Halsey gestured Mason to resume his seat. 'When I'm in a room with you, Mr Mason,' he said, 'I'll be the one doing the standing.'

# BIBLIOGRAPHY

Burrowes, Jim (OAM), Interview with former Coastwatcher by
    Michael Veitch, 23 May 2020

Clemens, Martin, *Alone on Guadalcanal: A Coastwatcher's Story*,
    Blue Jacket Books, Naval Institute Press, Annapolis,
    Maryland, 1998

Feldt, Eric A., *The Coast Watchers*, Oxford University Press,
    Melbourne, 1946

Feuer, A. B., *Coast Watching in World War II: Operations Against
    the Japanese on the Solomon Islands*, 1941–43, Stackpole
    Books, Pennsylvania, 1992

Gamble, Bruce, *Darkest Hour: The True Story of Lark Force at
    Rabaul – Australia's Worst Military Disaster of World War II*,
    Zenith/MBI, South Windsor, 2006

Gamble, Bruce, Target Rabaul: *The Allied Siege of Japan's Most
    Infamous Stronghold, March 1943–August 1945*, Zenith Press,
    2013

Harris, John, 'Simply a Question of Duty: A Coastwatcher
    in North Australia Part 2', Naval Historical Society of
    Australia, June 2016

Horner, D. M., *Crisis of Command: Australian Generalship and the Japanese Threat, 1941–43*, ANU Press, Canberra, 1978

Horton, D. C., *Fire Over the Islands: Coast Watchers of the Solomons*, A.H. & A.W. Reed Ltd, 1970

Leckie, Robert, *Challenge for the Pacific, Guadalcanal: The Turning Point of the War*, Hodder and Stoughton, London, 1966

Lee, Betty, *Right Man Right Place, Worst Time: Commander Eric Feldt, His Life and His Coastwatchers*, Boolarong Press, 2019

Lindsay, Patrick, *The Coast Watchers: The Men Behind Enemy Lines Who Saved the Pacific*, Penguin Random House Australia, 2011, Kindle edition

Lord, Walter, *Lonely Vigil: Coastwatchers of the Solomons*, Viking, New York, 1977

Macintyre, Donald, *The Battle for the Pacific*, Angus and Robertson, London, 1966

Mackenzie, Gregory, 'Coastwatching in the Pacific – Solomon Islands', Naval Historical Society of Australia, April 1993

Murray, Mary, *Hunted: A Coastwatcher's Story*, Rigby Ltd, Melbourne, 1967

Read, Jack, *Coast Watcher: The Bougainville Reports 1941–1943*, Papua New Guinea Printing Co., Port Moresby, 2006

Simpson, Colin, 'Never Be Taken Alive', *Sunday Herald*, 23 August 1953

Stevens, David, *Naval Networks: The Dominance of Communications in Maritime Operations*, Sea Power Centre, Australia, 2012

Thompson, Peter, *Pacific Fury: How Australia and Her Allies Defeated the Japanese*, William Heinemann, Sydney, 2009

Van Liew, Michael, 'The Coastwatchers: Intelligence Lessons Learned for the Future Single Naval Battle', Center for International Maritime Intelligence, March 2021

White, Osmar, *Green Armour*, Angus & Robertson, Sydney, 1945

White, Osmar, 'The Man in the Panama Who Mothered the Coastwatchers', *Pacific Islands Monthly*, 1 November 1957

Wigmore, Lionel, *The Japanese Thrust (Australia in the War of 1939–1945)*, Series 1 (Army), Volume IV, Australian War Memorial, Canberra, 1957

Williams, Henry Leslie, Interview, Keith Murdoch Sound Archive, Australian War Memorial, Accession Number SOO959

Winter, Barbara, The Intrigue Master: Commander Long and Naval Intelligence in Australia 1913–1945, Boolarong Press, Brisbane, 1995

Wright, Malcolm, *If I Die: Coastwatching and Guerilla Warfare Behind Japanese Lines*, Lansdowne Press, Melbourne, 1965

# INDEX